Mario Vargas Llosa

Mario Vargas Llosa

A Collection of Critical Essays

Edited by Charles Rossman and
Alan Warren Friedman

University of Texas Press, Austin & London

For Marcela: without your enthusiasm for Vargas Llosa a dozen years ago, and your insistence ever since that others should share your pleasure in his works, this book would not exist. Te agradecemos.

International Standard Book Number 0-292-75039-0
Library of Congress Catalog Card Number 78-50821
Copyright © 1978 by the University of Texas Press
All rights reserved
Printed in the United States of America

With the exception of "*La tía Julia y el escribidor*, or the Coded Self-Portrait," by José Miguel Oviedo, the essays in this volume were previously published in *Texas Studies in Literature and Language*, vol. 19, no. 4.

Illustration by Barbara Whitehead

Contents

Editors' Preface

Mario Vargas Llosa has become internationally famous as one of the major authors of the boom in Spanish American fiction. His work has become the subject of an increasing flow of scholarly investigation and critical commentary in Spanish. Yet, even though his three major novels and several shorter pieces have been translated into English, his work has received very little critical attention *in English*. This collection of essays—which reprints in revised and expanded form the Winter 1977 special issue of *Texas Studies in Literature and Language*—has been created to fill that void.

The following articles fall into two general categories: first a series of critical examinations of individual novels, arranged in the order in which the novels themselves were published: second, a group of more general discussions that range across the body of Vargas Llosa's work to explore pervasive themes and concerns. Two pieces by José Miguel Oviedo serve as a coda. In the first, he and Vargas Llosa discuss the genesis and nature of Vargas Llosa's most recent novel, just published under the title *La tía Julia y el escribidor*. Oviedo concludes with a critical discussion of that same novel.

Because this issue is intended primarily for English-speaking readers, who may not know Spanish, all quotations are from the English translations of Vargas Llosa's novels, when such exist. In the case of quotations from untranslated works, citations by page numbers are to the Spanish editions, with English translations provided by our respective authors. Following are the English and Spanish editions cited throughout this collection:

The Time of the Hero, trans. Lysander Kemp (New York: Grove Press, 1966)
The Green House, trans. Gregory Rabassa (New York: Avon Books, 1973)

Conversation in The Cathedral, trans. Gregory Rabassa (New York: Harper and Row, 1975)
Los cachorros (Pichula Cuéllar) (Barcelona: Editorial Lumen, 1967)
Gabriel García Márquez: historia de un deicidio (Barcelona: Editorial Seix Barral, 1971)
Pantaleón y las visitadoras (Barcelona: Editorial Seix Barral, 1973)
La orgía perpetua: Flaubert y "Madame Bovary" (Barcelona: Editorial Seix Barral, 1975)

Although we have asked our contributors to quote Vargas Llosa in English, we have not asked them to cite his novels exclusively by their English titles. Thus, the reader will discover that some essays refer to *The Time of the Hero, The Green House,* or *Conversation in The Cathedral,* while others refer to the Spanish originals, *La ciudad y los perros, La Casa Verde,* and *Conversación en La Catedral,* respectively.

Rilda L. Baker

"Of how to be and what to see while you are being"[1]:

The Reader's Performance in *The Time of the Hero*

> Reading is never a natural and innocent activity. The condition of the reader is to come after, to be constituted as reader by the repertoire of other texts, both literary and nonliterary, which are always already in place and waiting to be displaced by a critical reading.
>
> —Jonathan Culler[2]

In literary critical circles, a contemporary author's reputation customarily rests more on his recent works than on his earlier efforts, however well received they might have been. Too often we critical readers forget our initial enthusiasm for a work in our rush to assess more current pieces. We tend to establish hierarchies of quality across the works of a single author and, once such niches are fashioned, to ignore the works that occupy those artificial categories, concentrating instead on the creative publications as yet uncatalogued.

This, in brief, is the regimen to which all novelists, at least in Latin America, subject themselves as they write and continue to write. However, there are reactions to literature, and there are reactions. Of all of the novels published in Latin America since 1960 –during the period called the "boom"—no work that I know of has engendered more observable reactions than Mario Vargas Llosa's *La ciudad y los perros* (*The Time of the Hero*). Outside Peru the novel was well received, was heralded as a literary happening, and was even awarded a literary prize in Spain where it was published. Meanwhile, some Peruvian readers, especially residents of Lima, were aghast to find in that first edition a street map of their capital city (the setting of the action in the novel) together with a photograph of Leoncio Prado Academy (a prestigious paramilitary school that exists to this day in Lima). These two visual aids, along with the vividly portrayed cheating scandal that comprises the central narrative sequence of the novel, were perceived as nothing less than a brash insult to "the institution." Hence, with zeal worthy of any viceregal Inquisitor in colonial Spanish America, the cadets and officials of Lima's Leoncio Prado burned a pile of these "illustrated" editions in protest.[3]

Those visceral responses to his work must have delighted Vargas Llosa, who remarked during a round-table discussion dedicated to *The Time of the Hero*, "I do not admire novelists who keep the reader at a distance."[4] Clearly, Vargas Llosa's book-burning readers suffered not from excessive detachment from the created reality, but rather from what Erving Goffman terms *engrossment*, "the matter of being carried away into something."[5] Such total involvement in a fictive world calls to mind that paragon of reader-participants, Don Quixote, who destroyed the puppet theater of Master Pedro (Part II, chapter 26) in his zealous efforts to assist damsels in distress (puppets though they might be). Cervantes' beleaguered knight and Vargas Llosa's incensed readers share a lack of aesthetic distance, that is, "the reader's awareness that art and reality are separate."[6] Yet it is involvement, not aesthetic distance, that is the hallmark of most accomplished narratives. In fact, Vargas Llosa attributes the generic supremacy and the novelist's primary challenge to the possibility of such engrossment: "the novel is . . . the genre that installs the reader at the very heart of the reality evoked in the book. The author's obligation is to keep him there."[7]

My memory of the initial reactions to *The Time of the Hero*, together with my encounters with other texts in the intervening years, prompts this revaluation or re-vision of the novel. I want to focus particularly on this engrossment or involvement, to analyze what I perceive to be essential markers within the work that determine the reader's performance. As I begin the description of the reading process, I am reminded of Clifford Geertz's comment that ultimately critical reading is "not an experimental science in search of law but an interpretive one in search of meaning."[8]

The primary conceptual vehicle for considering this involvement is the notion of framing. Although "framing" is a metaphor appropriated from the pictorial arts, it and its consequences are fundamental to fiction. Boris Uspensky's comments on the frame are useful to our understanding of the organization of a novel and the ways we learn "how to be" readers:

> We may say that the frame of a painting (primarily, its real frame) belongs necessarily to the space of the external observer (that is, of the person who views the painting and who

occupies a position external to the representation)—and not to that imaginary three-dimensional space represented in the painting. When we mentally enter the imaginary space, we leave the frame behind, just as we no longer notice the wall on which the picture is hung; for that reason, the frame of a painting may possess its own independent decorative elements and ornamental representations. The frame is the borderline between the internal world of the representation and the world external to the representation.[9]

Following this logic, we can say that the boundaries of the narrative world are marked (and thus enclosed) by the narrator of a novel. Indeed, it is the narrating function that provides the reader with a psychological orientation toward the events recounted therein. However, in fiction the narrator is also the nexus between interior and exterior, between the demands of the created reality and the expectations that the reader brings with him to the act of reading. It is the successful structuring of this frame that induces the reader to accept the norms and premises defining the interior coherence of a novel. What is more important, as Goffman points out, "frame . . . organizes more than meaning; it also organizes involvement" (p. 345).

Though we virtually take it for granted, the title of a novel is often one of the first clues to the quality and direction of the reader's conceptual involvement and properly should be considered integral to the frame of the work. The ultimate meaning of the title, replete with connotations that the work can lend to it, is necessarily completely perceived only after the reading experience. In the case of Vargas Llosa's novel, however, the title provides an essential clue to one of the primary organizational principles in the work, a clue that is deleted from the frame of the English translation. Conversations with the novelist after the publication of this novel reveal that he debated at length over the title (a fact that confirms, to some extent, the importance of even that one line). Initially the work was to be called *La morada del héroe* (*The Hero's Dwelling*), whence the title for the English translation. Later that was changed to *Los impostores* (*The Imposters*), a more explicitly sarcastic reference to the problems treated in the novel. Finally, the Spanish edition was published with the title *La ciudad y los perros* (*The City and the Dogs*), a phrase, Monegal asserts, that highlights the tension between the characters and their environment (Monegal, pp. 52–53). Undoubtedly, that is one aspect of the significance of the title. I would suggest that, more than merely communicating a univocal message to the reader, the title as it finally appeared establishes very subtly the basic narrative format of the novel. Spatially, the episodes all occur either in the city or at the academy. The connection between the two major settings (ignoring the subsettings that actually exist within each) is always one of the "dogs," the cadets now in their fifth year who reacted to their third-year initiation into the academy by organizing all manner of subterfuge against the other cadets and the school officials. The term *dog* would normally refer to the third-year cadets, but for the reader it comes to designate the small group of cadets who are involved in the cheating scandal that results in one cadet's death. Essentially, the fictive present includes all of those events that follow chronologically the theft of the chemistry examination (the event that opens the novel), and the central narrative sequence ends with the cadets' departure from the academy. The Epilogue of the novel focuses once more on two of the cadets (Alberto and the Jaguar) after they have left the academy, and affords the only projection into the future, into the lives of the characters beyond the academy.

Not only does the Spanish title circumscribe the spatial aspects of the novel; in its duplicating construction it also hints at the temporal skeleton of the work. In addition to the alternation between those episodes set in the city and those which take place at the academy, there is a corresponding alternation between episodes that advance the central narrative sequence (the cheating scandal) and others that provide social backgrounds for three of the cadets (Alberto Fernández, the Jaguar, and Ricardo Arana). Each of these episodes belongs to a fictive past remote from the central action of the novel. Somehow one expects such background information to provide clues to or causes for the fundamental problems set forth in the novel. But the reader's expectations are not fulfilled, for the details of each cadet's earlier life outside the academy seem to pertain to individuals that hardly resemble those whom we meet inside the academy. Each of the narrations terminates with the youth's decision to enroll at Leoncio Prado: three cadets, and three distinct reasons for subjecting oneself to the discipline and rigors of paramilitary life.

Before I suggest the results of Vargas Llosa's contrapuntal narration, let me specify those units that I am calling *episodes*. *The Time of the Hero* consists of two lengthy sections, each having eight chapters, and an Epilogue. Heading each of the long sections is an epigraph, which is yet another means of orienting the reader toward the novelistic world. Each chapter in turn is divided into numerous subsections separated from one another by the typographical conventions of blank spaces and (in the Spanish edition) the capitalization of initial words in the following section. Only the last chapter of Part I is of one piece; it recounts the field maneuvers ("war games") during which Ricardo Arana is killed. Two of the chapters (chapter 4, Part I, and chapter 1, Part II) are divided into ten sections each. This organization into episodic sections within the larger chapter divisions facilitates the movement among multiple temporal and spatial settings.

The principal result of such temporal fragmentation is that the reader experiences a constant interplay between past and present, between actors in the primary setting (the academy) and others in the secondary location (the city). Throughout the novel the central narrative provides an axis around which all other events revolve. Flashbacks to earlier moments in the academic lives of these cadets and regressions to childhood memories both reflect the continuing problems provoked for cadets and officials alike by the theft of the examination. Through this contrapuntal rhythm the stress is placed on simultaneity, on the shifting center of the fictive present and the confounding effects of such movement. The ultimate result is the blurring of temporal and spatial categories, the interpenetration of time and space. Sharon Spencer's summary of this process is relevant to the narrative organization of Vargas Llosa's novel:

> The spatialization of time in the novel is the process of splintering the events that, in a traditional novel, would appear in a narrative sequence and of arranging them so that past, present and future actions are presented in reversed, or combined, patterns; when this is done, the events of the novel have been "spatialized," for the factor that constitutes their orientation to reality is the place where they occur.[10]

It should be noted that this structural format and its effects are not unique to Vargas Llosa's first novel. In *The Green House* (1966) and *Conversation in The Cathedral* (1969), this technique achieves its fullest development and becomes almost a trademark of Vargas Llosa's narrative style.

Beyond the title, which simultaneously heralds the reader's involvement and, in this novel, initiates that process, there are other markers that shape and determine reader response in *The Time of the Hero*. At least one critic has noted certain resemblances between this novel and the detective story format; in fact, the work is best viewed in the context of one long literary tradition of the riddle or puzzle.[11] Vargas Llosa refracts, even multiplies, the puzzle format until it not only contributes to the structural frame of the work but also affects the conceptual apprehension and ultimate interpretation of the novel. I would point out that this mystery/riddle/puzzle technique has received mixed responses from critical readers. Luis Harss, for one, regards it as bothersome and questions the effectiveness of such "seductions" of the reader. Harss goes so far as to assert that "Vargas Llosa has the bad habit of witholding vital information" (p. 355). To his complaint I would reply that this organization and expositional technique is successfully integrated into the system of the narrative world and performs both structural and cognitive functions, both of which contribute to the reader's comprehension of the significance in the novel. In Jonathan Culler's terms, however, my expectations of the work are tempered by a textual repertoire different from that of Harss.

Despite the fact that the initial impetus of the action is a misdemeanor (which the reader "witnesses") that results in the death of Ricardo Arana and prompts the investigation that occupies the second half of the novel, the most significant aspects of the puzzle frame relate only tangentially to those events. Structurally, the work draws on detective fiction but in fact moves well beyond the conventions of that genre. It is important to indicate that even in this little novel the conventions of detective stories, since they should be familiar both to reader and author, serve as another orienting device and lead the reader to expect "an ongoing continuity of values."[12] The detective story frame, however, is relegated to the background about midway through the novel. Thereafter the invention of the work takes over, and the reader is guided through a process that (in any good mystery) would lead to the resolution of conflicts, the answers to persistent questions, and a stabilized outcome favorable to most of the characters.

In *The Time of the Hero*, however, ambiguity and paradox remain unresolved. Rather than being lucid sources of illumination for the reader, the narrators in this novel generate conflicting meanings. Instead of one meaning or one truth, the novel provides clues to a range of meanings and possibilities of truth that call attention to the means by which we each arrive at our own personal worldviews. Ultimately, we are reminded in multiple ways that "imaginative truth" is often "a lie which [we] value."[13]

Returning to the puzzle frame, I want to present two examples of the questions that arise within the first two chapters of the novel, answers to which are only revealed in later chapters. The first concerns the identity of one of the characters, not himself a narrator, but rather an optic through which the reader views a sequence of events in the fictive past. After the initial narration of the theft

of the examination, the scene changes to Salaverry Avenue in Lima
and the childhood of someone named Ricardo. Until that moment
the reader has encountered no character by that name. Nor is any-
one revealed to be Ricardo in the section that follows. Among the
characters we have met, it could be the Boa, the Jaguar, or the
Slave, none of whom has been called by his given name up to that
point. Before the end of chapter 1 we can eliminate the Boa (we
think), since he performs a narrating function of his own utilizing
first-person pronouns. The final identification of this Ricardo is
made at the end of chapter 2, when the Slave gives his name as
Ricardo Arana.

I would underscore the fact that there is one characteristic of
that first episode (pp. 12–14) that persists throughout all of the
sections devoted to the Slave. The key to the temporal position
of these episodes is to be found in the phrase "El Esclavo ha olvi-
dado" ("The Slave has forgotten") and its variant "El Esclavo no
recuerda" ("The Slave doesn't remember"). The latter we find in
the section of chapter 1 that details the initiation of the cadets,
told indirectly through the eyes of the Slave before the reader can
positively identify him as Ricardo Arana. In a world of shifting
narrators and settings, the reader begins to search for connections
between the episodes, and an observant reader would probably
note the similarity between the two phrases. By the time we are
certain of his identity at the end of chapter 2, we have already encountered one oblique indication of Ricardo Arana's schoolboy
nickname.

Each of the sections concerning Ricardo begins with the phrase
"The Slave has forgotten" (my translation), which, by virtue of its
recurrence, becomes part of the narrative frame. (In a like manner,
those episodes dealing with Alberto's childhood tend to include an
early reference to Diego Ferré Street, and thus promote the reader's orientation within the narration.) It is interesting that one element of this framing device does not survive the translation process. Semantically, the frame remains unchanged; syntactically,
it is altered. The translator chooses to maintain the narrative past
tense in English and thereby deletes the verbal aspect of the phrase.
(Compare "The Slave *has* forgotten," my translation, with "The
Slave *had* forgotten," copyrighted translation.) What always follows these present-tense assertions by the omniscient narrator is
a past-tense account of Ricardo's childhood. What, then, is the
vantage of this narrator? There must be something in the fictive
present that permits him such statements as preludes to past narrations. The last episode in Ricardo's childhood recounts the day his
parents announced their decision to enroll him at Leoncio Prado.

That section is in the same chapter (Part II, chapter 1) in which the other cadets learn of the Slave's death. The end of his childhood memories coincides with his premature death at the academy. Therefore, if we maintain the introductory phrase in its present tense, the collective memories take on the repetitive qualities of a litany, a linguistic device that blends with the ongoing narration and still provides reinforcement of the cadet's death.

The second riddle, one which for many readers is unsolved until the Epilogue, is the identity of the narrator who is the friend of Skinny Higueras and is always around Bellavista Plaza. We encounter this first-person narrator in chapter 2, Part I. What we learn about him in this initial section is that he has a brother, that his father is dead, and that he studies with a girl friend named Tere. Again, a process of elimination is put to work, and we recall that, given the characters we have met, this person could be the Boa (unlikely) or the Jaguar. By this stage in the novel, however, it is clear that Alberto is to be one of the principal figures, and certain intuitions (perhaps a desire to give him a voice of his own instead of hearing him through the mediating omniscient narrator) lead us to suspect that these passages may be yet another view of Alberto's childhood. Conflicting information should allow the reader to eliminate this possibility by chapter 5 of Part I. This narrator's father is dead; Alberto's is not. The confusion is promoted by Alberto's involvement with Teresa. Are there two Teresas? Unlike the accounts of Ricardo and Alberto's childhood (both narrated in the third person), this account continues well into Part II of the novel. The final installment in this third series of flashbacks is in chapter 7, Part II. Like the other two, this series also terminates with the narrator's decision to enroll at Leoncio Prado. Still, no positive identification has been confirmed by information available in other sections of the novel. The reader can only surmise who this narrator might be. The Epilogue solves the riddle unequivocally; in fact, the answer is in the very last section of the novel. The Jaguar and Skinny Higueras are once again together, reviewing each other's experiences. This time the narration is third rather than first person, and the Jaguar's name is mentioned near the beginning of the section. The pieces fit; the problem is solved. Yet the solution to the narrator's identity only highlights how little these accounts of childhood experiences actually contribute to our understanding of the cadet's conduct within the academy. The vital information, which in a detective story would set one's mind at rest, only renews--even heightens—the reader's perplexity in *The Time of the Hero.*

For observant readers, however, this narrator's identity should come as no surprise. There are at least four clues lodged in other sections of the novel, minor details which, taken together, establish rather clearly that Skinny Higueras' friend is the Jaguar. First, Alberto admits at one point that he attended La Salle Academy before he came to Leoncio Prado (p. 142). The first-person narrator reports seeing the La Salle students on the street one day (p. 205). This narrator could not be a La Salle student, therefore not Alberto. Second, Alberto is from Miraflores (an upper-class suburb of Lima) while the narrator seems to be from Bellavista. We can thereby eliminate Alberto. (Now the reader's task changes from elimination to confirmation.) Third, the Boa remembers that the Jaguar once said that he was from Bellavista (p. 238), and in the same breath comments that the Jaguar uses his head and feet to fight. Fourth, the description of the Jaguar during the initiation (p. 56) emphasizes his fighting style (head and feet). The first-person narrator reveals (p. 305) that his brother taught him to use his head and feet to fight.

Such a detailed inventory of clues and counterclues might seem to digress from the central concern of framing and involvement. But it is precisely the presence of the detective-story frame and its operational modes with which the reader is familiar that encourages this quest for clues.

There is at least one more characteristic of the narrative frame in Vargas Llosa's novel that does not survive translation. I present this because I believe that it may be the key (at least *a* key) to the overt reactions to the publication of the novel in 1962. Earlier I mentioned the liturgical opening of all of the sections that recount Ricardo Arana's childhood. Recall that in Spanish the use of the present tense at the beginning of those passages creates a temporal texture that is absent from the passages cast in the narrative past tense in English. Several critics have noted that tense alternation— even indiscriminate usage of verb tenses—is a hallmark of Vargas Llosa's style. In *The Time of the Hero*, Vargas Llosa's tense alternation is not at all random or without purpose. There are, in fact, specific instances of narration in the present tense, passages that describe recurrent scenes (dawn and reveille at the academy, chapter 2, Part I) or present elements of the setting that may exist outside of the novel (the description of Diego Ferré Street [p. 29]). In the following paragraph, which is the translator's version, consider the perceptual effects of substituting the present tense which Vargas Llosa himself used, for each of the italicized past-tense verbs:

> Diego Ferré Street *was* less than three hundred yards long,
> and a stranger to it would have thought it was an alley with
> a dead end. In fact, if you *looked* down it from the corner of
> Larco Avenue, where it *began*, you *could* see a two-story
> house closing off the other end two blocks away. . . . At a
> distance, that house *seemed* to end Diego Ferré, but actually
> it *stood* on a narrow cross street, Porta.   (p. 29; my em-
> phasis)

Induced to accept the immediacy of the scene by the use of the
present tense, the reader accompanies the narrator on a walking
tour of Diego Ferré Street, not merely a setting for Vargas Llosa's
novel, but rather an apparently "real" neighborhood into which
one might venture at any time. In the first edition of the novel,
this attitude on the reader's part, or the facilitation of this attitude, was reinforced by the inclusion of the city map. This contrast between verbal tenses establishes the transcendence of the
setting and, at the same time, endows the events with a presence
and presentness that they might not otherwise display.

The product of this narrative technique is a double-edged sword.
Clearly, the reader is drawn into the world of the novel because of
this strategy. It also enlists the reader's capacities to visualize, thereby rendering the novelistic space more vivid. However, such a technique also leaves open the possibility of some spatial projection
beyond the realm of the novel, beyond the covers of the book or
the boundaries of the reader's imagination. For the cadets and officials of Leoncio Prado, the implied resemblance (and explicit coincidence) between Vargas Llosa's academy and their own prompted
an indignant public reaction designed (I would assume) to deny
any such relationship. Their demonstrated disapproval served more
to spotlight than to suppress that social critical possibility.

In *The Time of the Hero*, the success of Vargas Llosa's presentation depends, in large measure, on the careful implementation and
integration of familiar structural frames that induce the reader into involving himself in the created reality. The narrative stress patterns established by means of the alternating rhythm create an in-
terface, a zone of significance between two poles of meaning. The
reality of the novel is not a Manichean world; neither the reader
nor the characters are permitted the luxury of all-or-nothing attitudes, of yes-or-no answers. The reader's involvement points out
the existence of growing gray areas, actions that defy categoriza-
tion, social responsibilities that threaten individuality, and individual behaviors that menace the established social order. The moral

and social dilemmas that circumscribe the world portrayed in the novel are paralleled in the reader's experience by the subversion of the initial behavioral frame (the detective story, mystery, or puzzle) that was to guide him through the novel. While the frame overtly involves the reader in the novel, it also covertly affords him the experience of implication and deception that are integral to the social drama comprising the work.

Vargas Llosa manages to station both the characters and the reader in an interstitial, interstructural zone in which we struggle to discern the shadows and specters of behavioral demands that will operate within the world of the fictive academy and, perhaps, could extend beyond the experience of this novel. The narrative frame erected in *The Time of the Hero* is sustained by means of multilevel alternation: third-person narration vs. first-person narration, fictive past vs. fictive present, past-tense verbs vs. present-tense verbs, the city vs. the academy. Reading Vargas Llosa's novel becomes a retrogressive procedure in which the reader is required to retreat three steps and retrieve lost pieces of the chain of events in order to advance four steps in pursuit of the accelerating action. Frustrating and puzzling though it be, it is the reader's involvement in and response to the operational modes of the work that permit him to perceive its "configurative meaning." As Wolfgang Iser summarizes, the novel is "the genre in which reader involvement coincides with meaning production."[14]

University of Texas at San Antonio

Notes

1. Taken from the poem/song "Between the Lines," by Janis Ian (Mine Music, Ltd., April Music, Inc., 1974):

> In books and magazines of how to be
> and what to see while you are being
> Before and after photographs teach
> how to pass from reaching to believing
> We live beyond our means on other people's dreams
> and that's succeeding.
> Between the lines of photographs
> I've seen the past—
> it isn't pleasing.

2. Jonathan Culler, "Beyond Interpretation: The Prospects of Contemporary Criticism," *Comparative Literature*, 28 (Summer 1976), 254.
3. Recounted by Emir Rodríguez Monegal, "Madurez de Vargas Llosa,"

Homenaje a Mario Vargas Llosa, ed. Helmy Giacoman and José Miguel Oviedo (New York: Las Americas, 1971), p. 52 (my translation).

4. Quoted by Mario Benedetti, "Vargas Llosa y su fértil escándalo," *Homenaje a Mario Vargas Llosa*, p. 247 (my translation).

5. Erving Goffman, *Frame Analysis: An Essay on the Organization of Experience* (New York: Harper and Row, Harper Colophon Books, 1974), p. 347.

6. C. Hugh Holman, *A Handbook to Literature*, 3d ed. (New York: Odyssey Press, 1972), p. 8.

7. Quoted by Luis Harss, "Mario Vargas Llosa, or the Revolving Door," *Into the Mainstream* (New York: Harper and Row, 1967), p. 358.

8. Clifford Geertz, *The Interpretation of Culture* (New York: Basic Books, 1973), p. 5.

9. Boris Uspensky, *A Poetics of Composition*, trans. Valentina Zavarin and Susan Wittig (Berkeley: Univ. of California Press, 1973), p. 143.

10. Sharon Spencer, *Space, Time and Structure in the Modern Novel* (New York: New York Univ. Press, 1971), p. 291.

11. José Promis Ojeda, "Algunas notas a proposito de 'La ciudad y los perros,' de Mario Vargas Llosa," *Homenaje a Mario Vargas Llosa*, p. 291.

12. For a discussion of the concepts of *convention* and *invention* in popular literature, see John Cawelti, "The Concept of Formula in the Study of Popular Literature," *Journal of Popular Culture*, vol. 3, pp. 381–90. I have been guided by his definitions for the purposes of this study.

13. Morse Peckham, *Man's Rage for Chaos* (New York: Schocken Books, 1965), p. 45.

14. Wolfgang Iser, *The Implied Reader* (Baltimore: Johns Hopkins Univ. Press, 1974), p. xi.

Michael Moody

A Small Whirlpool: Narrative Structure

in *The Green House*

R. S. Crane, in his well-known article on the concept of plot, arrives at conclusions which are most convincing in their delineation of elements composing narrative structure and the role these play in a total literary experience. Of special interest here is Crane's broad definition of plot as a "particular temporal synthesis effected by the writer of the elements of action, character, and thought."[1] This idea will, to a considerable degree, inform subsequent discussion of *The Green House*. The present study will consider narrative structure primarily as a question of temporal synthesis. Patterns of structural design and the disposition of time will be viewed in their relationship to thematic issues and as unifying elements through which the novel achieves coherence and artistic form.

The quality of synthesis that Crane would look for in a literary work has also been a topic of commentary by Vargas Llosa in specific reference to *The Green House*. When asked during an interview to describe the subject of his novel, the author spoke first of the five lines of narrative that present the stories of the green house, the Mangachería, the mission at Santa María de Nieva, Jum, and Fushía. His concluding remarks then recapitulated salient features of structure within the novel as well as the literary goal shaping his efforts:

> These five stories occur over a period of forty years. They are interwoven; they have characters in common and the structure is discontinuous as much in time as in space. In each episode of the novel, things occur that have taken place in different moments of those forty years. There is no linear order. I have tried to give all of these worlds—so opposite, so different -as a totality.[2]

Implicit in the author's statement is an awareness that the novel's expressive power must ultimately derive from an artistic integration of diverse literary elements. The totality of which he speaks finally encloses a vision of man encompassing the complexity and relativity of human experience. Translating human features such as these into literary terms also implies a corresponding complexity in narrative structure.

The principle of discontinuity, however, when applied to the novel's structure, brings about a general impression of formlessness rather than integration. For the reader, vagueness and uncertainty are subjective values that arise inevitably when a constant disruption of temporal and spatial sequences obscures perception of larger formal designs. Yet, on a thematic level, this negation of omniscience on the part of the author, demonstrating an unwillingness to give a total interpretation of a world seen as multiple and diverse, is itself a statement underscoring the relative nature of reality.

A view of man that recognizes the irrational and chaotic structuring of both human and external reality has little use for a strict notion of causality. In consequence, the structure of the narrative appears to loosen and in general takes on a formless quality that corresponds to and depicts the author's world view. Thus, the impression of formlessness acquires functional meaning in the novel by its ability to communicate a sense of chaos and purposelessness in the lives of characters whose existence lacks order and direction.

In a discussion of spatial form, Walter Sutton has seen this kind of thematic implication closely united with structural fragmentation. Speaking of the fundamental difference he sees between classical and modern poetry, Sutton writes:

> It is the burden of time of twentieth-century man—his consciousness of his diminished place in the scheme of things and of his lack of qualification for the hero's role—that is a pervasive theme of the poetry cited here. And the juxtaposition of images from past to present has less the effect of establishing identity than of enforcing contrasts. . . . In this time perspective the lack of "syntactical sequence" or of transitions within the poem has less the effect of establishing a unified pattern of experience than it has of pointing up the meaningless and atomistic point of view of modern man . . . in contrast with what the disillusioned poet regards as the more orderly world views of earlier historical periods.[3]

Sutton, of course, is here describing the general effect often brought about in modern poetry by the selection of technique. But as given literary substance and particularity in *The Green*

House, the effect he describes is nonetheless associated with the thematic statements toward which the novel gathers its elements. Such an effect, however, need not be a true reflection of the deeper reality of the novel's form. To be sure, a work of art must have structure. As the following analysis will show, the quality of form-lessness in *The Green House* is, to a considerable degree, an artfully contrived illusion created for its particular power of expression in rendering the novel's thematic issues.

The novel is divided into four large chapters and an Epilogue. A rather lengthy episode, which Vargas Llosa calls an *umbral*, introduces each chapter wherein subchapters, varying in number from three to five, follow in sequence. Within the first two chapters, five fragments of narrative compose each subchapter. In the latter half of the novel, the subchapters are composed of four fragments. The Epilogue then brings the novel to a close with an *umbral* and four fragments.

Although the linear arrangement of narrative units shows a certain numerical balance across the first and last two chapters, the formal pattern reflecting a deeper structural figuration arises from the ordering of fragments on the subchapter level. Because the story lines display predictable arrangement after each chapter's introductory episode, the plots can be seen to rotate in sequence and, within each large chapter, to create recurring circular structures in a spiraling movement.[4]

When taken together, the time elements of all the plots enormously complicate the novel's structural design. At the beginning of the narrative, for example, five plot lines are started, and each involves not only a different time level but a different internal ordering of time. Moreover, at the novel's onset, two of the plots—those relating the stories of Bonifacia at the mission and Fushía's river voyage—contain counterpointing narrations that advance on different temporal planes and with varying rhythms. But with certain exceptions, the predictability of the individual plots also extends to their separate chronologies.

To demonstrate the predictable arrangement of the plots, their temporal sequence, and their circular character, it is useful to disassemble them from the order in which they are first perceived by the reader. Observed in isolation, the plots can be seen to fashion patterns of arrangement that show a basic unity underlying the novel's structuring of both form and theme. This approach to the problem of analysis, however, carries certain disadvantages precisely because it violates the character of the reader's experience. After a brief discussion of the separate plots, I will consider them in relationship and comment upon the special literary effects brought about by their fragmentation.

Following the introductory episode of each chapter, the first line of narrative encountered by the reader has as its major concern the story of Bonifacia. The first three episodes advance on two narrative levels: the direct presentation of Bonifacia's interrogation by the Mother Superior is interwoven with descriptions by a privileged narrator who presents, in successive scenes, views of Santa María de Nieva, the prisonlike routines of the mission, a moment of human contact between Bonifacia and the girls, and finally, in the fourth episode, the girls' actual escape. The tense, emotional, and fast-moving dialogue of the scenes is steadily counterpointed with the calm, measured prose of the outside narrator. The tones of the two levels are quite distinct, and a rising tempo produces in the whole a rhythm of alternating intensities that adds a considerable element of suspense.

In the fourth episode, the descriptions of the outside narrator end at a point in time just prior to the opening interrogation scene. Thus, the simultaeous portrayal of the two levels creates a circular or looping pattern in which the descriptive component takes the reader through a sequence of events the outcome of which he has already witnessed. In this process, he encounters in the last episode a third narrative line containing a conversation between Bonifacia and Sister Angélica. The time period here is somewhat uncertain but obviously occurs after the Chicais girls were brought to the mission and before their escape. It is in this conversation that Bonifacia seeks answers about her past.[5]

Moving in chronological sequence throughout the novel, this narrative line begins with a series of views of Bonifacia at the mission, then develops her relationship with Lituma, and ends with her marriage and departure for Piura. Within chapters 2 and 3, some of the fragments deal primarily with Lituma's search for the escaped Indian girls and his later pursuit of Fushía, but these events, while diverging from the main story line, are chronologically ordered in relation to it.

The second fragment of the novel's subchapters always presents the story of Fushía, which acquires shape and dramatic compression within the temporal and spatial limits enclosed in the portrayal of the river voyage. For thirty days Fushía and Aquilino talk to one another as they move slowly down the river toward their destination, the leper colony. Of the sixteen episodes focusing on Fushía's life, ten record this journey; and, except for a final scene set in the Epilogue, all belong within the internal time structure established by the conversations between the two men. Together the episodes reveal an organizing principle essentially the same as the one seen operating on a minor scale in the early views of Bonifacia at the mission.

The first episode opens Fushía's story at a point of personal crisis. Already involved in a sequence of ongoing dialogue, Fushía is seen responding to questions posed to him by Aquilino. While the primary focus follows the sequential portrayal of their conversations, Aquilino's questions activate another time dimension in which important events in Fushía's past are recapitulated. This second sequence shows some chronological arrangement through the many episodes, taking the reader from his earliest view of Fushía in Brazil to a time, on the island, just prior to his departure with Aquilino for the leper colony. The chronological direction of the second time sequence is not readily apparent, however, because events occurring on this level are normally, but not always, linked conceptually to the subject matter of the conversations. The last episodes also show a final parallel with the scenes of Bonifacia at the mission in that the earlier temporal level moves toward conclusion with an account of escape. On this occasion it is that of Adrián Nieves and Lalita from Fushía's island.

Again the author has chosen a circular or looping pattern to structure the internal disposition of time. With regard to a definition of Fushía's life, the structure has important thematic implications. At the point of looping, the portrayal of his past comes to an end, and, because his future has already been seen, an air of finality pervades the last episode. The linkage of time dimensions completes the design of a plot structure that had been unclear. But more importantly, the structural transition corresponds to the passage of Fushía's self to the state of being of an object.

The technique marks the point at which Fushía's will decisively loses the struggle with circumstance. By this juncture he has been overwhelmed by events. Pursued by the police, sick, and abandoned, Fushía has no recourse but to submit to Aquilino and leave the island. The transition that Fushía undergoes to a new state of being places his mode of existence outside the scope of time and action. His story, framed in such a context, takes on the timeless quality of myth. His voyage toward the dominion of death imparts to his life the special resonance and expressiveness of a prototype.

The third fragment of the subchapters narrates events associated with the story of Don Anselmo. Although lapses in time of some length separate the events contained in these fragments, their sequential order, through chapter 3, is chronological. The fact that future events are often anticipated within this line of narrative substantially heightens the reader's sense of mystery but does not alter the sequence of actual portrayal.

Only the three fragments that narrate the relationship between Don Anselmo and Antonio occurring in chapter 4 appear to be temporally dislocated. But insofar as this portrayal represents a *mangache* re-creation taking place near the moment of Don Anselmo's death, the time becomes contemporaneous with the event itself, which is narrated in the Epilogue. Thus the events of chapter 4 are not out of order in relation to the rest of the narrative but rather brought to a state of temporal suspension after Don Anselmo has been seen to merge with the collective existence of the Mangachería.

In the first half of the novel, the fourth fragment of each subchapter conveys events directly associated with the capture of Jum and Bonifacia at Urakusa. With one exception, the fragments composing this portrayal advance in a chronological movement. After beginning at Borja with Corporal Delgado's decision to go to Urakusa, the narrative then switches to a scene situated in Santa María de Nieva. The major issue here concerns Julio Reátegui's reaction to news that the Indians at Urakusa have set up a cooperative and will no longer sell their rubber to him. At the end of this scene, Reátegui is informed of an incident at Urakusa that took place the week before and involved a corporal from the Borja garrison. It soon becomes apparent that this fragment has been dislocated in time as well as space when subsequent scenes continue the line of chronology first established at Borja. Temporally, the succeeding fragments narrate the river journey undertaken by Corporal Delgado and Adrián Nieves, their arrival in Urakusa, and the ensuing attack. Still chronologically ordered, the next three scenes pertain to the arrival in Urakusa of Julio Reátegui with his raiding party and their seizure of Jum and Bonifacia.

Thus, in terms of temporal progression, the main story line is established in the opening scene at the Borja garrison. The participation of Julio Reátegui begins at a different point in time and space but immediately forms a tangent converging with the original line. With the capture of Jum and Bonifacia, this narrative comes to a close. It is for this reason that the original five plots contract to four in the last half of the novel.

The fifth fragment of each subchapter has as its subject events in the Mangachería and, principally, the outcome of the relationship between Lituma and Bonifacia that was begun in the novel's first line of narrative. At the center of Lituma's experience is one incident that drastically alters the trajectory of his life. His story provides an excellent example of how group values stimulated in a given situation deprive the individual of the independence of judgment, response, and feeling that are necessary to achieve autonomy as a personality. La Chunga's brothel is the setting for his deadly confrontation with Chápiro Seminario.

The methods employed to narrate the incident have much in common with those used to present the stories of Bonifacia and Fushía. A conversation taking place in La Chunga's brothel among a number of participants establishes a framework in the present within which the sequence of past events leading to Seminario's death is chronologically reconstructed. Similar also is the structural looping that ends Lituma's participation as an active character at a moment of personal crisis just prior to his return to Piura where his story as Lituma first begins.

This event, leading as it does to the death of Chápiro Seminario, to Lituma's incarceration, and to Bonifacia's ruinous liaison with Josefino and her entrance to La Chunga's brothel, has widening repercussions in many lives and illustrates how closely interwoven are the fortunes of the novel's characters. Additionally, there is, in the outcome of Lituma's act, the same strong element of disproportion between cause and effect that has been observed in other incidents. One impulsive gesture, generated by the kinetics of group values and a critical situation, brings catastrophe into the lives of many.

In this analysis, however, only the arrangement of fragments within the novel's first three chapters is immediately pertinent. In chapter 4, the events portrayed do not follow the temporal ordering of the preceding chapters. The first of the three fragments presented in chapter 4 begins a narration of events taking place shortly after the arrival of Lituma and Bonifacia in the Mangachería. The three fragments are in chronological sequence and narrate Josefino's advances to Bonifacia, her submission to him after Lituma is jailed, and finally her entrance into La Chunga's brothel. The period enclosed by these three fragments can be placed between the end of the first story in Santa María de Nieva and the beginning of the fifth narrative, which starts with Lituma's return from prison.

This study has shown how the organization of materials within separate plots creates a circular design of structural loops in the character portrayals of Bonifacia, Fushía, and Lituma. In each case, the looping occurs at a break in the narrative that corresponds to a decisive turning point in the trajectory of the character. The same pattern with the same rationale can now be identified in the formal relationships that exist between entire plot lines.

The point of departure from which a large internal design in *The Green House* can be traced is the scene at Borja situated within the novel's first cycle of fragments. The direction established in this line of narrative takes the reader to the events at Urakusa, which, in effect, supply the origins for the story of Bonifacia and Lituma in Santa María de Nieva. At Urakusa, the movement of time is broken and, within the spatial composition of the novel, brought into the shape of a loop when it is rejoined at Santa María de Nieva.

In a like manner, the novel's ordering of time displays yet another loop when, at the end of the first narrative, Bonifacia and Lituma leave Santa María de Nieva to have their story resumed in the fourth chapter of the *mangache* sequence. And in a final turn, the end of this chapter, which sees Bonifacia enter La Chunga's brothel, loops back to the beginning of the same line of narrative when Lituma returns from prison and finds that Bonifacia has become a prostitute.

The disposition of chronological time, then, quite directly unites three of the five plots in a spiraling structure that shapes their diverse elements into multiple and complex patterns of association. An extremely close correspondence can be observed between formal and thematic structure in that each major break in temporal sequence severs the characters from their past existence and each loop returns them to yet another experience of entrapment.

Rearranging the parts of the novel can be a useful procedure in order to see how unifying patterns of form and meaning are created within the several plots. But, as stated before, this procedure has limitations, for its concern with chronological sequence does not adequately show the true complexity of the novel's treatment of formal and temporal relationships. The novel is much more than the sum of its parts, and to see the synthesis it achieves ultimately requires that the reader's immediate experience be taken into account.

As he progresses through the novel, the reader does not perceive the internal temporal design that underlies the arrangement of each narrative and that thus serves as a source of unity for the many dislocated fragments. Instead, he observes the concurrent advance of all the plots, which produces a continual overlapping of temporal levels so that characters and events are simultaneously viewed from various perspectives and at different distances in time.

To structure the novel in such a fashion, with multiple plots rotating on different axes of time and at different speeds, clearly destroys the traditional novelistic feature of controlled progression in plot sequence and characterization. Certainly no single dramatic issue presents itself to hold together and unify the novel's accumulating body of incident. Following the spiraling, circular recurrence of plot lines, the reader experiences structure as a series of refracted views offering disconnected glimpses of a reality so fragmented that it can be only partially ascertained at any given point in the novel.

Such regulating concepts as conflict, climax, and resolution, in their normal temporal succession, have no application to the novel when it is viewed as one narrative entity. These elements, however, do play a significant role in the formation of structure, but not in their traditional manner. If their occurrence and treatment within the stories are duly noted, certain major principles of organization can be made evident and certain consequences identified that have important bearing on the quality of the reader's experience.

Because the plots advance simultaneously and in cycles, the resulting fragmentation of time levels brings about portrayals in which one salient trait emerges with regularity: incidents properly belonging to the preparation of conflicts as well as others pertaining to their resolution are revealed *before* the exposition of the major climactic moment in the trajectory of each character. In the reader's perception, a sequential rise and descent of suspense around a central climax does not occur. The traditional structuring of suspense, especially in plots where action tends to be the synthesizing principle, has been drastically altered.

In the case of Fushía, preparatory incidents in the form of an ongoing representation of his past life and the outcome of these events—the voyage to the leper colony—take place primarily within the same story line. The climax of his story, the occasion where Fushía decisively changes to a new mode of existence, culminates at the point of structural looping. As this event occurs shortly before the Epilogue, the ordering of materials allows the reader to perceive the past, present, and future of this character before experiencing the climactic event that divided his existence.

The same kind of structural looping also marks the climax in the portrayals of Bonifacia and Lituma. But these characters, like Jum and Don Anselmo, participate in more than one plot sequence, so that information and incidents involving different stages in their lives are presented in separate lines of narrative. Thus, the reader learns that Bonifacia has become a prostitute in La Chunga's brothel before the events at the mission are fully played out. Also unfolding in different stories, Lituma's experiences in Santa María de Nieva and his return from prison are seen before his confrontation with Chápiro Seminario. All the events of Jum's life are made known before the Epilogue presents the scene of his symbolic crucifixion. Don Anselmo's intense and lyric relationship with Antonia is narrated after he has been seen in both his youth and old age.

In all these stories, the arrangement of incident displaces the element of climax from its normal context. It should perhaps be added that even though the technique of giving characters different names in their different situations sometimes delays recognition of relationships between time levels, the moments of discovery and association on the part of the reader always precede the representation of a climax.

As a consequence of this method of displacement, climactic scenes within the several stories are distributed throughout the course of the novel. For the reader, the resultant effect is most complex. His progress through any given set of fragments within the cycle of a subchapter becomes an experience of numerous and conflicting tensions. His knowledge of events and character relationships varies in its completeness with regard to the immediate state of development of each plot. In every cycle, he will be in a different position in relation to each plot's movement toward or away from its central climax.[6]

Although the displacement of climax within a story might be thought to limit its possibilities of suspense, this is clearly not so in *The Green House*. When shifts to other plots interrupt scenes of growing tension, the reader's sense of expectancy actually heightens enormously. It is also the functional role of ambiguity—whether of fact or of character motivation—always to withhold key elements from a total design and, thus, to preserve doubt and mystery. Even when the reader knows both the antecedents and the outcome of an event, even when he knows the two ends of the situational trajectory of a character, incidents yet to be narrated continue to hold the promise of synthesis and meaning made coherent. A novel so constructed does not disclose its secrets until the last page is turned, and even then the reader's impulse is to begin again and to follow once more the cycles which yielded their direction and meaning with tantalizing equivocacy. With characteristics such as these, the novel's structure gives origin to intellectual and emotional appeals that are strong and consistent.

If the concept of plot is employed in a narrow sense to mean simply a framework of incidents, then it can be said of *The Green House* that none of the five story lines initiated at the novel's beginning constitutes a completely unified structure providing an encompassing view of its subject. Even when the many disconnected fragments pertaining to each line of narrative are taken out of their contexts and reassembled in sequence, they do not yield adequately developed plots. Almost immediately, the separate strands of the novel begin to mesh. The originally unrelated characters are soon weaving in and out of incidents that belong to stories taking place in different settings and time periods.

The juxtaposition of dislocated scenes frequently creates parallels and contrasts that relate the fragments across plot lines in terms of action and theme rather than through the causal relations within a single narrative. This effect, for example, is quite pronounced in the novel's opening scenes where all the fragments, including the introductory episode, narrate events associated with at least one phase of an existential cycle of entrapment and escape.

Many such examples can be found in the novel, but the most significant structural consequences brought about by this kind of portrayal relate to the total representation given to the incident at Urakusa. As mentioned above, the novel's first cycle of fragments contains the scene in which Corporal Delgado requests leave from the military garrison at Borja in order to return to his home. To gain favor of his Captain, who suffers from the bites of jungle mosquitos, the Corporal promises to make a stopover in Urakusa and bring back an ointment prepared by the Indians. This trivial agreement between the two men sets in motion a chain of events that will reach catastrophic proportions and eventually, either directly or indirectly, entangle the lives of all the novel's major characters.

With Adrián Nieves serving as guide, the party arrives in Urakusa. Disregarding prudent advice, the Corporal steals a few valueless articles from the deserted village and thus invites the attack from which Adrián Nieves escapes by throwing himself into the river. Some time later, he is picked up by Fushía and Lalita, who have established themselves on an island situated deep in the jungle. In this setting is forged the relationship between Nieves and Lalita that leads to their flight from Fushía's island, and which in turn takes them to Santa María de Nieva.

Julio Reátegui, finding vague reports of what happened at Urakusa an excuse to settle his personal dealings with the same group of Indians, leads an expedition against the village. After taking Jum captive, Reátegui allows his men to violate the Indian women and nearly devastate the community. When he returns to Santa María de Nieva, Reátegui displays a strange contradiction in his character by bringing along a new ward for the mission, Bonifacia. In this setting, the lives of both Jum and Bonifacia come into contact with Sergeant Lituma. After being expelled from the mission, Bonifacia goes to live in the home of Adrián Nieves and Lalita, and while there meets and marries Lituma. With his bride

of a few days, Lituma returns to the Mangachería; and, when he
is later imprisoned, Bonifacia—the girl from the distant village of
Urakusa —enters the world of La Chunga's brothel, a place with direct links to the early story of Don Anselmo.

This brief sketch, drawing information from all of the story
lines, gives an indication of how tightly interwoven are the many
lives activated in the novel's several plots. In addition, this close
interlocking of people and events sheds much light on the novel's
portrayal of causality. In the disproportion existing between the
origins of the conflict at Urakusa and its consequences, reality displays a capriciousness that implies a breakdown of causal relationships. After the decision reached at Borja, the fact that subsequent
events gather such momentum and reach such proportions underscores a view that the world is essentially chaotic. Operating here
is another kind of causality that is neither coherent nor rational
nor objective.

The true nature of this causality can be seen clearly in Jum's
experience. In the course of the novel, the many characters who
are caught up in the dynamics of the incident at Urakusa express
their varied and conflicting accounts of what actually happened.
Because Adrián Nieves never returns to the military garrison, it
is incorrectly assumed that he was killed. Because Corporal Delgado never divulges his own acts of provocation, it is generally believed that the Indians attacked out of hostility and savagery. As
it takes shape in Santa María de Nieva, the "truth" of the incident, the interpretation shaping the response of the authorities
and subsequent action, becomes a re-creation that in turn stabilizes
and acquires its own validity.

The process by which truth is transformed by subjective re-crea-
tions—a phenomenon having its special counterpart in the Mangachería —brings the nature of truth itself into question. In Santa
María de Nieva, Jum finds that the reality of his past experience
has been so altered and become so elusive that he will never find
justice among those who do not share his perspective. Jum struggles not only against men more powerful than he but against an
existential situation that has been warped and made relative by the
limitations of others and thus has no unity with the past. Already
in a position of weakness, he is further victimized by intangible
forces over which he has no control.

The peculiar behavior of causal relationships places in doubt
man's capacity to order the world through reason. A basic conflict
arises between man's needs and his ability to control and order the
forces that can supply his needs. He simply cannot cope with a

reality so fragile and unstable that it can assume new and unexpected forms and in so doing defeat his endeavors. The power and
importance of men, in the void between cause and effect, are lost.

The repercussions related to "action, character, and thought"
resulting from Corporal Delgado's decision at Borja give evidence
of how little autonomy the separate plots of the novel possess. As
the reader progresses through the narrative, receiving intermittent
insights into relationships that are unfolding in different story
lines, the scattered fragments begin to draw together and the separate identity of the plots becomes increasingly diffuse. It is soon
evident that each plot exists to contribute to the whole, to create
a totality in which each part acquires its full weight and value only
through its necessary relationship to a larger design.

Thus, the decision reached at Borja between two minor characters represents the center from which ever-widening circles of association and relationships move outward. Eventually their periphery
encloses the totality of the novel. At different distances from the
center, the characters are linked to one another across time and
setting in an intricately complex pattern of human relationships.

From this kind of portrayal, with its particular structuring of
experience, can be drawn a metaphor that is most expressive of
the author's method. Georges Poulet described this metaphor when
he found in it a key to an understanding of style and structure in
Flaubert's *Madame Bovary*:

> No doubt the image suggested here is the one of a stone
> dropped in a pool. From the point where it strikes the sur-
> face, concentric waves go out in all directions. The circles
> widen, multiply, get farther from the center. So an adven-
> ture, an accident, something unprovoked, uncalled for, may
> fall suddenly into the pool of life, burst into its stillness,
> produce circles of events going outward. The accident in it-
> self is nothing; just a piece of gravel thrown in the water.
> But the small whirlpool it creates breaks the limits of the
> still narrow circle of existence, to replace them by an infi-
> nite circumference. The most insignificant event may be the
> starting point of an immense future.[7]

The scene at Borja provides just this kind of nucleus in *The
Green House*. In several discussions, critics have clearly recognized
the circular character of the novel's structure. Luis Harss and Barbara Dohmann, for example, stated: "There are no advancing lines
in *La Casa Verde*, only closing circles that spiral into each other.
They meet and merge in a moment of violent interchange, then

spin off again on their dizzying course like particles in an accelerator."[8]

In an article notable for its sensitivity, Esperanza Figueroa Amaral repeatedly refers to circularity in order to describe the novel's patterning of both form and experience. While her discussion of time is most perceptive, the interpretation of river symbolism that she offers as the novel's nuclear element does not represent an analysis that can be accepted here. But it is interesting that her interpretation draws precisely on the kind of metaphor described by Georges Poulet: "The novel is a circle. Within it the characters move in waves conditioned by the rivers. A phrase is a stone that falls into the water and from it events and thoughts emerge concentrically, from one point to another, until meeting again. The characters disappear circularly in the distance while the river continues to wind."[9]

Although their discussions do not develop the structural role of circularity at any length, these critics have nonetheless correctly identified the essential design of the novel's structure. Comments such as these plainly indicate an awareness that just as the arrangement of parts within the narrative gives origin to an image of the circle so also do the several plots organize human experience in such a way as to evoke the same image in their representation of reality.

But the element forming the nucleus of structure within *The Green House* does not pertain to the level of symbolism. Something much smaller, something much less significant, falls into the novel's "pool of life" to break the surface stillness. The catalyst at the center from which expanding peripheries radiate in all directions is nothing more, nor less, vital than one trivial segment of raw experience, one small human act. To see what the scene at Borja represents, it is necessary to recall the original context:

> Corporal Robert Delgado fidgets a good while outside the office of Captain Artemio Quiroga and has a hard time deciding. In between the ashen sky and the Borja garrison, blackish clouds are slowly passing by, and on the nearby parade ground the sergeants are drilling the recruits: attention God damn it, at ease God damn it. The air is heavy with moisture. After all, a fine was the most he could get, and the Corporal pushes open the door and salutes the Captain, who is in his office, fanning himself with one hand: what was it, what did he want, and the Corporal a pass to go to Bagua could it be arranged? What was the matter with the Corporal, the Captain is now fanning himself furiously with both hands, what

bug had bitten him. But bugs didn't bite Corporal Roberto
Delgado, because he was a jungle boy, sir, from Bagua: he
wanted a pass to see his family. And there it came again, that
blasted rain. The Captain gets up, closes the window, goes
back to his chair, his hands and face wet. So bugs didn't bite
him, wasn't it most likely because his blood was no good?,
maybe they didn't want to get poisoned, that was why they
wouldn't bite him, and the Corporal agrees: it could be sir.
The officer smiles like a robot and the rain is filling the room
with sound: the large drops are falling like stones on the cala-
mine roof, the wind whistles in the chinks of the wall. When
had the Corporal had his last pass?, last year? Oh, well, that
was a different story and the Captain's face twitches. Then
he was due for a three-week furlough.   (pp. 28–29)

As the scene opens, Corporal Delgado paces back and forth before his Captain's office. Indecisively, he struggles for courage to
make the request that has brought him there. Around him the elements of nature impose their presence. Black clouds move against
an ashen sky blocking perception of distance. The air is heavy
with humid vapors and the caustic sounds of shouting men. On a
sudden impulse, he pushes open the door and enters the room.
The Captain sits at his desk fanning himself, trying to find some
relief from the stifling heat. Outside, the wind blows hot and burning. Rain begins to fall in drops that strike the roof like small stones
and fill the room with the noise of their impact. During the ensuing conversation, the Captain rises and closes the window.
    The scene could not be more oppressive or suffocating. In this
place and time, the elements brought together in the composition
of the scene convey a vision of human existence enclosed within
narrow bounds. Corporal Delgado has not had furlough for more
than a year. His leave from duty is equivalent to an escape from a
condition of entrapment and thus represents an expansion of his
existence.
    The direction of the incident is set. The agreement with the
Captain breaks "the still narrow circle of existence" and projects
Corporal Delgado as well as others toward new and unforeseen circumstances that bring into being a continuous spreading of outlying associations. Existence, as it is portrayed in this manner, becomes a spiraling accumulation of experience, eventually drawing
all of reality into a dialectic condition of interconnectedness in a
movement toward infinity.
    While Poulet's metaphor appropriately relates to the structur-
ing of human experience in *The Green House*, certain observations

must be made in order to distinguish important divergences in the way this metaphor can be applied to the works of the two novelists. In Poulet's analysis, it is Emma Bovary's subjective consciousness that represents the center of the spiraling structure he finds in Flaubert's novel. Poulet brilliantly uses the metaphor to demonstrate the complex relationships developed in the novel between Emma's inner consciousness and the surrounding reality in which she exists. When he speaks of "concentric waves," he is referring primarily to the manner in which her consciousness can be seen to expand. Later in the article, Poulet draws this conclusion: "Thus, what Flaubert intended to show in *Madame Bovary* is a life which at one moment contracts and at another unfolds; a life which sometimes is reduced to a moment without duration and a point without dimension; and which sometimes, from that moment and from that point, extends to a circular consciousness of all its duration, of all the depths of its dreams, of all the spatiality of its environment."[10]

It should be noted first of all that these comments also have a suggestive resonance in *The Green House*. Certainly, for example, Fushía's past unfolds within a framework where time and space are largely indeterminate. The portrayal of Don Anselmo's love affair with Antonia offers no precise measurement of temporal duration. But the crucial factor, the expansion of consciousness described by Poulet, is not entirely appropriate to Vargas Llosa's novel.

Within *The Green House*, a further complexity is brought about by those narrative methods which have been seen to dissociate the characters from their own existence. In the case of Don Anselmo, his expanded consciousness of love and the forms of reality is conveyed through the external voice of the Mangachería. With regard to Fushía, the methods of narration make uncertain just how much of his unfolding past has been re-created by Aquilino. In each portrayal, then, ambiguity introduced through style and structure makes it impossible for the reader to ascertain how the consciousness of these characters actually relates to objective experience so that as personalities they might be defined accurately. The kind of expansion of personal consciousness discussed by Poulet has, therefore, no direct parallel in *The Green House*. The reader of this novel faces a quite different problem inasmuch as the subjective, objective, and mythic components of reality are so blended that the concept of personality itself loses validity in the blurring of distinctions.

Thus, the portrayal of consciousness in the two novels simply cannot assume the same structural role. In *The Green House*, personal consciousness is too diffuse to hold the center the way it can in Flaubert's novel. The correspondence is achieved on another level, the level of human acts. The decision reached at Borja represents an expansion of existence not in terms of consciousness—which in the case of Corporal Delgado is nearly totally unknown to the reader—but in the multiplication of relationships that his act acquires with events that are external to him.

Other acts on the same order have already been identified in the novel. When Bonifacia releases the girls at the mission or when Lituma plays Russian roulette with Chápiro Seminario, these acts are like smaller stones dropped within the expanding ripples of the same pool, creating their own widening peripheries that meet and merge in interlocking patterns of experience. Ambiguity occurs on this level also, but it is an ambiguity directed inward, producing uncertainty in relation to character motivation rather than in the consequences that come about as a result of such acts.

One further divergence in the application of Poulet's metaphor must be commented on. Because the coordinating element at the center of *Madame Bovary* remains a single consciousness, Poulet is able to make these final observations: "Thus the main purpose of Flaubert's novel is to create relation and order. This order is formal. From the center to the circumference, from the circumference to the center, there are constant relations. These are the relations set by the sentient subject between each moment of its consciousness and its total environment."[11] Poulet has previously argued that, for the most part in Flaubert's novel, "the circumference does not lose its relation to the center,"[12] and the novel, therefore, primarily constructs a vision of existential coherence.

This ultimate relationship between structure and theme that Poulet finds in *Madame Bovary* does not apply to *The Green House*. Lacking the kind of integrated center that can hold the multiplying circles of experience in some form of equilibrium, Vargas Llosa's novel ultimately creates the opposite view of existence. A different handling of causality introduces a fundamental absurdity in the design of reality. The discrepancy between the size of the acts at the novel's focal points and the magnitude of resulting consequences underscores a vision of disorder and chaos. Even though the causal relations between center and circumference in the two novels are different, Poulet's basic metaphor is still appropriate because, in another context, it can fully express just such an elemental imbalance in the structure of human experience.

The human acts located at the several focal points of *The Green House* are only fragments of something larger. Man himself—understood as a circumscribed consciousness or as an integral personality

—has been displaced from these centers and superseded by a fragment of his existence. The novel's structure thus builds on an element that can be seen to represent a negation of man's integrity as a complete being.

The crucial acts in the lives of characters like Corporal Delgado, Bonifacia, and Lituma define them not so much in terms of their own personalities as in terms of their relationships to their surrounding world. In and of themselves these characters, as well as others, are not integrated or whole individuals. The organization of the novel's structure in multiple and fragmented plots leaves tremendous gaps in their existence. Like the novel's form, their lives have no temporal or spatial continuity.

Thus, the breakup of order in structural arrangement corresponds to a human condition in which man loses his identity as an organic being and exists only contingently, as one element of a larger pattern of relationships. A novelistic structure based on the principle of discontinuity can develop precisely this kind of thematic interpretation by its presentation of reality in individualized fragments that themselves have no independent value and gather meaning only through the relations they acquire with other fragments. In this way, the novel's structure evokes a human condition in which a larger definition depends entirely on the coherence created by multiple relationships.

Being logically unordered and discontinuous in time and space, the fragments of the novel create an impression that time has been reduced to one dimension. For the reader, all of the fragments seem to coexist within a framework where the point of reference is always the present. Even though many individual fragments contain time shifts of various sorts or counterpointing narrations that clearly refer back to past events, the impression conveyed is still one of presentness.

In his constant effort to reconstruct sequence and causality in the lives of the characters, the reader becomes increasingly preoccupied with the problem of time. Because the characters themselves only rarely comment on its passage, he must rely heavily on his own memory of events and interpersonal relationships. As more and more characters are brought into some kind of contact by the novel's spiraling structure, temporal relations among the several ongoing stories are both illuminated and obscured and must be continually readjusted. Clarity in these matters is almost always delayed, and sometimes never completely achieved. Eventually, for example, the reader becomes aware that events in Piura are associated with two different brothels, each belonging to a different period, but the distance separating these events never comes into final focus. Several characters, in fact, are seen to disagree and offer contradictory accounts of just when the original green house once flourished; and all the while, the aged Don Anselmo continues to deny its very existence.

Such vagueness in the treatment of time is a deliberate part of the author's method and quite essential to the novel's meaning. By dramatizing the content of the characters' memories as well as their present, he makes all of reality seem contemporaneous. Within each fragment of narrative, everything merges into simultaneity. Guided by this kind of portrayal, the reader experiences an immensely heightened sense of immediacy.

Yet even while a focus on the immediate aspects of their circumstance binds the characters to the present, a contradictory impression is also involved. The divergent effects build on something of a paradox. This eternal present, having been emancipated from linear and causal progression, exhibits no flow of its own. The disruption of formal sequence places the temporal reality of each fragment in suspension. Fused this way with a condition of timelessness, the present can no longer be a completely viable concept. The novel's elaborate portrayal of the moment occurs within a structure that invalidates divisional measurements in time.

In addition, the fragments must be defined not only in isolation but also in terms of their relationships. As the reader progresses through the novel, each fragment acquires a history and in turn becomes part of the history of other fragments. With the development of relationships, the reader perceives the temporal identity of the fragments as simultaneously both present and past. In context, the fragments display complex and multiple modes of temporal existence.

The illusion of simultaneity in *The Green House* and the multiple temporal values of its fragments are not the only features contributing to a structural and thematic negation of an objective and linear concept of time. Events themselves, as they are portrayed in each story, strongly suggest that human existence in all its facets is cyclic and, in a sense, timeless. While structural fragmentation underscores the breakup of individual personality in a disordered world, certain elements within the stories establish temporal continuity on other levels. Something humanly permanent exists beneath the fleeting, disconnected moments experienced by the characters. Although disassociated from themselves and from their personal histories, the characters enact human dramas that are framed by either generic or symbolic reference and, therefore, belong to the cyclic flow of an endless past.

In a number of instances, the repetition of like events through time indicates that the present is essentially a redefinition of the past. At the mission in Santa María de Nieva, Bonifacia and the other Indian girls relive a pattern of experience that has not changed in its basic structure since the early days of the colonial period. Each year for centuries has brought a new group of girls to the mission for whom the future has held an equivalent destiny. In the Mangachería, Lituma and Chápiro Seminario destroy one another in a prefigured confrontation that links them with the past and the unfinished conflicts of other men. For nearly all the characters, life represents an intolerable cycle of entrapment and escape that reduces their aspirations to thoughts of a sanctuary where, in the places of their origins, they might find some alleviation from the final experience of extinction.

On the level of symbolism, the cyclic quality of time acquires its full meaning in yet another dimension. In the stories of Don Anselmo and Fushía, the appearance of archetypal patterns suggests that man must relive the same conflicts and imperfections that compose the unchanging realities of human experience. That these realities are essentially tragic is an interpretation appropriate to both of their stories as well as to that of Jum. Jum's defeat—vividly portrayed in the novel's Epilogue—extends to all who would assert the independence of the human spirit. Identified with the martyred Christ, Jum hangs in the plaza of Santa María de Nieva, and his agony is eloquent testimony that man is forever destined to be recrucified across time.

The role and temporal values of symbolism move the ultimate definition of the protagonists beyond a strictly existential framework. If life compels the characters of *The Green House* to participate in forming their destiny, it also severely limits the possibilities available to them.

Through different aspects of structure, the characters are simultaneously related to chronological time and emancipated from its causality, so that their stories acquire formal coherence and reveal the timeless dimension of human tragedies. Circular designs in the disposition of the plots and their chronological sequence establish predictability and unity among the narrative fragments and create uncommonly close bonds between structure and thematic expression. But it is in the elaborate patterning of relationships between a central, catalytic incident and the expanding peripheries of its outlying associations that the novel achieves an ultimate synthesis linking all of the stories across time and setting and, in so doing, shows that all of their diverse happenings constitute a single human and literary experience.

University of Idaho
Moscow

Notes

1. R. S. Crane, "The Concept of Plot and the Plot of *Tom Jones*," in *Critics and Criticism, Ancient and Modern*, ed. R. S. Crane (Chicago: Univ. of Chicago Press, 1952), p. 620.

2. Elena Poniatowska, "Al fin un escritor que le apasiona escribir, no lo que se diga de sus libros: Mario Vargas Llosa," *La Cultura en México*, no. 117, supplement to *Siempre!*, 7 July 1965, p. 3.

3. Walter Sutton, "The Literary Image and the Reader: A Consideration of the Theory of Spatial Form," *Journal of Aesthetics and Art Criticism*, 16 (September 1957), 116.

4. For a partial list of the novel's sequence of fragments, see Emir Rodríguez Monegal, "Madurez de Vargas Llosa," *Mundo Nuevo*, no. 3 (September 1966), 69-70.

5. This discussion and those pertaining to Fushía and Lituma in subsequent pages draw upon and expand my earlier analysis, "The Web of Defeat: A Thematic View of Characterization," in *Hispania*, 59 (March 1976), 11-23.

6. This aspect of the novel's structure—with its overlapping of intensities —has led a number of critics to employ terms appropriate to musical composition as a means of describing the novel's emotional texture. Emir Rodríguez Monegal (p. 72) speaks of an orchestration of elements that he, as well as José Domingo ("Crónica de novela," *Insula*, 21 [June 1966], 6), have seen building *in crescendo*. This view derives its validity from the fact that several of the displaced climaxes occur in rather rapid succession either in or very near the Epilogue.

7. Georges Poulet, "The Circle and the Center: Reality and Madame Bovary," *Western Review*, 19 (1955), 252.

8. Luis Harss and Barbara Dohmann, *Into the Mainstream: Conversations with Latin-American Writers* (New York: Harper and Row, 1967), pp. 374-75.

9. Esperanza Figueroa Amaral, "*La casa verde* de Mario Vargas Llosa," *Revista Ibero-americana*, 34 (1968), 113.

10. Poulet, p. 258.

11. Ibid., p. 260.

12. Ibid., p. 257.

Luys A. Díez

The Sources of *The Green House*: The Mythical Background of a Fabulous Novel

Out of that glittering galaxy of Spanish-American writers to invade the western literary scene in the last ten years or so, none is more expansive or articulate about his own work than the Peruvian Mario Vargas Llosa. Despite his shy personality, loathing of the cocktail circuit, and general dislike of social exchange, Vargas Llosa became, from the beginning of his career, a natural for interviewers and critics—always accessible to the tape recorder, generous with his busy time, personable, and self-effacing.[1]

In the years between the instant success of *The Time of the Hero*, which launched Vargas Llosa as the young stormy petrel of Latin America's "new novel," and the publication of his second and more ambitious novel, *The Green House*, he granted a number of long interviews that were to become a must for those interested in a deeper knowledge of his writings. Indeed, his lengthy conversations in Paris with Elena Poniatowska and Emir Rodríguez Monegal are an invaluable corpus of information about the novelist's background, formative readings, working methods, narrative techniques, and, in general, his *Weltanschauung*.[2]

In these interviews of the mid-1960s, Vargas Llosa also revealed the fascinating link between his novels and personal experiences. Thus, the traumatic years he had spent as a cadet-student at a Lima military school were reflected in his first novel, *The Time of the Hero*. For his second novel, however, the rapport between life and fiction had acquired greater proportions and complexity. *The Green House* incorporated five impressions he had experienced at different times, between 1945 and 1958, and places as far apart as the city of Piura and the Amazon jungle.

In 1971, with his fame as a writer widened and strengthened after two new books, the novella *Los cachorros* and the mammoth novel *Conversation in The Cathedral*, Vargas Llosa went back to the story of those experiences behind *The Green House* and published it in the form of a writer's log book, titled *Historia secreta de una novela* ("Secret History of a Novel").[3]

This article will deal with the strange symbiosis between reality and fiction in *The Green House* by comparing the text of the novel with the interview material, the writer's log book, and my own personal impressions after visiting the locales of the action—where reality threatens to overshadow the novelist's power of imagination. It is aimed at the American reader of Vargas Llosa who enjoys his novelistic craft in translation but has no easy access to the material mentioned, except perhaps for Luis Harss's *Into the Mainstream*, where some of the items about the sources of *The Green House* can be found.[4]

Two Tales of One City

"I have always treasured those things that have emotionally affected my life." This statement by Vargas Llosa aptly summarizes the process of composition behind *The Green House* and the degree to which personal impressions have lent narrative substance to the stories that make up its plot.

> The novel is based on five experiences I lived at different times and far-off places. It is like a synthesis of those experiences from five moments in my life.   (Interview with Monegal)

To us, the interest of these experiences is threefold: for their intrinsic human fascination, for the way in which these disparate factual elements have been pieced together into a powerfully imaginative novel, and for the process of their poetic transformation from "experienced reality" into "novelistic reality" with some striking effects, especially in the Amazon stories.

The oldest and tenderest memories pertain to a northern town close to the Ecuadorian border, Piura, which Vargas Llosa had already used as the locale for three stories in the collection *Los jefes* (1959).[5] The city of Piura dominated two vital stages of his life. Despite the time hiatus between them, both stays in that city had blended and mingled in the novelist's mind by dint of the vivid impression this quaint northern town and its colorful people had made on him. Over the years, those perceptions, memories, and images of Piura would suffer the natural, albeit mysterious process of dimming and reluming.

> Two of them, however, would increasingly acquire greater form and shape until they became two inseparable companions, two secret myths.   (*Secret History*, p. 11)

These two images, *fons et origo* of the Piuran side of *The Green House*, were a strange brothel and a slum called Mangachería. The description of that house of pleasure, turned into a mythical place by the convergence of reminiscence and novelistic creation, epitomizes the continuous juxtaposition in the novel of reality and imagination.

> It was perhaps its lonely and humid look that first aroused mine and my friends' curiosity. There was something dark and enigmatic, a diabolic aura seemed to hang around this building, which we had named "the green house." During the day, it would remain quiet, peaceful, harmless—like a lizard sleeping in the sand. But at dusk "the green house" would stir alive, full of clamorous gaiety. We could see the lights and hear the music. Furthermore, from the Puento Viejo, I and my friends, could espy the visitors . . . and gleefully recognize most of them, including our brothers, uncles and even our fathers, as they stole through the bridge towards the brothel.   (*Secret History*, p. 12)

> Seven years later, in 1952, I returned to Piura to live there for another whole year—I was sixteen. The green house was still there, in the same place. But this time I could see by myself what mysteries lay behind those green walls. It was an underdeveloped institution, hardly comfortable but rather original. It consisted of a huge single room lined up with doors that led straight into the desert. There was a three-man band: an almost blind old man who played the harp, a very young fellow who played the guitar and sang, and a kind of giant, either weight-lifter or professional wrestler, who handled the drums.   (Ibid., pp. 20–21)

Just as the character Professor Fontana in *The Time of the Hero* represents the fictional metamorphosis of the famous surrealist poet César Moro, many of the above recollections can be seen skillfully developed into memorable pages of *The Green House*.[6]

> This is how the Green House was born. . . . When the house was finished, Don Anselmo had it painted green all over. Even the children laughed hard on seeing those walls covered with an emerald skin. . . . They immediately christened it "the Green House." They were amused not only by its color, but also by its bizarre anatomy. It had two stories, but the lower one barely deserved the name: a spacious room cut by four beams, also green.   (pp. 83–84)

The children of the city would sneak out of their houses at
night and, hiding behind the bushes, would spy on visitors
and listen to the music, the laughter.   (p. 90)

And opposite the bar, in a corner, there are the musicians.
Don Anselmo, settled on a bench uses the wall as a back rest
and holds the harp between his legs. He wears glasses, his hair
falls down over his forehead. . . . The one who plays the gui-
tar and has such a melodious voice is the shy, laconic Kid
Alejandro. . . . The one sitting in the fibre chair and manipu-
lating the drum and cymbals, the least artist, the most muscu-
lar of the three, is Jocko, the ex-truck driver.   (p. 123)

But as a close analysis of this novel shows, the transposition
goes much further than a simple fictionalization of personal memories. The narrative passages quoted above represent the confluence
and emotional coexistence of two novelistic "green houses": the
one of Don Anselmo, or "foundation house," is conveyed by the
first two passages; that of Chunga, his alleged daughter, by the last
quotation. Furthermore, it raises the question of a possible relationship between the two Green Houses in the novel and Vargas
Llosa's dual experience of Piura. For it seems appropriate to relate
that earlier brothel, founded by Don Anselmo to be soon shrouded
with a mythical aura, to the novelist's childhood memories of a
fabulous green building in the Piuran desert. The parallel also applies between Vargas Llosa's description of the picturesque, albeit
sordidly real interior of the brothel and the novel's second Green
House. In fact, in another passage of *Historia secreta de una novela*,
we find a description of the brothel's madam that strongly suggests
the character Chunga.

The bar was in a corner of the salon . . . tended by an ageless
woman with a sour and puritanic expression.   (*Secret
History*, p. 21)

She was a shapeless young woman, with scant humor, and
with rather dark skin and a steely heart . . . her lipless mouth,
her eyes that watched everything with an indolence that could
make merriment dissolve.   (*The Green House*, p. 268)

Piura is also the source of another narrative area of the plot,
built around four ne'er-do-wells who called themselves *los inconquistables* ("champs" in the translation) and their favorite stamp-
ing grounds—the district of Mangachería, a sort of Dumesquean
"Court of Miracles."

The other image that lived and grew on me, like "the green house," was that of a Piura slum . . . the gaiest and most original in the whole town. All the musical groups, all the orchestras in Piura had been born in Mangachería. . . . Every Mangache felt enormous pride in having been born and bred there, considering themselves Mangache first, then Piuran and, at last, Peruvian. . . . They hated the police and boasted of never having allowed a Civil Guard patrol to roam their street at night.   (*Secret History*, pp. 15–16)

The rich vein of legends and local folklore concerning Mangachería has been dispersed throughout the novel, mostly linked to the champs' exploits as they aimlessly and noisily drink their way from *chicha* bars to brothels and chili dives. A more concentrated narrative about this subject appears in Part 3 when, after the burning of his Green House, Don Anselmo rapidly recedes into a tramp who hangs around the teeming streets of Mangachería. His later emergence as the dignified and respected "harpist" (*el arpista*) who, together with Kid Alejandro and Jocko, works for his daughter's second Green House, brings together in the fragmented plot of the novel, the two "images" of Vargas Llosa's Piuran memorabilia.

As a bridge spanning both narrative areas, we find the highly fictionalized story of Toñita, the blind-mute girl who, after surviving the massacre of her whole family in the desert, was seduced by Don Anselmo and eventually died in childbirth. This melodramatic part of the novel (a veritable *feuilleton à la* Sue), greatly compensated for by the poetic texture of its prose, rounds off the Piuran side of *The Green House* with background descriptions of the desert, the river area, and Gallinacera—a rival slum of Mangachería.

What of Piura itself—does it really possess the fascination and interest that aroused Vargas Llosa's enthusiasm? The answer from most people who have visited it tends to be in the affirmative. I still remember the impression it made on me during a short stay in the summer of 1968. The Plaza de Armas, the dry riverbed, the *chicha* bars, and the people themselves seemed to me as colorful and fascinating as they must have been in the years remembered by the novelist. It is true that Mangachería had virtually disappeared to make way for a new urban development (just as one of the champs had sadly foreshadowed) and that the sand rain, checked now by artificial dunes and new estates, no longer blanketed the streets of the central district at night. If the famous "green house" is but a local memory and its former location a contradictory issue, there is still the Colegio San Miguel, setting of Vargas Llosa's short story *Los jefes*, as well as many other places mentioned in *The Green House.*

Two of the local characters mentioned in this novel deserve in themselves a passing commentary. Father García, whom Mangache children jeer as "firebug" (*el quemador*) for his alleged participation in the burning of Don Anselmo's "Green House," was in real life Monsignor Jesús Santos García, a Spanish priest of fiery temper when provoked, who had been one of Vargas Llosa's teachers at Colegio San Miguel, as well as twice mayor of Piura, and, according to popular talk, several times a natural father. Also authentic is the braggart character of Chápiro Seminario, member of a large and powerful local family, chosen by the novelist as the epitome of Piura's renowned sense of *machismo.*

Three Amazon Stories in Search of an Author

One of the most striking aspects about the sources of *The Green House* is the way these fascinating Piuran memories blend with a new nexus of experiences lived in another remote part of Peru— the Amazon jungle.

While Vargas Llosa was still toiling with the Piuran impressions, trying to render them into fiction, he was offered a chance, which few Peruvians from the coast wish for, to visit the Amazon part of the country.[7] This happened in the summer of 1958, when he was about to leave for Spain on a graduate scholarship. The trip to the Amazon would turn out to be that felicitous and infrequent event of a writer walking straight into his future work. Settings, atmosphere, themes, and characters would gradually emerge, or even spring up, as though rallying to a preordained meeting with the novelist: Santa María de Nieva and Urakusa; the Marañón and Morona rivers; Jum and Reátegui; the Spanish missionaries and the Aguruna girls; the Civil Guards and the Huambisas; Tushía and his harem of adolescent Indians; subhuman living conditions and exploitation of the most abject sort; the nuns' heroic dedication and the iniquities resulting from their humanitarian work.

All this fabulous and authentic story, which Vargas Llosa often recounted, in synthesis, to interviewers and critics at the time of the publication of *The Green House*, was first rendered into a detailed article, "Crónica de un viaje a la selva" ("Chronicle of a Trip to the Jungle"), drafted by Vargas Llosa soon after his return from the Amazon.[8] The more recent publication of *Historia secreta de una novela* reveals the circumstances surrounding that "chronicle" and the value that Vargas Llosa gives it in retrospect.

From the start I thought of writing something about all that
and I kept a book full of notes I had made during the trip.
After a week in Lima I started for Europe, via Brazil. I remember wasting a couple of days in the splendorous city of
Rio, shut up in a hotel room, writing a chronicle on my trip
for the journal *Cultura Peruana*. This silly article and the
novelty of Europe cooled off for a while my decision of turning that short but profound Amazonian experience into a
novel.   (*Secret History*, p. 47)

This contemptuous statement by Vargas Llosa about his chronicle would seem somewhat strange and rather harsh to those who
are familiar with it and the circumstances of its publication. It was
the novelist himself who alerted me in London, before my visit to
Peru, about its existence and the possible interest it might have for
my research. Not only did it prove to be very informative, but it
also provided a comparative yardstick. For, unlike the matter-of-
fact reporting on his jungle experience that we find in *Historia secreta de una novela*, "Chronicle of a Trip to the Jungle" is a vehe-
ment, blistering indictment of the cruelty, inhumanity, and rampant corruption blatantly at work in Peru's Amazon region. Its
publication produced both horror and skepticism within the professional circles in Lima. The angry retorts and denials on the part
of high officials supposedly responsible for ignoring or condoning
the abuses could be now considered, in hindsight, as a preview of
what was to happen, five years later, when *The Time of the Hero*,
Vargas Llosa's first novel, reached readers in Lima.

The chronicle includes many aspects of jungle life that would
later be skillfully incorporated into the novel as a subtle and convincing background: the *pongos* (rapids) and *caños*, or small streams,
connecting rivers and turning most of the jungle into a vast archi-
pelago that is continuously changing in configuration; the *lupunas*,
or sacred trees, fearfully revered by the Indians; the native economy based on rubber and hides bartered to white or mestizo factors for small wares before the Indians organized themselves in co-
operatives.[9]

The factor pays with machetes, shotguns, cloths . . . whose
price he himself determines. The Indian loses on three counts:
the pricing given to his rubber is three or four times lower
than its market value; he is again cheated on the weight of
his merchandise and, finally, he is paid with goods or wares
arbitrarily priced by the factor.   ("Chronicle")

This chronicle-exposé includes many other points of information about the region, the harshness of its climate, and the pitiful living conditions confronting all the jungle's inhabitants—officials, nuns, army personnel, exploiters, and exploited. But the possible superiority of the "Chronicle" over the more pondered reporting in *Historia secreta* is the distribution of the material that gives fictional life to the three Amazon stories (of Bonifacia, of Jum, and of Fushía) that, together with those set in Piura, make up *The Green House*. Each of those three jungle stories, in their early versions in the "Chronicle," is preceded by an expressive head-title, a method Vargas Llosa often uses in earlier drafts of his novels. Their direct relationship with the novel hardly needs any commentary or interpretation.

Tushía, Bluebeard of the Jungle

The intricate plot of *The Green House* and its uncanny unfolding could be likened, metaphorically, to the fluvial web in the Amazon with its maze of main rivers, tributaries, and small streams, now joining unexpectedly, now virtually disappearing in the thick undergrowth. In this intravenous mesh of meandering narratives, Tushía's story should be viewed as the main artery where all the others (Jum, Bonifacia, Lalita, Nieves, Lituma) converge at a certain moment to veer away again toward new unhappy junctions.

Despite his importance in the novel and the vividness of his characterization, Tushía (later changed to Fushía) is only an oblique reference in Vargas Llosa's chronicle. At that time he was a living legend, an aggregate of rumors and hearsay—the locals often talked about him in awe, but few, including the novelist himself, had ever met that fabulous Japanese.

> The first concrete reference I had about any *patrón (i.e.,* factor) was in Chicais where we heard about a famous one who seems to have come out of a macabre novel. His name is Tushía, of Japanese origin, and lives on an island he owns by the Santiago River. In that inaccessible region, Tushía rules like a feudal lord. He has a private harem of women (eleven, we were told) captured by his army of desperados from Huambisa or Aguaruna villages. One of them, a girl of twelve, had fled from the island and passed through Chicais when we were there.   ("Chronicle")

Seven years later, in his conversation with Elena Poniatowska, Vargas Llosa alludes to a second journey to the jungle settings of

The Green House, after he had already completed a "final draft" of the novel: "I went in May to see what had become of Fushía and the other characters." Then he talks about "Fushía's" recent death from an almost extinct disease (*viruela negra*) and of a letter he had written during his agony to the Nieva clergy begging absolution for his crimes and requesting to be married by letter ("Cásenme por carta") to the last girl he had met and whose particulars he pathetically described.[10]

Fushía, as the readers of *The Green House* know, dies of leprosy (an almost equally anachronistic disease), and his last days at a jungle hospital are filled with sadness and a kind of remorse. The runaway girl could have inspired the character of Lalita, and some of the data about Fushía's horrendous fate was incorporated into the final version of the novel already written.

Jum of Urakusa, "Hombre Flagelado"[11]

The story of Jum was "awaiting" the novelist at the Aguaruna village of Urakusa. What the travelers learned is a familiar chapter of history—the banal degradation of primitive people by others at a higher stage of technology.

The sequence of events as stated in the "Chronicle" becomes clear in the novel only after multiple readings. As the "Chronicle" relates the sequence, it all hinges on an army corporal from the Borja garrison, Roberto Delgado Campos, who sets out by boat for the locality of Bagua to enjoy a furlough. He puts up at Urakusa for the night, and finding the village temporarily deserted (the inhabitants having taken to the woods for good measure upon his approach), he plunders it. But as Delgado and his escort are resuming their journey, they are set upon by the Aguarunas who bring them back to Urakusa as prisoners. At that point their leader (*alcalde*), called Jum, returns from a hunting trip and orders Delgado and his men to be set free and even lends the corporal his own canoe. This is what follows from Vargas Llosa's irate report:

> A few days later, a punitive expedition arrived at Urakusa, led by the Governor of Santa María de Nieva, Julio Reátegui. Jum came down to the river landing to greet, cordially, the Governor. Without any warning, Reátegui struck him on the head with his lantern. Jum and other five Indian men were arrested, whipped and kicked around by the soldiers. . . . Two women were raped—one of them, eight times in the presence of her children. Later Jum was taken to Santa María. He was stripped and hanged by the arms from a tree in the

main square. He was flogged senseless and, as a macabre touch,
they burned his arm pits with hot hard-boiled eggs. The torture was followed by humiliation—they cropped his hair.

("Chronicle")

The sober and pithy style makes the reporting of these horrors all
the more oppressive. In marked contrast, their treatment in the
novel, through the techniques of fragmentation and montage, tends
to smooth the harrowing edges and gives the reader a greater sense
of objectivity. Furthermore, in the "Chronicle" Vargas Llosa was
so incensed by the existence of such vile conditions that he pro-
ceeded dauntlessly to point his finger at all active and passive perpetrators.

> The material authors of this infernal deed are: the Lieutenant-
> Governor of Santa María de Nieva, Julio Reátegui; the Justice
> of the Peace, Arévalo Benzos; the Mayor, Manuel Aguila. . . .
> After three days of torture, Jum was allowed to return to his
> village. The Lima authorities have had knowledge of these
> events for some time. Yet, incredible though it may sound,
> none of the culprits has been indicted or suspended from his
> duties. The incident with corporal Delgado does not entirely
> justify such an outpouring of cruelty. The main reason . . .
> seems to have been the Aguaruna efforts to organize a coop-
> erative and thus escape the factors' exploitation. The Nieva
> authorities are themselves factors or middlemen. The rest
> needs no explanation.   ("Chronicle")

Years later, in reflecting on the ghastly occurrences, he would
state in the interviews and in *Historia secreta* that such abuses could
not be judged, let alone understood, as matters of individual right
or wrong, but only as part and parcel of a socioeconomic system
that thrives on corruption and injustice.

> When I went to the Upper Marañón, I discovered that Peru
> was still a more vast, more tremendous and more frightening
> place than what I gauged through my experience at Leoncio
> Prado.   (Interview with E. Poniatowska)

Yet all these brief reports on an incident he only knew through
third parties contain the whole story of Jum in the novel: the excuse of the Urakusa incident, the punitive party, the sadistic pun-
ishment of Jum, his humiliation. . . . Even the names of the places
and of the participants have been religiously preserved in the novel.

Vargas Llosa had to contrive, however, ways to link up Jum with Fushía, Bonifacia, Lalita, and Nieves. And this is one of the greatest *tours de force* in *The Green House*, depending as it does on a complex concatenation of human destinies: Nieves is forced, after the Aguaruna attack on Corporal Delgado, to find refuge in Fushía's island; his entanglement with Lalita, Fushía's woman, will lead both of them to flee the island and settle down in Santa María de Nieva; meantime, Bonifacia, who had been taken to Santa María as Jum's alleged daughter, has been brought up by the nuns; she'll be expelled from the mission and go to live with Nieves and Lalita; through them she will meet a police sergeant who courts her and eventually takes her to Piura as his wife; misfortune strikes again when sergeant Lituma is sent to a Lima prison and Bonifacia becomes one of the "inmates" at Piura's second "Green House," where she feels filially attracted to a semiblind harp player.

Two necessary additions to Jum's story are his subsequent repeated trips to Santa María to claim the goods stolen from him after he was arrested and tortured by Reátegui, and the story of two mysterious Lima teachers who indoctrinate the Aguarunas about how to form their own cooperative. Both narrative items are enacted obliquely in the so-called Porticos or *narrativas flotantes* (to use the novelist's terminology) that open each of the novel's four parts and the Epilogue.

In spite of the richness of all this material and Jum's apparent importance in the plot, the reader will not be exactly overwhelmed by his presence in the novel. In fact, by one of those mysterious quirks in literary creation, Jum suffers a diminishing process to the point of being reduced to a mere shadow, while Fushía, a more improbable character at the start, is felt with the true vividness of a full-fledged protagonist.

> I tried many times to reconstruct what might have been the course of his life, from the time he was thrown into the world in the bush or on a river beach up to that barbarous moment when he was hanging from a tree. . . . But every attempt sounded artificial, phoney, clumsily folkloric. . . . Finally I yielded to the evidence: I was not sufficiently able to present the world, the abject injustices, the other men, through the eyes and conscience of this man whose language, costumes and beliefs I ignored. I was forced to reduce Jum's importance in the novel and broke down his story into several short episodes which were retold, not from Jum's viewpoint but through the perspective of intermediaries or witnesses.
>
> (*Secret History*, pp. 65–66)

The Fate of an Aguaruna Girl

The character of Bonifacia, the Aguaruna pupil from the Nieva mission whose bitter destiny ultimately leads her to the second Green House, is another interesting example of narrative symbiosis. The genesis of this character results from the union of two experiences during Vargas Llosa's first trip to the jungle. The first experience is his encounter with an Indian girl who had been forcedly transported to Lima to work as a domestic and was later miraculously returned to her Aguaruna family by one of Vargas Llosa's traveling companions.

> Esther Chuwik is about ten-years old. She is tall, delicate, with light eyes and a fine voice. . . . She was, like many other jungle children, kidnapped three years ago and taken to Lima. E. M. Best was able to locate her and bring her back to her own family. Now she is a student at the Chicais bilingual school where she shares a desk with her father. In Chicais alone there is evidence of twenty-nine kidnappings. The factors, the engineers, the army officers and even the missionaries take away the girls for domestic work. There are cases of taking several of them for friends and relations in the cities. All this I would have found too incredible if I had heard about it in Lima.   ("Chronicle")

When I read this part of the "Chronicle" and the particular way the girl was remembered by Vargas Llosa, I could not help thinking of Bonifacia in the novel. It is her pronounced light green eyes and endearing vague sadness that distinguish her through the different stages of character development: as a little child clinging to Jum's leg in the boat; as Bonifacia, the trustee at the mission house; and as Wildflower (*Selvática*) in Chunga's establishment. Her entire story exudes a strong note of melancholy and nostalgia, from her early appearance arguing her case with the Mother Superior up to that section of the Epilogue where she is overcome by the death of Don Anselmo—himself the symbol of a lost father-figure, more desired than actually remembered. Hence the ambiguous references in the novel to Jum's paternity and Don Anselmo's vague allusion to his Amazon origin.

This part of the "Chronicle" and the following section dealing with the forced recruitment of Indian girls to be "civilized" by the nuns at their Nieva school, corresponds to the novel's opening: the arrival at Chicais of the missionaries and their escort of Civil Guards.

Thus the story of Esther Chuwik and the dubious humanitarian work of the nuns becomes the fifth source of *The Green House.*

> In Urakusa we learned, too, of the methods used by well-meaning people to "impose" civilization on the Indians. Santa María de Nieva has a mission and a Catholic school for the Upper Marañón area. Due to the travelling difficulties, along the river, the missionaries make recruiting excursions every so often in search of students. The enrollment of pupils acquires at times the aspect of a kidnapping. The recruiters are accompanied by soldiers to neutralize any possible resistance by the Indian parents to giving up their little daughters. . . . I have seen photographs of the kidnapping of two girls at Urakusa—aboard a boat one could see two nuns with taciturn faces, surrounded by soldiers and, by their side, the kidnapped girls.   ("Chronicle")

The real tragedy in this process of education inevitably happened when the girls grew up. Since they were by then estranged from their old indigenous habitat, and since the mission could not provide for further education or training, they were placed as maids in the cities. Unfortunately, many of them are eventually snared into prostitution (cf. Bonifacia).

After his second journey to the Amazon, in 1964, Vargas Llosa stated in several interviews, and at greater length in *Historia secreta,* that the overall situation regarding the missionary work and the fate of the Indian pupils appeared to have improved considerably. Not only did the Spanish nuns who run the mission now appear to him in a more humane light ("the personal case of these missionaries deserved respect and admiration"), but also the forced recruitment of pupils had given way, in his view, to the voluntary entrusting of the girls by the parents. All these changes in evaluation were incorporated into the last draft of the novel.

The Fortunate Union of Two Conflicting Novels

The five experiences that give novelistic substance to *The Green House* could ultimately be viewed as a sample of the social ailments afflicting countries like Peru. None of them, however, has found its way directly from real life to novelistic reality, nor can they be considered at the same level as the "fictionalized anthropology" of the prewar Indigenist writers.

What we have in *The Green House* is a paradigm of true narrative transposition. Each of those images or experiences, once recorded in the sensitive mind of a talented novelist, underwent an intensive process of germination, surfacing at times to blend with newly acquired impressions. Such was the case, for instance, of Fushía. Devoid of a concrete past in Vargas Llosa's Amazon memorabilia, Fushía was provided with a biographical background from two unexpected sources: a faded recollection the novelist had of one of his Bolivian uncles who, at the time of the Second World War, dealt in contraband strategic material; and Vargas Llosa's own impressions of the Brazilian capital of Mato Grosso, Campo Grande, during a stopover in his flight from Lima to Rio (cf. *Secret History*, p. 63).

But the most fascinating aspect of the convoluted composition of *The Green House* has to be the convergence of Piuran and Amazonian themes—something that has captivated readers as much as critics. For a while, the novelist himself seemed reticent when asked about this point. Thus, he evasively answered Rodríguez Monegal:

> In actual fact . . . the five stories are linked together by their atmosphere and by sharing some of the same characters, who move from one to the other story.
>
> (Interview with Monegal)

The truth is, however, that *The Green House* had a dual composition. Vargas Llosa, rather tired and discouraged over a novel he was writing on his Piuran memories, decided at one point to alternate it with another novel on the events he had witnessed in the Amazon. The confluence of both narrative areas was virtually a Pirandellian phenomenon as several characters seemed to force their way from one to the other area.

> In point of fact I did not succeed (with the alternate writing). . . . Every day I had to confront a horrendous confusion. Absurdly enough, my greatest efforts were directed at keeping every character in its right place. The Piurans were invading Santa María de Nieva; the jungle characters were determined to slip into "the green house." It became increasingly harder to hold all of them in their respective worlds. . . . In the end the whole thing was foundering in a sea of chaos. . . . I decided then . . . to merge both worlds and write one single novel that would absorb all that mass of memories. It would take me another three years and plenty of tribulations to sort out such a disorder. *(Secret History*, pp. 51–53)

As we all well know by now, this happy encounter of the desert dunes and the jungle undergrowth, of *inconquistables* and *selváticos*, of "the green house" and the mission, of Fushía and Don Anselmo, of Chunga and Bonifacia, turned this novel into a jewel of imagination and narrative craft. But if I were forced to make a choice, I fancy that it would be Piura that would come to the rescue of the jungle and win the day. It is the Piuran stories that add the yeast of poetic sensibility to the dazzling techniques so arduously wrought to chart the quavering Amazonian chaos.

Queens College of CUNY
Flushing, New York

Notes

1. It would be hard to compute all of Vargas Llosa's interviews in the last seven years. José Miguel Oviedo, in his all-inclusive bibliography, records some forty. See J. M. Oviedo, *Mario Vargas Llosa. La invención de una realidad* (Barcelona: Barral Editores, 1970).

2. Elena Poniatowska, "Al fin un escritor que le apasiona escribir," *La Cultura en México*, 117 (Suplemento de *Siempre!*), 7 July 1965, p. II–VIII. Emir Rodríguez Monegal, "Diálogo con M. Vargas Llosa," *Ercilla* (Santiago de Chile), 6 July 1966, pp. 34–35, 39.

3. Mario Vargas Llosa, *Historia secreta de una novela* (Barcelona: Tusquet Editores, 1971). Fittingly, it is printed in green ink.

4. Luis Harss, "The Revolving Doors," in *Into the Mainstream* (New York: Harper and Row, 1967), pp. 342–76. Interested readers will find Harss's book an excellent mixture of interview and sobering, original criticism.

5. The three stories with Piuran settings are *Los jefes* (Colegio San Miguel), *El desafío* (Mangache-like atmosphere) and *Un visitante* (vivid description of Piuran desert, featuring a policeman called Sargento Lituma).

6. Cf. Nelson Osorio Tejada, "La expresión de los niveles de realidad en la narrativa de Vargas Llosa," in *Asedios a Vargas Llosa* (Santiago: Editorial Universitaria, 1972), pp. 67–88. Mario Vargas Llosa himself has evoked, in a poignant article, Moro's ordeal as instructor of French in Leoncio Prado: "Notas sobre César Moro," *Literatura* (Lima), 1 (February 1958), 5.

7. Virtually half of Peru's area is jungle. Yet, most Peruvians live close to the coast or in the Sierras, oblivious of the true physical nature of their country.

Vargas Llosa's journey to the Amazon was organized by "Instituto Lingüístico de Verano," a missionary-linguistic organization from Oklahoma University that has been working in the entire Amazon basin for several decades. They compile Indian languages and train Indians as bilingual teachers. During my visit to Chicais, I was able to talk to Jum through one of his sons who is an accredited bilingual teacher.

8. Mario Vargas Llosa, "Crónica de un viaje a la selva," *Cultura Peruana*, 123 (September 1958), no pages recorded.

9. In his *Historia secreta*, Vargas Llosa recounts, with his usual candor, the difficulties he encountered in achieving the right background and atmo-

sphere for the novel, without falling into the usual excesses of the *novelística de la selva*, a veritable subgenre with many practioners in Peru itself.

10. Vargas Llosa admits (*Historia secreta*) having read the letter in Nieva and having been deeply touched by its pathetic tone. It would be interesting to find out if the poetic, moving passages, describing Fushía's wretched last days, were part of the final rewriting after this second journey to the jungle.

11. For this subtitle introducing the second jungle source (or theme), I have retained the original Spanish of Vargas Llosa's phrase introducing the corresponding section of the "Chronicle." To translate "hombre flagelado" as "flagellated man" or "flogged man" would be to lose the symbolic overtones of Vargas Llosa's phrase.

Alan Cheuse

Mario Vargas Llosa and *Conversation in The*
Cathedral: The Question of Naturalism

Where have the critics gone wrong? The astonishing success during
the past decade of Latin American novelists who accentuate the
technique of "magical realism" seems to have blinded most readers
to the persistence in the work of Mario Vargas Llosa of a hardy
strain of naturalism. But as any reader, new or initiated, of the
stunningly broad, expansive context of Vargas Llosa knows or soon
discovers, he is not merely roaming around in a traditional nineteenth-century novelistic "world," immersed in the fiction of the
most proficient Flaubertian or Balzacian in Lima. While apparently true to the naturalistic code that characters are basically determined by heredity and environment, Vargas Llosa questions the
very idea of environment. The juxtaposition of jungle and city
forges a new vision that leads us, at least as we read, to become
aware of the inscrutable forces behind each of the figures in the
various social groups that comprise the main actors in the novel.

In *The Green House*, Vargas Llosa added a new "context" to
the geographical regions of city, desert, mountain, and jungle:
this is the "region" of time past and the "region" of time present.
This addition creates a "three-dimensional" narrative in which the
traditional display of naturalistic principles cannot be separated
from the modernist outlook. With regions of *time* overlaying regions of *geography*, the reader finds new and innovative time-spaces
in which to ponder the activity of men and women under the internal pressures of psyche. Some of these land and time spaces unknown to traditional nineteenth-century fiction are city-present,
city-past; desert-present, desert-past; jungle-present, jungle-past;
and, to add to the deepening sense of uncertainty that abounds in
the supposedly concrete "environment" of the naturalist's world,
city-past as narrative present, city-present as narrative past; desert-
past as narrative present, desert-present as narrative past, jungle-
past as narrative present. In the massive *Conversation in The Ca-*
thedral, Vargas Llosa's contexts or zones of time and being appear
in paradoxical but equally striking form. Instead of associating

time with various geographical locations as in *The Green House*,
we find here temporal zones that imply specific kinds of topological presences. In other words, in *The Green House* space seems to
take priority over time whereas in *Conversation* time takes priority
over space.

For those, like myself, who found much that was persuasive in
Ronald Christ's important article on Vargas Llosa's "film sense"
(which appeared in the Spring 1976 issue of *Review*), the time
scheme within the fiction of *Conversation* must be invoked as evidence against Christ's view that Vargas Llosa is wholly "filmic" in
his use of rhetorical "montage" at the expense of linear progression. *Conversation* opens in the narrative present ("Santiago looks
at the Avenida Tacna without love"), in the middle of the life of
Santiago Zavala, son of the late Peruvian industrialist Don Fermín
Zavala. Lima is under the thrall of an epidemic of rabies. Zavala,
a communist during his university days, is writing editorials attack-
ing the sloth of the city administration's handling of the stray dog
problem for the muckraking pages of *La Crónica*. The first chapter (of the first of the novel's four sections) carries the reader along
for many pages in a single tense and plane (the present, in Lima).
Zavala sets out in quest of his wife's dog, which has been dragooned
by dogcatchers anxious to earn their commission (ironically, part
of the city's response to Zavala's own editorials). He encounters
Ambrosio, a black man, now a dogcatcher, who once drove his
father's limousine as well as the limousine of the notorious Cayo
Bermúdez, Minister of Security under the regime of the dictator
Odría (during Santiago's university days). Only then does the
epic "conversation" commence in "La Catedral," the bar-restau-
rant-brothel where Santiago and Ambrosio retire for drinks and
reminiscences.

Nearly twenty pages of linear narrative in the present tense prepare the way for the limited "montage" effects, those sequences
in which the narrative shifts from present conversation (ostensibly
moving forward in time present) to the scenes out of the past (various levels of the past to be exact). This linear present-tense "over-
ture" to the more complicated main body of the novel enunciates
clearly Vargas Llosa's naturalistic assumptions. Following the epi-
gram from Balzac ("le roman est l'histoire privée des nations"),
Zavala's opening interrogation ("At what precise moment had Peru
fucked itself up?") seems almost programmatically naturalistic
both in diction and ethos. The association between the epidemic
of rabid dogs and the deterioration of the psychic lives of the city's
inhabitants, the main motif of the opening sequence, further establishes the novel's roots in the naturalistic tradition. The every-

day details of Zavala's progress, his encounter with one of his fellow reporters, his passage across town to discover that his own dog has been snatched, his arrival at the dog pound (where he witnesses the brutal murder of the stray dogs), all reinforce the naturalistic atmosphere. The scene is degraded, enervating, the spirit bowed. When Zavala and Ambrosio retire to La Catedral, the metaphor of the world as brothel (which Vargas Llosa plays on in *The Green House* by superimposing the image of the brothel called The Green House and the jungle in all its green and lushy decay) emerges as the central image of the novel, an image clearly naturalistic in meaning and texture.

What then distinguishes Vargas Llosa's relentless attention to the smell and feel of the actual world from the nineteenth-century models of Balzac, Flaubert, and Zola? Or from the twentieth-century American novelists whose pages his seem to resemble, John Dos Passos and Dreiser? One immediate response must be that, as Ronald Christ has suggested, his "meaning" lies not so much in the nature of the materials as in the nature of the presentation of the materials. The habitual use of the "montage" effect, or, as I would prefer to regard it, the manipulation of the "environment" of time itself, clearly separates *Conversation in The Cathedral* from the methods of conventional naturalism (which presumes a steady, linear, temporal progression and a cause-and-effect relationship between past and present, action and actor).

Consider the opening of section seven, Part I, where Vargas Llosa juxtaposes the discussion between Bermúdez and an assistant against the flight of a desert buzzard and its subsequent demise at the hands of a hungry peasant.

It was noontime, the sun fell straight down onto the sand, and a buzzard with bloody eyes and black plumage was flying over the motionless dunes, descending in tight circles, his wings folded back, his beak ready, a slight glimmering tremor on the desert.

"Fifteen were on file," the Prefect said. "Nine Apristas, three Communists, three doubtful. The other eleven had no record. No, Don Cayo, they haven't been interrogated yet."

An iguana? Two maddened, little feet, a tiny, straight-lined dust storm, a thread of gunpowder lighting up, a rampant invisible arrow. Softly the bird of prey flapped his wings at ground level, caught it with his beak.   (p. 111)

The reader seems to perceive the conversation about subversion at the university, which is the subject of the Prefect's remarks, and

the flight and death of the bird of prey simultaneously. This lends
the text a spatial quality. However, with respect to the novel's
chronology, the scenes are widely spearated in time. The former
takes place early in the novel's time scheme (when Zavala is still
at the university), and the latter occurs around the time of Bermúdez' downfall. Thus cause and effect cease to hold in this atmosphere in which time past and time near-distant stand in relationship to each other as hill to pond, dune to ocean shore—in
"geographical" rather than causal positioning.

One time block reflects back or forward upon the other (in the
manner, as Ronald Christ has accurately pointed out, of the "wandering rocks" section of *Ulysses*). For example, in the scene just
prior to the one from which I have quoted, there is a three-time-
tiered passage in which Santiago and Ambrosio in the present in
La Catedral evoke by means of their discussion Zavala's infatua-
tion with the proto-communist student Aida during his days at the
University of San Marcos. *At the same time*, the reader stumbles
on one of the mysterious patches of dialogue between Don Fermín
and Ambrosio which threads its way through the novel. This micro-
conversation refers to Ambrosio's murder of Bermúdez' mistress
"La Musa" in order to end the possibility of her blackmailing Don
Fermín, whose homosexuality remains as much a mystery to the
uninitiated reader as the murder itself:

> "I don't know what to do, I feel confused, I have doubts,"
> Aida finally said. "That's why I called you, I thought all of a
> sudden that you could help me."
> "And I began to talk about politics," Santiago says. "See
> what I mean?"
> "Of course," Don Fermín said. "Getting away from the
> house and Lima, disappearing. I'm not thinking about my-
> self, you poor devil, I'm thinking about you."
> "But what do you mean when you say that," as if startled,
> he thinks, scared.
> "In the sense that love can make a person very much an
> individualist," Santiago said. "And then he gives it more im-
> portance than anything, the revolution included."
> "But you were the one who said that the two things weren't
> incompatible," hissing, he thinks, whispering. "Do you think
> they are now? How can you be sure you're never going to fall
> in love?"
> "I didn't believe anything, I didn't know anything," San-
> tiago says. "Just wanting to leave, escape, disappear."

"But where, sir?" Ambrosio said. "You don't believe me, you're kicking me out, sir."
"Then it's not true that you have doubts, you're in love with him, too," Santiago said.   (pp. 108–09)

In Zavala's quest to discover at what point he, like Peru, has "fucked himself up," this juxtaposition of conversations about love—love between himself and Aida, between Aida and Jacobo (another member of their radical group at San Marcos who is the cause of Aida's "confusion" and the referent of the pronoun "him" in the last statement), and love between Don Fermín and Ambrosio—dramatizes the fluctuating nature of meaning with respect to the relationship of past and present. For one moment it seems that Don Fermín is telling Santiago to leave town; in another it appears that he is advising Ambrosio (after the murder the black driver commits as an act of love for his employer) to "disappear." The love that Santiago speaks about in relationship to his thwarted feelings for Aida (and her masked affection for the hypocritical Jacobo) also refers the reader to Don Fermín's feelings for Ambrosio and vice-versa.

The effect here clearly sets Vargas Llosa's pages apart from those of conventional naturalism where any confusion of the intellect or the senses must belong to one or another of the characters but never to the reader or the "character" of the text itself. The reader senses here, as he does in *The Time of the Hero* and *The Green House*, a kind of psychic leak in which emotions abound that may or may not be attached to any single character, thus lending the text or scene a sense or feeling as though it were a character itself. This dispersal of individual character for the sake of the success of the text is not a new invention. Joyce lends *Ulysses* a "character" above and beyond that of either Dedalus' or Bloom's. Call it tone, mood, or whatever, clearly the totality of the narrative's language takes on a "life" that the reader cannot easily forget. We can go back to Flaubert, mentor of both Joyce and Vargas Llosa, to find the first serious instances of the "character" of the text becoming a salient feature of the narrative. With this in mind, we can consider that psyche itself becomes a geographical or topological "location"—mind turns into landscape, a "spatial" phenomenon as well as a temporal one in which the reader may "roam" about and ponder the "view."

Time, in these parts, becomes not so much a major constituent as the entire complex of time-plus-space and character-in-context; it functions as a musical key, or as color in a painting, a defining

but not a definitive factor. This is hardly the sustaining metaphys-
ic of a programmatic twentieth-century naturalist. Rather, it stands
as a major revision of the naturalist belief in the substantiality of
nothing but the physical and chemical world. What is natural as
well in a world of processes is the way in which the feeling imagination works on the materials of the past. Yet even the feeling
imagination working through the links between present and past,
and the relationship of one mind to another in the present, may
be seen in a larger "natural" context, the context of "society," a
complex tapestry of geography, tribes, and time. Among modern
novelists with a naturalist's disposition, only Dos Passos comes
close to effecting such a major revisioning of the nineteenth-century novelistic aesthetic.

There is yet another problematical element that arises out of
a reading of Vargas Llosa as a pure naturalist. As Luis Harss has
pointed out (elsewhere in this issue), individuals tend to get lost
in Vargas Llosa's vast landscapes. Add the vastness of the "time-
scape," and one might wonder how, if at all, Vargas Llosa's characters manage to survive in our memories (where all books finally
live or die). Here we must admit the presence of myth, and the
notion that myth, usually considered antithetical to the naturalistic novelist's disposition, plays an important role in these dramas
as well. For how else do we recall the fascinating criminal Fushía
of *The Green House*, a figure as memorable as Balzac's Vautrin, if
not by the paradoxical means by which the environment itself
forges characters who represent it as a way of being? And how
then can one separate the question of Vargas Llosa's "naturalism"
from his critical awareness of twentieth-century "modernist" issues, which he expresses in techniques quite alien to the nineteenth-
century narrative mode? What Harss describes as the "tidal movement of shadowy figures up and down the river of life and death"
rises up from the text as river fog emanates from the moving wa-
ters, suggesting to the reader that it is not for the facts but for the
mystery rising from the facts that he reads.

The creation of myth and mystery might at first seem antithetical to the naturalist's purposes. Balzac's quest, and Flaubert's, we
assume, was to enlighten us about the patterns made by human
figures as they dance to the music of the Bourse. How does society
in its plenitude function? How does it "work"? As Erich Auerbach
suggested in *Mimesis*, Balzac's methods may be intelligently compared to those of nineteenth-century zoology. But is the generation of myth and mystery finally alien to the naturalistic writer?
Not if the reader recalls Balzac's lifelong interest in the occult. Not
if we consider Flaubert's pursuit—through the figure of Emma

Bovary—for meaning beyond the actual things of this world. Not if we recall the attempt to lay bare the mysterious driving forces of life in the best work of Dos Passos or Dreiser.

Vargas Llosa stands then in the tradition of the great practitioners of the nineteenth-century novel, presenting the world as it appears to the senses while at the same time extending the form by using the feeling imagination with the same extraordinary results as the so-called magical realists. His extraordinary effects thus upset the critical reader's customary notions of naturalism, realism, and fantasy. They bring to light once again—as does all important narrative fiction—the knowledge that beneath the smooth flowing surfaces of the text a vitality abounds that no method or rubric can either quantify or control.

Bennington College
Bennington, Vermont

Jean Franco

Conversations and Confessions: Self and Character

in *The Fall* and *Conversation in The Cathedral*

Vargas Llosa's early novels, *The Time of the Hero* and *The Green House*, both dispensed with the traditional practice of representing character as developing organically over a period of time. His characters are thus susceptible to abrupt changes of identity when removed from one context to another. For instance, the Sergeant and Lituma of *The Green House* are genetically one and the same but seem different persons. First as soldier and then as a member of a gang of *machos* (and hence inscribed successively within different times and different realities), the Sergeant and Lituma respond to different codes of behavior. Unlike the classical-realist novelists of the nineteenth century for whom moral responsibility was often related to the gradual unfolding of a personal identity, Vargas Llosa projects a self radically separated from any continuity with the past and only able to acquire ethical status by the conscious reinvention of a project. His third major novel, *Conversation in The Cathedral*, is a striking illustration of an attempt to constitute character through activating conscious recollection.

At this point, it is perhaps worth recalling that individualized fictional characters developing over a period of time have traditionally constituted a locus for the novelist's moral concern and for the projection of attitudes to the self. Despite the slightly different significance between the English "character" and the Spanish "*personaje*," both have connotations of individual and constitutive roles in the spectacle of life.[1] Originally derived from the term for an engraving instrument, "character" came to refer to distinctive features or traces and hence both to that which distinguished one self from another and to the moral strength and discipline that involved acting according to coherent principles. Since we refer to a "good" and a "bad" character, the term also carries strong moral connotations, so that it is hardly surprising that a substantial body of English criticism should have judged characters as it would living people, and has viewed great novels as existing to "reveal and explore character."[2] On the other hand, the Spanish

"personaje" (and the French *"personnage"*), which derives from
persona (mask), is, like the English "personality," closely associated with the phenomenal, with the individual as viewed from the
outside and distinct from an essential self. However, both "character" and *"personaje"* suggest strong individualized traits whose
very uniqueness is a mark of their "truth to life."[3]

As Fredric Jameson points out, however, a literature of consciousness—and existentialism is this—demands a quite different
configuration. To begin with, consciousness is not the unfolding
of an inner self but a project to be realized and the existentialist
character's relation to the past is not a continuation of a linear
process but something to be reinvented at every instant.[4] Further,
since existentialism places the onus of freedom on the reader and
not necessarily on the characters, the author must offer as little
mediation as possible in the way of value-loaded descriptions and
comments. Thus, Sartre's "orchestration of consciousness" was
elaborated to enable the reader to enter the character's mind "as
into a windmill."[5] It is also clear that a literature of consciousness
no longer needs strongly individualized characters, for it is not the
accidental variety of personal histories that are important so much
as the more generalized potential for feeling and understanding in
a common world.[6] Sartre's *The Reprieve* is, perhaps, the best example of the kind of novel I am speaking about.[7] In it, the Munich
crisis of 1938 is refracted through the reactions and statements of
a number of people, and consciousness becomes generalized throughout the text rather than concentrated and intensified in one or
two protagonists.

Conversation in The Cathedral obviously owes something to
The Reprieve since it, too, presents us with an orchestration of
consciousness around a single historical moment—in this case, the
years between 1948 and 1963, which includes the entire Odría
regime (1948–56), a regime noteworthy for its repressiveness and
corruption. Indeed, as in *The Reprieve*, there are moments when
the "characters" are named but then dissolve back into the chorus
of the text so that their discourse is identifiable only when new
information becomes available to the reader. However, unlike *The
Reprieve*, which plunges the reader into a kind of multitudinous
and simultaneous consciousness, *Conversation in The Cathedral*
makes time a silent agent. It is this unnamed presence that dislo-
cates the identity of the characters and mocks the intentionality
of the conversations that form the bulk of the text. Given the basic difference between these two novels, it seems to me that *The
Fall* by Albert Camus offers a more significant comparison with
Vargas Llosa's novel, for here, too, time forms the ironic under-

current to the manifest text. Further, the irony also allows critical scrutiny of the speech act—confession—which constitutes "character" in the two novels.

As a narrative, *The Fall* consists of a confession made by the judge-penitent, Clamance, before a silent listener whose generic characteristics (he is an educated bourgeois) are those of any cultivated reader. The "church" in which he begins his confession is the Mexico City Bar in Amsterdam, a setting that anticipates the cathedral-bar of *Conversation in The Cathedral*. Clamance is, by implication, confessing in a world without perfection, without a God authorized to dispense absolution and forgiveness. What substitutes for God and the Sacred is a contract between the silent bourgeois listener (who is analogous to the reader) and Clamance who will provide efficient bar service (he has a hold over the barman) in exchange for telling his story. Considering himself superior, because of his education, to the barman who does not even speak his language, for the barman is Dutch and Clamance French, the judge-penitent must waylay a listener who shares a common culture and language. At this level, *The Fall* can be read as an allegory of literature which is a marginalized activity within bourgeois society.

The sin to which Clamance confesses is one all too familiar in the modern world: it is that the self which is formed by and responds to social approval and standards is out of joint with some more authentic self. Borne along by public approval of his charitable activities as a lawyer, Clamance is one day awakened by a mocking laugh to the fact that his words do not coincide with his deeds. The laughter that comes out of nowhere appears to be the only language left to the real self. Thus made conscious of a maladjustment, Clamance ceases to be a contented citizen and, instead, anxiously tries to line up his social image with his authentic self, first by acting out his real feelings in court and then in his relations with women. Finally, he becomes an "empty prophet for shabby times," a "judge-penitent" in Amsterdam, whose canals circle the city like the circles of Dante's hell. He is now aware that the "keenest of human torments is to be judged without a law" and anxious, for this very reason, to implicate his listener in the common guilt. This does not mean that Clamance is now authentic; only that he has found a way of reconciling personal pride and public morality by controlling others and enslaving them to their human condition. He has discovered that he can avoid the isolation of guilt by *telling his story* and confessing. Thus, when eventually confined to his room by sickness, he confesses that he is hiding a stolen Van Eyck painting, *The Just Judges*, and also symbolically reveals the inauthenticity of that inner room of the self where he is "king, pope and judge" and where he still, nevertheless, poses and postures for a public. It is at this point, however, that he also explains his storytelling technique, which has mischievous similarities to Sartrean practice.

> I choose the features we have in common, the experiences we have endured together, the failings we share—good form in other words, the man of the hour as he is rife in me and others. With all that, I construct a portrait which is the image of all and of no one. A mask, in short, rather like those carnival masks which are both lifelike and stylized, so that they make people say "Why, surely I've met him." When the portrait is finished, as it is this evening, I show it with great sorrow: "This, alas, is what I am."[8]

There is an analogy here between Clamance's self-portrait and the fictional characters in some of Sartre's earlier work—for example, *Nausea*—and an implicit criticism of the moral exhibitionism involved in such fictional projections. "Committed" literature is shown to be a subtle instrument for implicating the reader in the author's manipulation of power. Clamance thus becomes a kind of parody, a confessor who can act as a God by making everyone feel as guilty as himself, and who then stands back to watch their Last Judgment:

> They rise slowly: I already see the first of them arriving. On his bewildered face, half hidden by his hand, I read the melancholy of the common condition and the despair of not being able to escape it. And as for me, I pity without absolving, I understand without forgiving and above all, I feel at last that I am being adored.   (p. 143)

The Fall is, however, more than a parody of Sartrean commitment, for it also reveals the ambiguity of confession. The baring of the soul *in extremis* (Clamance is old and ill) supposedly guarantees the revelation of a self free from posturing. However, the very rules of confession, which are structured according to moral abstractions, make nonsense of sincerity. Confession only permits revelation to be filtered through the grid of precoded categories. That is why that inner self which Clamance tries to call into being through confession is the mirror image of the "other" he addresses whilst this "other" is, in turn, the externalized image of the only self he recognizes. Confession is thus tautological, confirming that which is already presupposed by the confessional structure, which in turn is produced by social law and power. Thus, even though Clamance gives up his success within the system when he feels that his sense of individual worth has been undermined, his solution is to rearrange matters according to another plan in which he still exercises power but in a different way. He becomes a rebel whose rebellion confirms and does not challenge the system. And he is able to maintain this role because of the very fact that tautological confession prevents the intrusion of otherness. The "other" can only be divined through silence, laughter, and in the incidental visions of nature. The beauty of the canals and the falling snow glimpsed fleetingly by Clamance constitute counterpoints within the monotone; and they mark, in Blanchot's term, "a secondary progression" that silently accompanies Clamance's babble.[9]

> See the huge flakes drifting against the windowpanes. It must be the doves, surely. They finally made up their minds to come down, the little dears; they are covering the waters and the roofs with a thick layer of feathers; they are fluttering at every window. What an invasion! Let's hope they are bringing good news. Everyone will be saved, eh?—and not only the elect.   (p. 145)

Clamance, who prides himself on preaching servitude in order to force others to share in the common guilt of the human condition and thus escape judgment himself, here represents the snow as the paraclete. In the religion of nature, there can be no elect few, no privilege, however, so that both he and his discourse, by contrast, seem vain and superfluous.

Camus once described the technique of *The Fall* as dramatic monologue and implied dialogue.[10] As Maurice Blanchot rightly points out, however, the dialogue is imprisoned within the monologue, for the debate is always in Clamance's consciousness.[11] Further, the more Clamance speaks of his "self," the emptier and more ambiguous that self becomes. Thus Blanchot concludes:

> The impersonality of his features, the general nature of his characteristics, the details that have nothing unique about them and even the remorse which seems borrowed from one of Stendhal's letters, this "disdainful confession" which confesses nothing that is recognizable as a lived experience, all that which, with classical discretion depicts man in general and the great impersonality of all is presented here only to

make us await the presence of someone who is almost no-
body, the alibi in which he traps us so that he might escape.[12]

Thus Camus makes confession the supreme form of evasion and
speech the instrument of self-concealment. Such evasion, however,
seems to stem from the very nature of the system for the place of
the individual is already decreed and delimited by law. Yet law
cannot be based on an absolute, for God the Father no longer un-
derwrites it. Hence, we are left with an empty rhetoric that allows
the individual only the self-assertion of a personal style (*parole*).
Since rhetoric (*parole*) is always motivated by the need to persuade
and hence to exercise power over others, it leaves no space for a
self outside the system. Only nature stands as a bulwark against
human intentionality; only nature is unaltered by discourse. Thus,
if we are to find a human *nature* that escapes the corruption of
power and the posturings of rhetoric, it must be grounded in this
reality in which the "human" is contingent. And here lies the paradoxical axis of the novel. For Clamance's very consciousness, his
apparent frankness and lucidity protect him against profounder
truths to which nature and time bear testimony.

The deceptive frankness of Clamance's confession is analogous
to the deceptiveness of the conversations in Vargas Llosa's novel.
As I shall show, both novels reveal discourse to be the exercise of
power. What takes place in *Conversation in The Cathedral* is not
a true dialogue between the journalist Santiago and the ex-chauf-
fer Ambrosio, but rather separate recollections that take the form
of dismembered dialogues with other people in the past. As each
man evokes different incidents in the past, these come together to
form new and revealing patterns and connections that, however,
can only be totalized by the reader.[13] However, in contrast to
Camus's novel, which is written as a monotone, *Conversation in
The Cathedral* presents a polyphony of voices, an "orchestration
of consciousness." At the same time, the architectonic brilliance
of the narrative with its multiplicity of interwoven dialogues seems
designed to conceal, behind the dense texture, the fundamentally
reiterative patterns of life. The conversation, like Clamance's confession, thus hides where it appears to reveal and reveals only through
silences and gaps.

Where *Conversation in The Cathedral* differs most significantly
from *The Fall* is in having precise historical references.[14] Set in
the 1960s, when Santiago, in search of a lost dog, discovers his
father's ex-chauffeur, Ambrosio, working in the dog pound, the
novel takes us back to the eight years of General Odría's presidency.

At this time, both the protagonists were young men on the verge
of becoming independent of their families. Both have fathers who
are closely connected to the corrupt regime. Santiago's father, a
businessman, is deeply involved in deals with the government strong
man, Cayo Bermúdez. Ambrosio's father works as a member of
a goon squad. Both Ambrosio and Santiago attempt to separate
themselves from the inevitability of settling into the family mold,
and of becoming mere repetitions of their fathers. Both come to
recognize themselves as social failures.

Yet the very concreteness of the historical setting is deceptive.
For the novel shows that neither history nor human agency pro-
motes change, which is, rather, the work of time. It is time that
imbues recollections with the irony of afterthought and pries open
secrets with its revealing fingers to finally expose characters to the
nakedness of truth. Thus, the very passage of time frames youthful
hope in the aura of disillusionment and inevitably makes conversation a kind of posturing when seen from the vantage point of
the future.

What separates Ambrosio and Santiago from other characters
in the novel is that both attempt to free themselves from the burden of repetition and reiteration. They thus directly confront what
Sartre calls "facticity," that is, all that is unchangeable in their
lives—Ambrosio's blackness, Santiago's middle-class background—
and in the process they acquire some degree of consciousness.[15]
Consciousness thus becomes a kind of retroactive process practiced
on the given and transcending the individual. In this sense, Ambrosio and Santiago are brothers under the skin. However, there is a
Cartesian abyss between their manners of apprehending reality,
which helps to account for the fact that their four-hour conversation does not produce mutual understanding. Of the two, only
Santiago is given any extensive inner monologue, though this could
more properly be described as dialogue within consciousness. Ambrosio is the more instinctual and opaque since he seldom verbal-
izes his motives. This difference is subtly underlined by the fact
that, in The Cathedral, Santiago drinks whereas Ambrosio eats.
There can be no real reciprocity since their circumstances, their
natures, and their needs are different. In the conversation, they
are therefore at cross-purposes. Santiago thinks that he already
knows what he has come to find out—namely that Ambrosio had
been his father's (Don Fermín's) lover and had murdered the
prostitute Hortensia to protect him—but he wants to hear Ambrosio confess his motives. Ambrosio, for whom Don Fermín's wealth
had signified liberation from necessity, finds Santiago's reasons for
breaking with his father lame. Santiago is unworthy of Don Fermín.

Their separate acts of self-understanding acquired through recollection do not lead to mutual understanding, and their separate consciousnesses can never constitute the whole truth, which must be totalized by a third person (the reader). Consciousness transcends the individual because each person is blinkered by class and cirumstance.

Conversation, in any case, does not of itself reveal truth since discourse is essentially instrumental, and is projected into relationships already weighted by inequalities of power. Speech is bound up with the social structure, which is predominantly paternalistic. The father-son relationship, in which an authoritarian figure whose power seems to be "natural" dispenses rewards and punishments, becomes the paradigm of the network that constitutes the nation itself. Conversation is the verbal transaction in which the varying status of these relationships is perpetually reviewed. Thus, for instance, the following apparently disconnected conversations are bonded by the common paternalistic metaphor:

(a) "Is that all you've got, Ambrosio?" Trifulcio asked. "Only twenty soles, a driver and everything."[16]

(b) "Why don't you send him abroad to study?" Bermúdez asked. "Maybe with the change in surroundings the boy will straighten out."   (p. 131)

Both conversations show that fathers are necessary functions of the socialization process. Trifulcio, for whom force is the only law, has just made his son give up his money at knife point. Although he immediately shows remorse, his spontaneous action demonstrates the desperately primitive level on which he has struggled for survival. Apparently he is worlds apart from the wealthy businessman, Don Fermín, yet their function is analogous, for the latter is also anxious that *his* sons learn the law of survival. Thus, in (b), Cayo Bermúdez answers an unvoiced question, "How can I straighten out my son and make him accept the dominant values?" The son of whom they are speaking is not Santiago but an elder son, Sparky, whose school record has been poor and who resists going into the family business. Like Trifulcio, Fermín is expected to use his paternal authority in order to reinforce the social system and hence to reproduce it. Its values are, in turn, inscribed within a chain of dependency relationships that extends from the humble Trifulcio to Odría himself who is dependent on the support of the United States. Thus, Cayo's apparently harmless suggestion that Sparky be sent abroad in order to be straightened out underlines not only the authoritarian role of the father, but also the fact that this is not the ultimate authority. Should he fail to discipline his son, there is always a higher authority "abroad."

Different classes are, of course, socialized in different ways. At the lowest level, physical force schools the child in the dominant patterns of adult life. The middle classes play the survival game in a different manner. They are schooled into believing that their superiority to the poor is natural and justified. Doña Zoila, Santiago's mother, embodies this ideology in its purest and least conscious form. But Santiago himself feels no compunction at trying out an aphrodisiac on the maid, something he would never have done with a "decent" girl. The family—already stratified into masters and servants and into older and younger generations bonded by a system of rewards, punishments, favors, and bribery—is thus the microcosm of society. This is made explicit in the continuation of the Cayo Bermúdez-Fermín conversation and the Trifulcio-Ambrosio confrontation mentioned above:

> (a) "You make me a little jealous listening to you, Mr. Zavala," Bermúdez said. "In spite of all the headaches, being a father must have its compensations."

> (b) "But it's all right, I do think it just happened like that and that you will pay me back," Ambrosio said, "Now forget about it, please."   (p. 132)

The main significance of these exchanges is that they reveal that a system of recompense is the glue that holds society together. Each person is bound to others by debts or favors that put the debtor in the power of the giver. In (a), Cayo voices the common assumption that sons exist in order to prolong the father's life and compensate him; (b) adds an ironic comment. A father has stolen from his son and is unlikely ever to repay him. In both cases, the exchange is unequal because fathers and sons do not hold the same power, and this is true for all social relationships, as is clear in the following sequence:

> (a) "You're a good son, I hope everything works out for you in Lima. Believe me, I'll pay you back, Ambrosio."

> (b) "They sent me from one place to the other, they made me wait here for hours, Don Cayo." Ambrosio said, "I was ready to go back to Chincha, I tell you."

> (c) "Generally the Director of Public Order's chauffeur is

someone from the Police Department, Don Cayo," Dr. Alcibiades said. "For reasons of security. But if you prefer."

(d) "I've come back to look for work, Don Cayo." "I'm sick of driving that broken-down old bus. I thought that maybe you could help me get a job." (p. 133)

Here the paternalistic network of favors and rewards is shown to extend beyond family relationships and to be part of the national structure. In (c), Alcibiades recognizes that custom is no match for power, and he therefore accedes to Cayo's request that Ambrosio be given a position as a chauffeur. In (d), Ambrosio exacts (without direct allusion to Cayo's "debt") his reward for having helped him years before to kidnap the girl he would marry. In yet another example, this social bonding is shown at an even higher level:

(a) "Do you need some money?" Espina asked. "Yes, sure, I'll lend you some now and tomorrow we'll get them to give you an advance in the payroll department."

(b) "What bad luck happened to you in Pucallpa?" Santiago asks.

(c) "I'll find a small hotel in the neighborhood." Bermúdez said, "I'll come by early tomorrow."

(d) "For me, for me?" Don Fermín asked. "Or did you do it for yourself, in order to have me in your hands, you poor devil?"

(e) "Someone who thought he was my friend sent me there," Ambrosio says. (p. 57)

In (a) and (c), General Espina, who had earlier participated in the kidnapping of Bermúdez's future wife, is trying to get Cayo to take a job as Director of Security in the newly formed Odría government. In (b) and (e), Santiago is interrogating Ambrosio in The Cathedral about his life after the downfall of Bermúdez. The immediate effect of intercalating these dialogues is to telescope time, but it also underlines the repetitiveness and sameness of social intercourse. It is only by reading later episodes, however, that the irony of the passage can be appreciated. For, as Espina's second-in-command, Cayo will catch him plotting against Odría and will betray the plot, thus freeing himself from his initial debt. At the same time, precisely because he has been indebted to him, he is obliged to save Espina from imprisonment and have him sent abroad. This apparent "generosity" is repaid later when Cayo, in his turn, is allowed to leave the country quietly after yet another palace revolution. Ambrosio's "bad luck" offers an ironic counterpoint to this effective network. He had been banished to Pucallpa after murdering Hortensia in order to free Fermín from the threat of blackmail. Yet Fermín does not repay his devotion with trust and cannot believe that his servant's motives were disinterested. Ambrosio's relationship with the friend who sent him to Pucallpa also ironically underscores Espina's relationship to Bermúdez. Ambrosio had helped Ludovico to find regular work as Don Cayo's chauffeur, and hence puts him in his debt. When Ludovico becomes a member of the police force, he is able to cover up Ambrosio's responsibility for Hortensia's murder but has him sent to his uncle in Pucallpa where the murderer's savings will quickly find their way into the uncle's pockets. Debt and repayment thus bond master and servant, thug and politician, businessmen and Ministers, Ministers and bureaucrats. Yet because the system is built on inequalities of power, it is also susceptible to treachery and betrayal. Each of the relationships alluded to—between Fermín and Ambrosio, between Ambrosio and Ludovico, between Cayo and Espina—is exposed to drastic shifts of loyalty. These do not overturn the system, however, since they merely redistribute power within the network without altering its fundamental characteristics.

We can now appreciate why *conversation* (literally "a turning around") is so functional to this sytem. In the context of power, conversation is instrumental, motivated by what the other wishes to hear or what it is convenient for him to hear. This explains not only why it is repetitive but also why people of different class backgrounds and situations often seem to be eerie echoes of one another. In the following example, the generic nature of the conversations is supported by making two different speech acts, uttered at different moments of time by different speakers, appear to be part of the same syntactical structure.

(a) "It's precisely because they're filthy trash that these newspapers are a great stimulant," Jacobo said, "If you feel demoralized, all you have to do is open up any one of them to bring back your hatred for the Peruvian bourgeoisie."

(b) "So you might say that with our scatography we're stimulating eighteen-year old rebels," Carlitos said. "So don't let your conscience bother you so much, Zavalita. Look, even though it's indirect, you're still helping your ex-buddies." (p. 144)

The Communist's denunciation of the yellow press is couched in terms similar to the journalist's self-denunciation. What differentiates the conversations is the contingent viewpoints of the speakers, although the basic similarity and continuity of their thinking is supported by the syntax, since Carlitos begins his reply with the conjunctive "so." Instead of individuation through personal styles of speaking or accent, as was often the practice in traditional realist novels, speech here serves as an instrument that is always ambiguous and depersonalized, unless it can be directly attached to a set of motives or conditions. That is why so much of the novel is concerned with trying to interpret the discourse of the other in ways that serve the interest of the speaker, as is illustrated in the following interrogation of a community leader.

> (a) "Everything comes out in this life of ours," Ludovico said, "The police are beginning to think that you're a subversive."
>
> (b) "Nothing of the kind, that's a lie." A good actor, sir. "Let me explain it all to you."
>
> (c) "That's fine, people with brains get to understand each other by talking." Ludovico said.   (p. 210)

In this episode, Ambrosio and Ludovico, as members of a goon squad, enforce a wavering organizer to bring his men out for a rally on behalf of Odría. Yet precisely because his adhesion is exacted by threats of violence and repression, the answers cannot be accepted at their face value. Hence, in (b), the speaker is assumed to be lying. However, (b) is not attributed to any named speaker. We deduce only that he is an inferior speaking to a superior because of the use of "sir." The words might be spoken in a completely different context, for instance, in the prison cell in which Ludovico had earlier assisted at the torture of the textile worker, Trinidad López. Interrogations are always based on the supposition that whatever confession is produced is probably a lie. "You're a sissy, friend, we haven't touched you and you're lying already" (p. 134), Ludovico remarks on that occasion. The phrase "a good actor" could be Ludovico's description of Trinidad or even Ambrosio explaining his participation in a goon squad to Don Fermín. What is important, however, is not the correct attribution of the speech so much that it is depersonalized and instrumental. Thus Ludovico's comment, "People with brains get to understand each other by talking," ironically underlines precisely the reverse of what he is saying.

Since speech is depersonalized, it is often possible for the reader to identify addressees only because of a title or mode of address. These situate the speakers and addressees socially, racially, and according to generatiòns, thus reproducing, on the linguistic level, the social stratifications and distributions of power. For instance, Ambrosio always addresses Santiago in the polite third person form and refers to him as *niño* or *niñito* (son, sonny). This helps the reader identify Ambrosio's conversations with Santiago and distinguishes them from his conversations with Don Fermín, whom he always addresses as *don* (sir). However, the English translation can only convey the generational connotations, whereas the Spanish *niño* also connotes a master-servant relationship in which the masters are eternally children to their servants. On the other hand, the servant's inferiority is shown through the use of the familiar *tu* form. Thus, the maid, Amalia, addresses Santiago in the third person but is addressed as *tu* by her masters. Hence, the modes of address are not merely props for the reader by also indications of the balance of power within a relationship. The shoeshine boy, for instance, refers to his customers as "boss," and Santiago addresses the taxi driver as *"maestro"* to indicate the driver's momentary command of the situation. Family nicknames—Sparky, Skinny, Freckles, Superbrain—establish the grounds of familiarity between people of the same social group and distinguish each member according to physical or mental characteristics. Then there are the racial, sexual, and class epithets. Ambrosio and Trifulcio are *zambos* (a mixture of black and Indian) but are often addressed as *"negro"* or *"negrito."* Amalia and Cayo Bermúdez are both described as half-breeds (*chola* and *cholo*). Both Amalia and Santiago's wife, Ana, are regarded as *huachafitas* by Santiago's family (this is a contemptuous term that conveys the vulgarity of the lower classes).[17] The city whores ironically refer to the homosexual Don Fermín as "Golden Ball" and nickname Cayo "Shithead." Such epithets and modes of address serve both to stereotype characters and also to compress individuality into facticity (i.e., that which determines a person's situation and cannot be altered). They also show that the majority of the characters in *Conversation in The Cathedral* not only are trapped within the given, but actively reproduce and continue the abuses of class and power through their very use of language.

The reason that people fall so easily into reproducing the system is that they are lured by the bait of immediate satisfaction and consumption. Earlier, in *The Green House*, Fushía had exemplified the attempt to short-circuit duration in order to make satisfaction simultaneous with need. In *Conversation in The Cathedral*, this impatience is generalized throughout the novel and represented concretely through a series of symbols—the dog pound, Santiago's work in the newspaper office, The Cathedral bar, and Lima itself. Indeed, the bar where Santiago and Ambrosio meet becomes their church, and the congregation is composed of sweating, devouring humanity viewed at animal level. Among the *graffitti* on the wall is the name "Saturnina," an allusion to Saturn, the god of time who devoured his own children. The pattern of quick consumption that The Cathedral symbolizes can only produce excrement, which is the color of Lima itself. This is also the only product that Santiago sees in his work: "I get in early, they give me my topic, I hold my nose and in two or three hours all set, I pull the chain and that's it."[18] He describes his work as a journalist as:

> "Piling up shit with a great deal of enthusiasm, a small pile today, a little more tomorrow, a fair amount day after tomorrow . . . until there was a whole mountain of shit. And now to eat it down to the last crumb. That's what happened to me, Carlitos."

The dog pound is simply a different representation of the same process. The dogs are snatched from their owners and then given back to them on payment of a fine. Thus, the workers earn their money more quickly and safely than if they captured dogs with rabies as they are supposed to do. As one of the workers pointedly observes, the dogs invariably shit as soon as they are freed, and this, in turn, indicates the metaphoric connection between this animal freedom (which is simply liberation from an immediate need) and the activity of most people in the novel.

The short-circuit between need and satisfaction, which prevents real production, also seems to telescope time. Of all the time-cycles in the novel, that between need and consumption is the shortest. A longer time-span is needed for the redistribution of rewards, debts, and favors that governs the social system. And there is a third, even longer cycle that encompasses the lives of Ambrosio and Santiago and that is structured around certain rites of passage —adolescence, marriage, birth. The four major books of the novel are thus like planetary cycles of rites of passage in which the shorter cycles revolve. Yet, plainly, to be caught in one of these cycles is *not* to be an individual, but is merely a function of the particular process involved, whether the primitive economy of the dog pound, whether the primitive social exchange of debt relationships, or whether the apparently natural institution of the family whose rituals cement and maintain social stratification. To assert any kind of individuality, a person must interrupt these depersonalized circuits by a conscious act of negation.

This is, in fact, how Ambrosio and Santiago try to constitute their selves, first by refusing to become what their fathers are and then by radically breaking with their fathers' life-styles. In this initial stage, Santiago enters the lower-class atmosphere of San Marcos University against his father's wishes and flirts with communism because it is the reverse of capitalism. Ambrosio chooses to work as a chauffeur, and his first boss, Cayo, who is Director of Security, seems the very reverse of his criminal father. Santiago becomes a marginalized déclassé both because of his work as a newspaper reporter and because of his marriage to a woman of inferior social status. Ambrosio becomes Don Fermín's lover because he venerates the comfortable middle-class style of Santiago's father. His dream is to stand on his own feet and be independent, and he appears on the verge of attaining this when he starts his own business in Pucallpa, just as Santiago appears to be on the verge of independence when he refuses his father's inheritance. One event—Hortensia's murder—decisively alters the future of the two men. It is this act that is the silent vacuum around which the conversations form, since it is never directly described and never sufficiently explained by the motives attributed to Ambrosio. As such, it constitutes a kind of enigmatic core. After the murder, nothing is quite the same. Ambrosio is doomed to failure, to returning to a marginal social status and occasional work in the dog pound, "and after that here and there, and then, well, after that he would have died, wasn't that so, son?" (p. 601). Yet this act, which alters the course of his life, never seems to have been consciously assumed and always appears as something alien to him, almost as if it had committed itself. For his part, Santiago confronts the father's scandalous homosexuality as both his shame and as a revelation since he discovers that Fermín can be pitied as a person while rejected as a social function. He is consequently able to divorce his refusal to receive his father's inheritance from his feeling of understanding. Hortensia's murder is thus on a different level from all the other activities in the novel. It is not just that it exposes the corrupt underbelly of the Odría regime but that it allows us to envisage beneath the automatized surface of the conversations some scarcely defined human quality, the baffling possibility of a real event.

The event is timeless, and hence it configures an important aspect of the novel, which involves the relationship of the text and the reader. For the differences between Ambrosio and Santiago are now seen to be contingent, and the reader alone possesses the information that enables him to move to understanding at a more complex level. As in Sartre's and Camus's novels, this means that the characters are not so much mimetic as thetic, or positionings within the totality. They are, as it were, agents for the reorganization of the past in a way that will allow it to be seen as neither natural nor inevitable. Because this also involves the relationship between author, text, and reader, it implicitly suggests that the activity of writing/reading (creativity) can be made to interrupt the automatized cycle of social life. The individuality and independence that Ambrosio and Santiago fail to achieve becomes invested in the Utopia of art.

Critics often refer to Vargas Llosa's reinvention of the past as the "creation of another reality," and indeed he encourages such a view of his work.[19] On inspection, however, what he achieves is not so much the invention of another reality as the activation of the reader's consciousness by preventing automatic responses. Like Sartre and Camus, therefore, his attention is focused beyond the creation of character to the reader. This has, of course, become one of the commonplaces of contemporary literature. Yet in the case of the writers under discussion, it seems to lead to an interesting paradox. For all of them publicly stress the role of the individual in society. At the same time, because they view the individual in terms of consciousness, they create literary projections of the individual that verge on impersonality. Thus, in *The Fall*, an individual who might be Everyman postures before the silence of nature. In *The Reprieve*, characters sink deeply into the undifferentiated crowd of history. And in *Conversation in The Cathedral*, they attempt to assert themselves as individuals only to be revealed as agents in the reader's act of self-awareness.

Stanford University
Stanford, California

Notes

1. This discussion of "character," "*personaje*," and "hero" is part of ongoing research initially funded by a grant from the Guggenheim Foundation. On "*personaje*," see also Noe Jitrik, *El no existente caballero: la idea de personaje y su evolución en la narrativa latinoamericana* (Buenos Aires: Megápolis, 1975).

2. W. J. Harvey, *Character and the Novel* (Ithaca: Cornell Univ. Press, 1965), p. 23.

3. For a "deconstruction of character" in the traditional novel, see Roland Barthes, *S/Z*, trans. Richard Miller (New York: Hill and Wang, 1974).

This analysis of the linguistic codes of a Balzac novel shows how character is configured in the act of reading.

4. Fredric Jameson, *Marxism and Form* (Princeton: Princeton Univ. Press, 1971), p. 212.

5. Jean-Paul Sartre, *What Is Literature?*, trans. Bernard Frechtman (New York: Methuen, 1951), p. 229.

6. Fredric Jameson, *Sartre: The Origins of Style* (New Haven: Yale Univ. Press, 1961), p. 61. See, also, pp. 191-92 for a discussion of character.

7. Jean-Paul Sartre, *The Reprieve*, trans. Eric Sutton (New York: Knopf, 1959).

8. Albert Camus, *The Fall* (New York: Vintage Books, 1956), pp. 139-40. All further references are to this edition.

9. Maurice Blanchot, "La confession dédaigneuse," in *Les critiques de notre temps et Camus* (Paris: Garnier, 1970), pp. 91-97.

10. Albert Camus, "Dernière interview d'Albert Camus," *Essais critiques* (Paris: Gallimard et Calmann-Levy, 1956), p. 1927.

11. Blanchot, p. 97.

12. Ibid., pp. 93-94.

13. Camus's thought only seems to have been seriously studied by Mario Vargas Llosa after he had written *Conversation in The Cathedral*. See his essay, "Albert Camus y la moral de los límites," *Inti*, 4 (Autumn 1976), 7-21.

14. For some comments on *Conversation in The Cathedral*, see José Miguel Oviedo, *Mario Vargas Llosa: La invención de una realidad* (Barcelona: Barral Editores, 1970). For a discussion of character in this novel, see Marvin Lewis, *The Novel and Society: Vargas Llosa's Literary Interpretation of Peruvian Reality* (Ann Arbor: Xerox University Microfilms, 1974).

15. Jameson, in *Sartre*, pp. 13-14 and pp. 87-88, discusses facticity.

16. The *sol* (plural *soles*) is a unit of Peruvian currency.

17. The English translation incorrectly translates "*huachafa*" as "half-breed."

18. This is my translation. The English translation has "unbuckle my chains," which is incorrect.

19. See, for instance, his *Gabriel García Márquez: historia de un deicidio* (Barcelona: Seix Barral, 1971).

Raymond L. Williams

The Narrative Art of Mario Vargas Llosa: Two Organizing Principles in *Pantaleón y las visitadoras*

The publication of *Pantaleón y las visitadoras* marks a change in the novelistic trajectory of Mario Vargas Llosa. Whereas the previous novels demonstrate a progressive development of structural complexity, the most recent work represents a movement toward traditional storytelling.[1] It also includes humor, a characteristic notably absent from Vargas Llosa's previous fiction. The more traditional, or at least less demanding, narrative technique, and the presence of humor relate *Pantaleón y las visitadoras* more closely to works of this decade like the Mexican Gustavo Sainz's *La princesa del palacio de hierro* (1974) and the Colombian Gustavo Alvarez Gardeazábal's *El bazar de los idiotas* (1974) than to the Vargas Llosa of *La Case Verde* or *Conversación en La Catedral*. Just as Sainz and Alvarez Gardeazábal have encountered critical disapproval of their popular, accessible, and humorous works, the vitality of *Pantaleón* and its "facile" humor have been questioned.[2] In the present study, I will consider two organizing principles that point to specific humorous and critical effects in this novel. The first principle of organization concerns the novel's content; the second involves the novel's structure according to the organization provided by the narrator. A basic assumption here is that these two organizing principles are fundamental to an appreciation of Vargas Llosa's narrative art both as a humorous entertainment and as a work subversively critical of the society it describes.

By utilizing Gérard Genette's concept of the nuclear verb, we can see the novel as an expansion of the basic sentence "Pantoja organizes prostitution for the military in Perú."[3] The verb essentializes what happens in the story. The verb "organizes" stresses Pantoja's methodical creation of an operation that supplies prostitutes for the military. The first chapter, written entirely in dialogue, introduces the "organizing" by having Pantoja receive his assignment, and the chapter particularly underlines his ability as an organizer. He is characterized by others in dialogue as an "innate organizer," with a "mathematical sense of order, executive capacity," and an "organizing brain." Midway through the novel and at the end are chapters that employ dialogue as in the first, and the remaining chapters describe Pantoja's "organizing" by means of military documents, messages, letters, and conversations. These communications appear in addition to short narrative passages by the omniscient narrator. In the second chapter Pantoja describes the intimate details of his organization via official communiqués. He supports his description with scientific experiments and data. By the third chapter Pantoja's mania for organization has reached such extremes that he uses a watch to make calculations of his own sexual relationship with his wife. Approximately halfway through the novel, Pantoja's failure is precipitated by his success as organizer: his operation has acquired its own dynamics, which the military fears it will not be able to control. A turning point in Pantoja's operation, a public denunciation on the radio by a local commentator and one of Pantoja's ex-prostitutes, also underlines his capacity as an organizer. The prostitute explains: "He has everything well organized, another of his manias is order. We all used to say this doesn't seem like a whorehouse but a barracks" (p. 199). At the end it is his success as organizer that causes a reaction: he loses his position and is sent on another remote assignment.

If we consider the expansion of the basic verb "organizes" in more detail, it becomes apparent that Vargas Llosa articulates social commentary by use of narrative techniques through which the incongruities in the process of "organizing" are observed. Vargas Llosa consistently juxtaposes sexual proclivity with the military repression of such impulses. The point of departure for this type of juxtaposition is the initial conversation between Pantoja and his wife Pocha in the first paragraph of the novel:

> —Wake up, Panta, says Pochita. It's already eight o'clock. Panta, Pantita.
> —Already eight? My God, I'm really sleepy, yawns Pantita. Did you sew my stripe on?
> —Yes, lieutenant, Pochita salutes. Oh, pardon me, my captain. Until I get used to it you'll have to be a lieutenant, honey.
> (p. 11)

Even in a playful conversation such as this, the initial confluence of the personal intimate life and the military code appear. A basic incongruity of the novel is thus established by its juxtaposing the military "lieutenant," "Pochita salutes," and "captain" on the one hand, and "honey" on the other. A similar technique, and effect, can be observed in the first communiqué sent by Pantoja. Pantoja's mathematical calculations of the length of time involved in the sexual act and the number of monthly sex acts necessary to enable the men to perform their military functions are a similar humorous juxtaposition of the military and the intimate. Once the operation has become a quasi-official part of the military superstructure, the effect of the juxtaposition loses its humor. This is the point at which Pocha observes that Pantoja now cherishes his assignment ("But now I notice that you love the Secret Service" [p. 114]) and the military becomes aware of the immanent dynamism of this operation. From approximately this point, the novel's vitality and movement are based on the conflict between Pantoja and his opponents, and on Pantoja's affair with La Brasileña. The juxtaposition no longer offers the humorous potential that it did before the prostitution became integrated into the military superstructure—it is no longer incongruent. It is notable, for example, that the commentator Sinchi uses the juxtaposition as the basis for his campaign against Pantoja: "this is Pantoja's lucrative business: to convert the garrisons, camps, bases, and border installations into miniature Sodom and Gomorrahs, thanks to his floating and aerial whorehouses" (p. 190). Although similar to Pocha's original statement in the sense that it juxtaposes the military and the intimate, the humor of the contradiction now becomes rhetorical bombast that, in effect, is a criticism of the juxtaposition itself.

These incongruities become apparent through the emphasis placed on the values and mentality of the military. An important example of this emphasis is a statement by Pantoja at the beginning of the novel when, upon receiving his orders to "organize" as a civilian, he affirms: "But always to think like a military man" (p. 26). His actions, and those of his colleagues, should be understood precisely as such, a manifestation of a military mentality. Technically, the predominance of the military is communicated through the novel's style, both in the use of official communiqués and in the actual choice of vocabulary in the message's content. Pantoja's actions are an expression of military ideals because his characterization consistently associates him with them. He finds it undesirable to disguise his military identity for this special project: "despite the sadness he feels having to hide his position as an officer in our Army, of which he is proud . . ." (p. 38). Besides his obsession with orderliness, his dependence upon and idealization of common sense reflects his military way of thinking. Thus, he explains his actions with the use of proverbs:

> That he is aware of his obligation to initiate the Service, setting modest and attainable goals, taking into account the reality

and hidden philosophy in proverbs such as "good things
come to those who wait" and "each thing in its own time."
(p. 45)

Similarly, his explanation for the lack of lighting in a house is that
"in the dark all cats are grey" (p. 47). Pantoja apologizes because
a hymn invented by the prostitutes does not include mention of
the navy. He explains that the hymn was not planned by military
authorities, but rather was a "spontaneous creation of the personnel." In accordance with the military code, the fact that it is spontaneous accounts for its deficiencies. The prostitute Maclovia explains how Pantoja organized prostitution along military lines:
"He made us cry, I tell you, saying now you're in a different category, you're our call girls and not street walkers, you serve the
country, you collaborate with the Armed Forces" (p. 195). For
Pantoja, the highest honor he can bestow upon La Brasileña is to
describe her as a "soldier killed in action."
 Another significant aspect of the values apparent in the novel is
its exaltation of *machismo*. The focal point of the anecdote is the
degrading and mechanized sexual practices that Pantoja institu-
tionalizes. The point of departure for such mechanization is Pantoja's initial scientific investigation. The actual operation functions
on the basis of the mechanical quality of the sexual act; for example, soldiers who behave well are assigned to the attractive Pe-
chuga, and others are punished by having to accept the less desir-
able Sandra. Again, the time of the act in this incident is calculated
to provide for maximum "efficiency."
 The fundamental incongruities in the social processes observed,
then, must be understood as an expression of a military mentality.
The values set forth in the novel, as part of the military superstructure, are not those of Mario Vargas Llosa as author, but those of
the military he is describing. This is especially apparent if we recall
once more Pantoja's characterization as the ideal military man and
his affirmation "But always to think like a military man." Although
the sexual act, for example, is degrading in the novel, it reflects
the values and mentality that Pantoja represents. As far as the first
organizing principle is concerned, we note that the nuclear verb
"Pantoja organizes prostitution for the military in Perú" is expanded through the development of incongruities in the social
processes. These processes are particularly representative of the
military values that the novel questions. Organizing, as the first
principle, is the basis for this incisive study of Peruvian society.

The second organizing principle, the formal means by which the nuclear verb is expanded, is based on the author's organization of the anecdotal material. Both the basic structure—the organization of the chapters within the novel—and the structure of the individual units themselves are functional. The basic structure develops ten chapters into what can be considered a four-part structure. The four parts are as follows.

I. Chapter 1 (Dialogue)
   Chapter 2
   (a) Parte número uno (Pantoja)
   (b) Section by omniscient narrator
   (c) Parte número dos (Pantoja)
   Chapter 3
   (a) Letter from Pocha
   (b) Section by omniscient narrator
   Chapter 4
   (a) Resolución confidencial (Carrillo)
   (b) Parte número tres (Pantoja)
   (c) Anotación (Collazos)
   (d) Resolución (Sarmiento)
   (e) Report (Quispe Salas)
   (f) Report (Santana)
   (g) Letter (Rojas)
   (h) Letter (Beltrán Calila)
II. Chapter 5 (Dialogue)
   Chapter 6
   (a) Instrucciones (Pantoja)
   (b) Parte estadístico (Mendoza)
   (c) Parte número quince (Pantoja)
   (d) Anotación (Collazos)
   (e) Message (Casahuanqui)
   (f) Letter (signed XXX)
   (g) Parte número dieciocho (Pantoja)
   (h) Anotación (Collazos)
   (i) Letter (Carrillo)
   (j) Anotación (Scavino)
   (k) Letter (Soma, Quilca, Sansho)
   (l) Parte número veintiséis (Pantoja)
   (m) Parte estadístico (Dávila)
   (n) Letter (Maclovia)
   (o) Letter (Calila)
   (p) Anotación (Scavino)

Chapter 7
(a) Voz de Sinchi
(b) Section by omniscient narrator
III. Chapter 8 (Dialogue)
Chapter 9 (Newspaper accounts)
IV. Chapter 10 (Dialogue)

According to this four-part structure, each part begins with a chapter of dialogue; the sections that follow the dialogue chapters develop and elaborate the situation set forth in the dialogue. The four parts develop four stages in Pantoja's organizing: (1) the establishment of the operation, (2) the expansion of the operation, (3) the downfall, and (4) an epilogue.

Part I, the establishment, consists of the first four chapters. The first chapter, containing dialogue on various temporal levels, suggests much of the plot that will be developed in the remainder of this part. We note in the dialogue between Pantoja and Pocha that he is dedicated to his military profession and that they have started on a new assignment. In dialogue on a different temporal level, we observe him actually receiving his assignment and establishing the operation. Here the initial investigation is carried out and no problems are encountered. Vargas Llosa will make the reader an active witness to the outcome of the conversations interspersed in the initial dialogue chapter.

Part II marks the expansion of the operation. Like Part I, it begins with a dialogue between Pantoja and Pocha, and this dialogue is soon intercalated with other dialogues, making the chapter progressively more complex. Two important changes of Part II, which will be further developed, are suggested. In the dialogue between Pantoja and Pocha, she states: "But now I notice that you love the Secret Service" (p. 114). Also, in the intercalated dialogue among the military, it is suggested that "Now it won't be possible to stop the avalanche" (p. 123). In the last section of Part II, the section narrated by the omniscient narrator, it is evident that Pocha has left Pantoja. The apprehension suggested in "Now it won't be possible to stop the avalanche" of the dialogue is fulfilled when the operation later becomes problem-laden. Pantoja receives an initial threat in an anonymous letter signed "XXX." Maclovia writes to Pocha to ask for her aid in returning to Pantoja's operation. The expansion noted in Part II is exemplified in these letters; they indicate that the expansion has meant an increasing *public* knowledge of the operation that culminates in the last chapter of Part II with Sinchi's radio program.

Part III, consisting of chapters 8 and 9 and identified as the stage of Pantoja's downfall, describes various problems. The dialogue chapter opens with a conversation between Pantoja and Leanor, his mother, replacing the departed Pocha. The operation has meant the end of his family. The intercalated conversations among the military officials indicate other problems. Sinchi's radio program, Pantoja's public speech in honor of La Brasileña, and the series of articles in the newspaper mark the complete public revelation of the operation and Pantoja's demise.

Part IV, chapter 10 functions as an epilogue because the organizing is now a *fait accompli*. It only remains to be seen what will be Pantoja's outcome. Pantoja's life acquires once again the initial order and harmony of the first chapter. In the last paragraph it is evident that Pocha has returned to him in his new assignment in Pomata. Her comment that he is a maniac in his work in Pomata suggests that he is again obsessed with military order and discipline.

The novel's basic structure functions as a piece of precision clockwork that recalls the dramatic structure of a traditional three-act play: Part I establishes the conflict, Part II complicates it, and Part III resolves it. The dialogue chapters function as an introduction to each part, marking those changes in the novel's development that the reader will experience directly in the narrative materials provided. Three factors provide for a circular structure: (1) General Scavino's warning at the beginning of the novel is fulfilled with Pantoja's failure; (2) Sinchi's presence in the first chapter culminates in his key role at the end of the novel; and (3) the opening dialogue between Pantoja and Pocha is complemented by the reestablishment of harmony when they return together, and she repeats, as in the opening conversation, "Wake up, Panta."

As has become evident in this general discussion of the structure, Vargas Llosa's organization employs a variety of narrative materials to relate Pantoja's story. These materials offer a wide range of types of discourse and narrative situations, including first-person narratives, third-person narratives, and chapters of mimetic dialogues. As a manner of considering the structure of the individual chapters in more detail, we might take into account Jakobson's model[4] for the situation in any communication act:

context
message
addresser_____addressee
contact
code

Taking this basic model one step further, we might consider the following scheme as a basic communication or narrative situation in a novel:[5]

context
"story"

narrator_____implied reader

series of printed pages
language used

Although the communication situation can, and often does, become more complex in novels, this basic model will provide a point of departure for considering the various situations Vargas Llosa creates in this novel.

Four basic models (variations of the model above) describe the narrative situations that are offered by the variety of materials in this novel. The four models are (1) communication situations that involve direct dialogue that the implied reader experiences as an outsider distanced from the story; (2) communication situations in which a written message is directed to a specific reader within the story; (3) a communication situation common in the traditional nineteenth-century novel—an omniscient narrator outside the story relates the events to an implied reader outside the story; and (4) a communication situation in which a narrator within the story directs a message to a general public, or broad audience, within the story. Each of the narrative segments in the novel can be placed into one of these four categories, and the models offer the possibility of analyzing the organization of Vargas Llosa's discourse in more detail.

Within the first model, communication situations that involve dialogue, are chapters 1, 5, 8, and 10. A controlling narrator provides occasional short phrases to indicate the speakers in the dialogue, and the reader observes the conversations as they occur. Thus, the stage directions by the narrator are all in the present tense ("he says"). The actual content of these dialogue chapters becomes more complex than the description of the communication situation might suggest because the "present" in these dialogue chapters involves simultaneous juxtaposition of various conversations. In the first chapter there are three basic groups of speakers. First, we note the dialogue among the members of Pantoja's family—Pantoja, Pocha, and Leonor. The time and place of this dialogue changes from Lima at the outset, to the initial days of the new assignment, and finally to his return home, drunk, at the end of the chapter. The second group is the religious cult of brother Francisco. A third group includes Pantoja outside his immediate family—first with military authorities, and at the end of the first chapter in a bar gathering information for his new mission. The communication situation in this chapter provides a distanced reader with the opportunity to observe Pantaleón's actions—chapter 1 is, for the most part, a behaviorist study—both on an interpersonal basis within his family and as the professional military man. The fact that the entire chapter develops on a synchronic level, a continuous present, has the effect of offering the reader the opportunity to compare the different intercalated dialogues. Thus, the confluence of the personal and military is attained by technical means. The continuous present suggests that Pantoja is not a character in different stages of development, but one who will act differently in different contexts. The context of the Jakobson scheme varies in chapter 1 (as it does also in chapters 5, 8, and 10), that is, "family" and "professional." The reader must, through his own organization, determine these contexts in his role as observer. It should be noted that this behaviorist presentation of Pantoja in the first chapter provides the reader with an understanding of the character not available to the other characters in the story. The intercalations provide a wider range of observation for the reader.

In the second model, a written message is directed to a specific reader within the story other than the implied reader of the novel. The sections that form this model include the military messages and reports. Also within this category are some nonmilitary communications, such as the letter Pocha writes and the letter from Maclovia to Pocha. As far as the military documents are concerned, they provide the implied reader of the novel with an inside view of the military superstructure. They offer us the opportunity to interpret the military mentality that pervades the novel. The context in the Jakobson scheme is "military," as is the language employed in these messages. This communication situation reveals Pantoja's military persona. Vargas Llosa employs this context to satirize military language. It is the total context that makes such phrases as "the institution's good name" ironic in these passages. Exclusive focus on the military provides detail that is not possible in the more general scope of the first chapter. Humorous and satirical effects are created when the detail surpasses normal expectations. Thus, we find humor in Pantoja's observation that the room he is investigating contains exactly 1,323 square meters. In summary, context and language are vital to the experience of those sections of the second model. Because he has read the first chapter, the reader of the novel has access to a broader context than that in which these messages are being written, and thus he becomes organizer himself when he integrates these military messages and letters into the total novel.

The third model, which involves an omniscient narrator outside of the story who relates the narration to an implied reader outside of the story (the traditional communication situation), is found in only three sections of the novel. They describe Pantoja during three different evenings—two in August of 1956 and one in 1958. This model adds elements to Pantoja's characterization previously absent from the novel. First, these sections provide the only psychological penetration of Pantoja in the novel. The reader becomes aware of aspects of Pantoja's character that none of the characters are able to observe. A factor that these sections have in common as far as the analysis of Pantoja is concerned is his feeling of horror and extraordinary fear toward the world. He is observed as terrified and helpless in his circumstance, even though it is different in each of the three chapters. These sections provide an obvious contrast to the military persona characterized in the second model. Further, these sections offer the only diachronic study of Pantoja in the entire novel, evoking key moments in his past that the reader may use to appreciate his present circumstance more fully. Here, for example, we note Pantoja's fears during a military ceremony when he was a cadet. Such past events appear as flashbacks that occur during the three evenings. In this communication situation, the role of the narrator and implied reader changes from the other models. The reader appreciates the "context" and "story" of the model as a passive agent: they are directly explained by the controlling narrator. These three sections provide order and unity to the overall novel, situate the reader, and add credibility (a human dimension) to the characterization of Pantoja.

The fourth model, in which a narrator within the story directs a message to a general public within the story, is expressed in the sections involving Sinchi on the radio and in the newspaper reports. This communication situation is employed only near the end of the novel. The context is now Peru: the moral codes publicly violated and publicized are those of the entire country. The communication situation in the first section of this type, Sinchi's radio program, changes throughout the chapter. It begins with Sinchi's words on the radio. His opening comments of self-characterization —describing his interest in public welfare—are ironic for the reader of the text (although not necessarily for the public to whom the broadcast is directed) because the reader has a larger context in which to judge him. The development of the program is effected through the use of Sinchi's metalanguage, explaining changes in the focus of the comments to his projected listening audience. After creating the proper atmosphere with a section he calls "a little culture," he formalizes his denunciation of Pantoja's operation in his "Commentary of the Day." Then the speaker changes when, in the part entitled "Interviews and Reports," Maclovia tells her story of life as a military prostitute. Her story is based on the anecdotal material of which the reader is already aware from the sections of the second model (the military documents). Given the change in context, the story loses its humorous effect and functions as part of Pantoja's drama. It now has a dramatic, and at time melodramatic, effect. The newspaper articles of chapter 9 have a similar audience, but the role of the reader of the text is changed. By reading Pantoja's funeral elegy, the reader, like the general public, becomes more aware of Pantoja's relationship with La Brasileña. The reader takes the role of organizer once more, coordinating the details revealed in the newspapers to formulate the total story in all its details. As in *Conversación en La Catedral*, Vargas Llosa employs one of his most favored techniques (common in the mystery novel), the surprise revelation of key details at the end of the novel. The use of his fourth model allows the reader to discover such details as an active participant in the novel.

These two organizing principles suggest that *Pantaleón y las visitadoras*, although perhaps a less demanding reading experience than Vargas Llosa's previous novels, exemplifies the precise control of narration that is a consistent mark of the author's work. This brief consideration of Pantoja's organization (the novel's content as described by use of a nuclear verb) and of Vargas Llosa's organization (the novel's structure) makes the novel a parody of military organization in both form and content. This correspondence between content and form, or theme and technique, creates a vital experience for the reader and implies the function of the work within Peruvian society. These observations also suggest that the essence of Vargas Llosa's fiction may be found in its organization as it has been described, rather than in the pure invention, or "magical realism," notable in a writer such as García Márquez. The transformation of reality is associated most closely with Vargas Llosa's manipulation of discourse and may be appreciated in this particular novel on the basis of these two principles of organization.

University of Chicago
Chicago, Illinois

Notes

1. See José Miguel Oviedo, *Mario Vargas Llosa: La invención de una realidad* (Barcelona: Barral Editores, 1970).
2. See Joseph Sommers, "Literatura e ideología: el militarismo en las novelas de Vargas Llosa," *Revista de crítica literaria latinoamericana*, 1 (1975), 87–112.
3. See Gérard Genette, "Discours du récit," in *Figures III* (Paris: Seuil, 1972). In the introduction, Genette suggests the possibility of considering a story as the expansion of a verb. For example, Genette notes that in the *Odyssey* the verb would be "Ulysses returns to Ithaca" and for *A la recherche du temps perdu*, "Marcel becomes a writer."
4. See Roman Jakobson, "Linguistics and Poetics," in *Style and Language*, ed. Thomas A. Sebeok (Cambridge, Mass.: MIT Press, 1960); reprinted in *The Structuralists from Marx to Lévi-Strauss*, ed. Richard and Fernande DeGeorge (Garden City: Anchor Books, 1972).
5. See John S. Brushwood, "Mexican Fiction in the Seventies: Author, Intellect, and Public," a paper read at the Comparative Literature Symposium of Texas Tech University, 27 January 1977. Currently in press.

William L. Siemens

Apollo's Metamorphosis in *Pantaleón y las visitadoras*

Pantaleón y las visitadoras is one of those deceptively simple novels that tend to unnerve people, perhaps because their appeal is on a level inaccessible to simple analysis. At a writers' conference in Guayaquil in 1975, the novelist Gustavo Alvarez Gardeazábal found that everyone there seemed to have enjoyed reading the book but that no one was willing to admit its value as literature, seemingly because they possessed no readily available traditional form to which to relate it. Furthermore, there appears to be a certain prejudice against the humorous novel in Latin American literary criticism—this despite the overarching presence of *Don Quixote* in the Hispanic novelistic tradition. Certainly this prejudice has prevented certain works of a profound seriousness beneath the surface, such as Guillermo Cabrera Infante's *Tres tristes tigres*, from being analyzed thoroughly enough to reveal their full import.

In fact, *Pantaleón y las visitadoras* represents one of those cases in which the artist is carried far beyond his original intention by the developing work. One is reminded of Alberto Giacometti's alarm as his sculptures became smaller and thinner.[1] At the IV Congreso de la Nueva Narrativa Hispanoamericana in Cali, Colombia, in 1974, Vargas Llosa spoke of first having written his work in his usual serious style and then realizing that it was a failure. As he wrote it a second time, some humor crept in, and the third and final writing resulted in the thoroughly humorous text that was ultimately published.

Humor is founded on anomaly and incongruity, and these are of the essence of the situation developed in the novel. The writing had its inception in Vargas Llosa's asking himself, upon reading of the actual events in Peru, what sort of military man could operate a prostitution service for the troops.[2] The result, oddly enough, is one of those novels in which Classical forms are taken apart for analysis the way a child takes a fine watch apart to see what makes it tick. In the case before us, however, the components are reassembled into something reminiscent of the Classical watch only in some very strange ways.

It appears that Vargas Llosa has grasped the essence of Classical concerns and played the ludicrous Peruvian situation off against them. The Greek writers were preoccupied with the preservation of order against the encroachments of ever-threatening chaos, and one of the most fundamental elements in the process must be the orderly arrangement of male-female relationships. The question posed by the style and forms of a book such as *Pantaleón y las visitadoras*, then, is what happens when the very antithesis of marital propriety runs amok in the jungle. The tension between order and chaos is increased even more by the fact that it is precisely for the sake of ending the chaos that the army, which should be the prime representative of order in the country, instigates the process, euphemistically styling the situation "an extended biologico-psychological problem among the troop leaders and men" (p. 85). Moreover, the officer chosen to organize the service is a model of efficiency and control, as is the unit he organizes—the most efficient in the entire Peruvian army (p. 225)—but he, the organization, and, to a great extent, the nation as a whole become victims of the chaos inherent in the project.

Into every system of thought based on a cyclical view of time is built the assumption that as the cosmos moves away from the point of creation the power that holds it together is dissipated, in a sort of social entropy, so that eventually the advent of a period of chaos is inevitable. The chaos is often institutionalized, as for example in the Latin "carnival" that precedes Lent, itself a preparatory period for the new creation represented by Easter. Mircea Eliade states that in premodern societies the end of a temporal cycle is characterized by orgy, which he feels indicates a "desperate effort not to lose contact with being."[3] In the Classical world, this tradition took the form of the replacement of Apollo by Dionysus in the temple at Delphi for a period of three months out of each year.

Delphi was a sort of *axis mundi*, a Center of the Classical Greek spirit, and the alternation of the two very different deities is an acknowledgment of the fact that man cannot live by reason alone, not even in the Age of Pericles. Thus it is that at the appropriate season of the year and the sun god Apollo, representative of the rational order of the cosmos, made way for Dionysus, a god of fertility and therefore related more closely to the dark, somewhat disorderly powers of the moon.

It is important to take note of this fact because it is my contention that underneath all the zany occurrences and transformations of Vargas Llosa's novel what is really going on is a process analogous to that replacement of Apollo by Dionysus at Delphi. What is striking, aside from the fact that in the present case Dionysus' rule lasts three years instead of three months, is the fact that both gods seem to be incarnate in a single character, so that a large part of the impact of the work—including the comic aspects—is a function of the ironies inherent in his metamorphosis from the one to the other.

As the narrative opens, it becomes clear that Pantaleón Pantoja is related to Apollo in a number of significant ways, notably in his preoccupation with maintaining rational control of all that is entrusted to him. It is this, no doubt, that has led him to dedicate his life so totally to military service that he prefers demotion and exile to leaving it. It might be noted that Apollo as Archer is something of a military figure also. The military is the most visible preserver of order in a society such as that of Peru, and Pantaleón is its highest expression within that context. Apollo is a solar diety, and it is especially appropriate that a theme involving him implicitly should show up in a novel from Peru, former center of the sun-worshipping Inca empire.

Solar deities and heroes are often associated with the lion, and there are probably at least two good reasons for this. Not only is the lion viewed as supreme in his realm, as is the sun, but it has been speculated that his mane suggests the sun's rays. The biblical Samson, whose glory, like that of the lion, is in his long hair, bears a name (*Shimshon*) that means "sun's man" or simply "solar," and he appears around Beth Shemesh, or "house of the sun," and kills a lion in one of the better-known episodes of his story.[4] The name "Apollon" itself, in fact, means "from the depths of the lion."[5]

Although the name Pantaleón is common in Peru, it was no doubt chosen by Vargas Llosa for reasons other than its mere realism. The combination of the Spanish *león* ("lion") with what can be taken as the neuter plural form of the Greek *pan* ("all") would make him "a lion in all things," which in fact he is. At one point, in the dream in which he is purified of his past sins by an enema (in order to plunge into his "heroic" adventure and, ironically, to become a spotless sacrificial victim), he roars like a lion (p. 84). In addition, he is associated with two women named Leonor: his mother and the madam who aids him.

At the risk of being accused of engaging in the facile reduction of all myth to solar myth, I wish to show how Pantaleón's trajectory does seem to follow the solar hero pattern, but only up to the point at which, rather than simply being temporarily overcome by the forces of the underworld and then emerging triumphant, he is *transformed into* one of the most important representatives of those forces, and then sacrificed. The occasion of all this would seem to be the onset of that period of sterility and chaos that appears when the cosmic cycle nears its end. The troops in the jungle have no sexual outlet, so that when they do arrive in a populated area the result tends to be mass rape. The measured, reasonable order of Apollo's solar reign has broken down (if it ever existed in fact), and even the military officers are forced to take refuge in a Dionysian solution to the problem. Bacchus is to have his day in that prime Jungian symbol of the collective unconscious known as the Amazon jungle.

One cannot help but wonder at the psychological implications of Vargas Llosa's having chosen a supremely Apollonian character to play the role of Dionysus. On the part of the military, Pantaleón is chosen because it is felt that he will be discreet in his handling of a highly irregular situation—will be able to prevent its dissolution into an uncontrollable state of affairs, and, just as importantly, to maintain this as a secret operation. It is tantamount to an attempt to make Dionysus subordinate to Apollo, whereas in the nature of the case it would appear to be an either/or proposition. On those psychological implications, Joan Cirlot's comments on Dionysus are enlightening: he is

> an infernal deity, and a symbol of the uninhibited unleashing of desire, or of the lifting of any inhibition or repression. Nietzsche drew attention to the antithesis between Apollo and Dionysus as symbols of the extreme views of art and life, drawing man, respectively, towards either order or chaos; or, in other words—in accordance with the Freudian death-wish—towards either existence and eternal life, or self-annihilation. The insatiable character of the Greek god . . . is apparent. . . . According to Jung, the Dionysus myth signifies the abyss of the "impassioned dissolution" of each individual, as a result of emotion carried to the extremes of paroxysm and in relation to the urge to escape from time into "pre-time," characteristic of the orgy; the myth is therefore representative of an unconscious urge.   (p. 78)

Cirlot also points out that two of the animals associated with Dionysus are the serpent and the he-goat, both of which become important in Pantaleón's trajectory, as we shall see.

It is normal for the solar hero to descend into the dark underworld, but for the express purpose of overcoming the dark forces there and emerging triumphant with new creative power brought up from the depths—not to be transformed into an infernal deity, as appears to be the case with Pantaleón Pantoja. In his methodical manner he descends into the jungle where he is to carry out his assigned task, and dutifully begins to frequent the places associated with prostitution. Not content with that, he begins experimenting with various local aphrodisiacs, first and significantly in a night spot known as "Las Tinieblas" ("darkness," but with definite overtones of something infernal and actively sinister; Lat. *tenebrae*). It is in another place, called "La Selva" ("the jungle") that he tries the most potent of them: "Something even worse [than the previous one] and *really satanic* is the potion known as *viborachado*," a mixture of the potent alcoholic beverage *aguardiente* and a pulverized poisonous snake (p. 90). It should be noted that in this passage he has revealed his descent into darkness and the jungle, and the beginnings of his association with the "uninhibited unleashing of desire" of which Cirlot speaks. Pantaleón remarks in his memo to his superior officers that the *viborachado* "produced in him an ardor and a stiffening of such ferocity and urgency that, with a regret as yet undiminished, he was compelled to retire to the uncomfortable rest room of the aforementioned establishment and engage in the solitary vice which he had believed extinct since the days of his childhood, in order to recover a certain measure of temperance and calm" (p. 91).

It is significant that the drink which produces what is for him a shameful loss of sexual inhibitions is specifically the one containing the body of the snake that can symbolize Dionysus as well as the breakdown of order in general (as related to Leviathan and other serpentine monsters that represent chaos in world mythology). It is in this unwitting Dionysian rite of communion that he becomes one with the god and is drawn gradually away from his Apollonian character. Like Adam, he experiences his encounter with the serpent and his fall in a place perceived as Paradise (p. 13), and it is, of course, no mere coincidence that the boat involved in his project is christened "Eva," after the woman who served as an instrument of the snake in the original fall from grace, order, and reason.

The airplane that is pressed into service is then named "Dalila," after another biblical devouring female, this one with a Hebrew name that may be a pun on a word meaning "night" (*Interpreter's Dictionary*, IV, 200), since she brings down the solar hero Samson just as Calypso (whose name is also associated with darkness) detains Odysseus. The archetypal role in question is actually carried out in the novel by the prostitute Olga, known as "La Brasileña," with whom Pantaleón has a torrid affair. It is her death that provokes Pantaleón into committing what takes on the proportions of an act of *hamartia*, since his "fatal flaw" appears to be a remnant of the idea of decency and order. At her funeral rites, Pantaleón appears back in his military uniform (in which, according to his aide, he is a different person [p. 181]), delivers a eulogy in honor of the prostitute that places her alongside the more traditional Peruvian military heroes, and reveals the true nature of the mission he has been carrying out (pp. 252–54).

What is taking place here is rather complex. It was out of the Dionysian rites that Greek tragedy sprang, and the catharsis experienced by the public as it viewed the sacrifice of the hero was associated with the human sacrifice of the more ancient Dionysian celebrations: as A. Le Marchant points out, Dionysus' "altars flowed with the blood of men."[6] Thus, Vargas Llosa's Dionysian hero, having unknowingly taken on the role of that god, slips quite naturally into the role of tragic hero as well. He is told at the outset by General Scavino, "The only way to avoid having this backfire on the institution is for you to sacrifice yourself" (p. 26). Pantaleón is destined to take on the sins of the common people and be sacrificed—though it is his alter ego, Brother Francisco, who actually dies, while Pantaleón, like the tragic hero Oedipus, merely goes into exile.

The transformation is carried out by the symbolic entrance of the infernal lunar serpent into the solar lion. Joseph Campbell comments, "The serpent . . . is symbolic of . . . the lunar mystery of time, while the lion is the solar power, the sun door to eternity,"[7] so that within a single character we now have a conflict between the eternal, idealistic values and those related to the periodic regeneration of the earth's fertility. The result is initially a series of those anomalies upon which the humor of the novel is built, and ultimately the hero's sacrifice. In this connection there is a bit of imagery the meaning of which might be cleared up by our pursuit of it beyond the obvious. It arises in Pantaleón's report to his superiors on the banquet held by his personnel on the occasion of the first anniversary of the Service. At first sight it looks like a simple parody of the Last Supper, and that is what it fundamentally is. The impression is strengthened by the fact that Pantaleón ingenuously refers to it as an "ágape" (p. 153). The word itself is the most noble of the Greek terms for love in the vocabulary of the Church, which became a technical term to designate the eucharistic meals of the early Christians in memory of Christ's Last Supper with the twelve disciples. Furthermore, just as the latter group sang a hymn before leaving the room, Pantaleón's employees have composed a "Visitors' Hymn" that they sing at the meal (p. 155).

The fact may be, however, that Pantaleón and his group have unwittingly gone *beyond* the Last Supper to something that underlies
it. That is, the Last Supper itself has been compared to a Dionysian
ritual meal, consisting as it did of several strikingly similar elements,
notably the stress on the wine, which is the item most often associated with Dionysus, and on the partaking of it as the essence of
the god. Thus, we may have still another connection of Pantaleón
with that deity.

As the transformation begins to take place, there is revealed in
Pantaleón an odd combination of a previously unknown sexual
passion and an attempt to control it in a thoroughly businesslike
manner.[8] No sooner has he arrived in the jungle than he becomes
a sexual fury with his wife, who has been accustomed to his very
proper sexual behavior (pp. 21–22), but then she finds him *timing*
their acts of intercourse in the interest of planning his program for
the troops (p. 70). At this point, his true position is ambiguous,
and to Pochita's comment, "I don't recognize you, Panta," he
adds, "I don't know who I am any more" (p. 22). This is the appropriate position for a hero in the process of transformation, as
in the case of Odysseus, who becomes "Noman" for a time. Never-
thelesss, in one of those instant cinematic scene changes that are
used to such good effect in the novel, the next line is uttered by
General Scavino: "I know very well who you are and what you've
come to Iquitos for." The general seems to have perceived his subordinate's incipient transformation into the god of revelry before
Pantaleón has.

One still wonders how objective and businesslike Pantaleón is
when he asks his orderly, "How can a person organize a Visitors'
Service without ever having had any contact with visitors in his
life, Bacacorzo?" (pp. 28–29). It may be either embarrassment or
insincerity that causes him to fumble around with his words when
he arrives in the red-light district: "I'd like to check on something,
ahem, hmm, hmm . . . , if possible. Solely for informational purposes" (p. 30). When introduced to the pimp, he still insists, "Don't
get me wrong, my interest in this is not personal, but rather technical" (p. 31). Even much later, when it has been remarked that
as the highly successful manager of a traveling brothel he is "finally
in his element" (p. 223) (in complete contrast to his own earlier
statement [p. 27]), and he has been told, "You've gone to the
other extreme" (p. 216), he protests that his behavior is only that
which his assignment calls for. To La Brasileña, who informs him
that he wears her out more than an entire regiment, he remarks,
"What's happening to my birdie is the fault of this job" (p. 214).
To her incredulity and argument that no man's libido is stirred up

on the basis of obligation, his reply is, "I'm not like everybody else, that's my problem. Things don't happen to me they way they do to other people" (p. 217). Insofar as this is true, it represents the fact that Pantaleón is the elect hero and must follow a predetermined course.

I have referred to Brother Francisco as Pantaleón's alter ego, and there is abundant textual evidence to indicate that Vargas Llosa intends him to be taken as such, but in just what way the two are to be connected in the reader's mind is more difficult to ascertain. More than once, Brother Francisco's religious movement is associated with Pantaleón's Service as one of the two "calamities" (p. 221) or "nightmares" (p. 304) of the jungle, and it is to be noted that both characters achieve their fame and success largely as leaders of groups of women. It would seem that the least one could say is that a rather grotesque revolution is taking place in that region at the two extremes of religion and prostitution, which should represent the good and evil propensities of man, respectively. Of course, it fails to work out that way: whereas Brother Francisco ends up by crucifying people—taking their lives rather than saving their souls—Pantaleón, involved in what would normally be the cynical exploitation of unfortunate women, is so thoughtful and efficient that they are delighted with their work; as his Chinese pimp puts it, "After Blothah Flancisco, Pantaleón is the gleatest" (p. 293).

It may be that the key to the relationship lies in the fact that when Dionysus reigns at Delphi there must be a priest to officiate at the rites, and by the same token, when Dionysian revelry prevails in the Amazonian region of Peru, someone must appear to take the role of priest from the more Apollonian Catholic clergymen. Someone must handle the religious aspects of the revolution, and he must do so in the spirit of the ancient rites, which of course end inevitably in human sacrifice. It is a curious point, and one pertinent to the thesis of this article, that the movement of these two characters is progressively backward in terms of civilization. With regard to animal sacrifice, we may note the irony of the name Francisco, which belonged to the saint who was known for his gentleness to all living creatures. The rites must, however, end in the more ancient human sacrifice if the Dionysian pattern is to be followed. There is, first, the case of the crucified infant, a tremendous shock to all initially, but later the occasion for the child's veneration and eventual deification. As in the Dionysian rites, in which sacrifices are offered to the god to ensure that the earth will continue to function properly, the perpetrators of this act "believed that with the sacrifice God would postpone the end of the world" (p. 131).

The question that arises is why disgrace and exile should be the final lot of a man who looks at first like a candidate for the role of solar hero. Even the Classical tragic hero typically follows the traditional steps of departure, penetration to the source of power, and life-enhancing return before he commits his sin and is sacrificed. Sophocles presents even the defeated, broken, and blinded Oedipus in the Colonus play as the greatest of men and makes his death a veritable apotheosis. Our question is one that applies to too many works of Spanish American prose fiction to be ignored. What is it that causes Rulfo's Juan Preciado in *Pedro Páramo* to descend into a Mexican Hades and never return? What of the hero-figure in each of the seven stories comprising García Márquez's *Eréndira* book, who seems to be endowed with the power to rescue the people, and who in every case turns out to be physically or morally disqualified? How is it that the Oliveira of Cortázar's *Rayuela*, at the end of a long search for the Center, may or may not attempt to dash his brains out on the chalked-in "Heaven" of a children's game?

The authors in question appear to be attempting to go home again and finding themselves unable to do so. There seems to be a definitive rejection of the linear concept of time and an acceptance of the cyclical variety, which normally includes the more or less firm expectation of periodic renewal. But each time a hero-figure descends to the primordial roots of the cosmos in search of power, either he lacks the ability to obtain it and return with it to renew his world, or the power is not there at all, or both (as in the case of Pedro Páramo's having slain his world and then having died himself). So the prophetic artist, speaking to his generation and for it, appears to be telling us that we are not quite ready yet to believe in the regular renewal that premodern man takes for granted. We have not seen it work yet, and perhaps we never will.

And perhaps *Pantaleón y las visitadoras* is speaking to just this issue in a subtle and somewhat complex way. Seemingly having raised his hero from his status as a common man and allowed (or forced) him to play the role of one god who is metamorphosed into another, Vargas Llosa then seems unwilling either to let his character be the totally successful hero typical of much of the world's mythology or to make him the tragic but still great Classical hero in his exile. All this in spite of the fact that the novel reveals elements of comedy and tragedy, both of which were derived from Dionysian worship. That is, the hero is exiled in disgrace as in tragedy, but at the end he *is* reunited with his wife, as in both comedy and narrative works such as the *Odyssey*. (His career is called a "black odyssey" at one point [p. 205].) In my opinion, the message implicit in all this is that in his arrival at Classical Greek forms modern man has not yet reached far enough into his primordial mythic roots to be able to begin again. It is as if the author and his characters were attempting to plant their feet on the bedrock of those Classical traditions only to find themselves falling through to the murky and uneasy depths of even more primitive thought.

My basis for this hypothesis is the fact that, even in his seeming transformation from the rational Apollo into the more primitive fertility god Dionysus, who "comes with his leopard skin upon his shoulders, for the beast is still part of his being" (Le Marchant, p. 18), Pantaleón seems unable to stop at the relatively civilized rites of the age of Pericles and finds himself in an age returning to human sacrifice.

Then the *dénouement* of the novel reveals at least two more very primitive motives. As mentioned above, one of the animals associated with Dionysus is the goat, in part, no doubt, because it was a sacrificial animal. The word "tragedy" means "goat song" and is rooted in the Dionysian rites. But there is an even more primitive way in which Vargas Llosa's characters are related to the goat. At the end of the novel we find the twin disasters of the jungle, Pantaleón and Brother Francisco, meeting their destinies at about the same time. Brother Francisco, finding that he is about to be recaptured, has himself crucified, rots on the cross, and is thrown into the river by soldiers. In the other case, it is stated that "it is imperative that the people forget the very existence of the famous Captain Pantoja" (p. 308), and he is exiled from the hot jungle to the very borders of the land, at cold Lake Titicaca. The point is that these ostensibly unrelated events take on significance in the careful manner in which the two are connected as doubles by the author, in that they reproduce one of the key features of the Hebrew Yom Kippur, or Day of Atonement:

[Aaron] is to receive two goats for a sacrifice for sin . . . from the community of the sons of Israel. . . . He is to draw lots for the two goats and allot one to Yahweh and the other to Azazel. Aaron is to offer up the goat whose lot was marked "For Yahweh" and offer it as a sacrifice for sin. The goat whose lot was marked "For Azazel" shall be set before Yahweh, still alive, to perform the rite of atonement over it, sending it out into the desert to Azazel.   (Leviticus 16:5–10, *Jerusalem Bible*)

Wilhelm Möller states that "Azazel" may simply mean "lonesome-ness" or "desert," but may be personified as a demon of the wilderness, in which case the word may be translated—significantly for our purposes—as "he who misleads others." It is noteworthy as well that "the two goats together are to be regarded as a single sin-sacrifice." They "represent two sides of the same thing."[9] As for the "rite of atonement," it is ironic how much greater an extension is here given to the early declaration to Pantaleón that he must sacrifice himself to avoid allowing the project to backfire on the army. At the end, he is moved to say, "The full responsibility is mine and mine alone" (p. 279).

In a very real sense, both of the characters are sacrificed for the sins of the people—Brother Francisco for their sin of lusting after a spectacular, bloodthirsty religion, and Pantaleón for their insatiable desire for illicit sex, as well as the sin of the military officers who conceive the quixotic plan in the first instance. As one of them says, "We have set an infernal machine in motion" (p. 241) —and of course, in the process, transformed one of their best officers into a primitive fertility god and then into a human scapegoat.

In fact, it is with this figure that we have broken through to perhaps the most primitive level of all, for there is in ancient mythology "the widespread institution of the human scapegoat, usually a misshapen person or one already under sentence of death, upon whom is saddled the taint of all sins and offenses which might otherwise be visited upon the community."[10] The fact that the name "Dionysus" means "lame god" may be pertinent here, but Pantaleón, of course, is "misshapen" only in that he himself has been thoroughly infected with the sexual madness he has been forced to set in motion, and by his act of glorification of La Brasileña, which is motivated only in part, it seems, by a sense of the rightness of the act, and partly by his blinding grief at the loss of the woman with whom he had become so deeply involved.

But there is more to the scapegoat theme as it is worked out in this novel. Within the range of primitive thinking—and I take for granted that many of its patterns survive in modern man—a king is the ideal subject for transformation into a scapegoat, since he is viewed as embodying the total essence of his people and the land to which they belong. Thus, when Oedipus violates the principles involved in the orderly succession of generations, both the people and the land become infertile. By the same token, once he is sent into exile and replaced by a virtuous man, all is well again. It is worth noting in this connection that the cynical journalist Sinchi tends to apply epithets of royalty to Pantaleón: "modern Babylonian sultan" (p. 188), "emperor of vice" (p. 190), and the like, so that in his being "polluted" by the prostitution project he seems to bring a plague upon both himself and his land, a plague that is removed only with his exile.

I have compared Pantaleón several times to Oedipus, but there is one particularly notable difference between them. Whereas Oedipus falls unknowingly into sin while engaged in a powerful effort to avoid it, Pantaleón becomes contaminated only gradually and in the full knowledge of what he is about. In addition, when the results of his acts are fully evident, instead of Oedipus' agonizing repentance, we have from Pantaleón the words, "I don't regret anything I have done" (p. 278). His *hybris* lies in his sense of duty, slightly tainted by his no longer suppressed libido.

Neither does he properly exhibit the Dionysian spirit he is forced to incarnate, for, although Dionysus is a spirit of disorder, his behavior leads ultimately to the order of a world renewed in its fertility; he uses only as means those chaotic, telluric forces of the cosmos which are associated with his name. The flat, hard ground must be broken up before it can produce new crops. For Pantaleón, on the contrary, the "fertility rites" are necessarily an end in themselves, and as such are paradoxically sterile. When one of the prostitutes does marry a customer, the result is a tremendous row, and the reversal of values that has taken place in Pantaleón's world of an orderly brothel is manifested in her plaintive question, "You mean it's a sin to get married?" (p. 197).

So it is that, even while corresponding superficially to some Classical patterns, Pantaleón's career violates them in their essential intent, which is the establishment and renewal of an orderly cosmos on the foundation of family life. It is for this reason, I believe, that he is unable to play the hero's role to the end, either as the untainted and triumphant hero of most of the world's mythology or as the tragic hero, noble though sacrificed.

In terms of psychology, our author seems to have recognized and done a masterful job of portraying what the Greeks already appear to have perceived in their myth involving Daphne's transformation into a laurel to avoid the pursuing Apollo—that there is a bit of Dionysus even in that god of rational behavior. Vargas Llosa has taken that recognition and caused it to function as the metamorphosis of Apollo into Dionysus, which in turn relates to Hegel's thesis that contrary forces may be fused in a synthesis simply because there is something essential that they share—a little yin in every yang.

West Virginia University
Morgantown

Notes

1. Alberto Giacometti, "A Letter," *Surrealists on Art*, ed. Lucy R. Lippard (Englewood Cliffs, N.J.: Prentice-Hall, 1970), p. 148.
2. Vargas Llosa's oral comments, IV Congreso de la Nueva Narrativa Hispanoamericana, Cali, Colombia, 13 August 1974.
3. Mircea Eliade, *The Myth of the Eternal Return, or Cosmos and History*, trans. Willard Trask (Princeton: Princeton Univ. Press, 1971), p. 92.
4. "Samson," *Interpreter's Dictionary of the Bible* (New York and Nashville: Abingdon, 1962), IV, 198–200. Hereafter cited in the text as *Interpreter's Dictionary*.
5. Joan E. Cirlot, *A Dictionary of Symbols*, trans. Jack Sage (New York: Philosophical Library, 1962), p. 14. Hereafter cited in the text by page number.
6. A. Le Marchant, *Greek Religion to the Time of Hesiod* (Manchester: Sherratt and Hughes, 1923), p. 18.
7. Joseph Campbell, *The Masks of God: Occidental Mythology* (New York: Viking, 1970), p. 467.
8. At the Cali conference referred to in note 2, I asked Vargas Llosa if he had read Vance Packard's *The Organization Man*. His reply was, "No, but I can tell what you're getting at from the title."
9. Wilhelm Möller, "Azazel," *International Standard Bible Encyclopedia*, ed. James Orr (Grand Rapids: Eerdmans, 1929), I, 343.
10. Theodore Gaster, *Myth, Legend and Custom in the Old Testament* (New York: Harper, 1969), II, 581.

Luis Harss

A City Boy

I find it hard to write about Vargas Llosa; there is simply too much of him. And I cannot say, "this or that is what counts"; one must take his work as a whole, at flood tide, as it were. One can, perhaps, even skip a book or two; the driving force is still there. To me, in short, he means a certain kind of concentrated energy. Surely no Spanish American writer is more devoted or more successful in his Flaubertian singlemindedness. Looking over his work, one finds no blind gropings, no brilliant failures, only a constant flow, straight from the source. Few writers in our highly intellectual literature appear less self-conscious (in spite of his critical rationalizations). In his work everything seems immediately "given" at face value. A comfortable "social relevance" obscures the element of private fantasy. Yet there are those famous demons—the cadet hero's Romantic inner voices—raging to be heard.

My struggle with Vargas Llosa began in 1965, with *La ciudad y los perros*. We both lived in Paris; we met in his two rumpled rooms near the Odéon to tape an interview. He wore a dark mustache, had slightly buck teeth, seemed rather dour. A kind of shadow came with him. The wife of a well-known Argentine writer also living in Paris at the time had, in a peevish moment, dismissed his work as "fine for a writer from an underdeveloped country." I knew that *La ciudad y los perros* had won some kind of prize in Spain. I had mixed feelings about it (those were the early days of the "boom"). The mechanics annoyed me; I thought they were an ostentatious display of faddish "technique." I had heard, somewhere, that Vargas Llosa wrote "straight" and then split up his episodes and jumbled them (as if that made any difference). Then there was his rather unexpected rehabilitation of dog-eat-dog Naturalism. I thought -being the survivor of a tough though nonmilitary boarding school myself—that it was a terror tactic disguising a childish shock at the fact of human cruelty. As in *Los jefes* (whose title inevitably recalled Sartre's "Enfance d'un chef"), I though I detected a nostalgic glorification, and even an aesthetic,

of the gang code. In a word, I suppose I found the novel powerful but in some ways rather silly. I couldn't get upset, for instance,
over adolescents torturing sick dogs or raping chickens (in my school
it was sheep). The characters, in spite of their tough stance, seemed
basically sentimentalized (and I think there remains this soft core
in Vargas Llosa's work). Further, they were drawn along such simple lines as to be mere walking puppets on the one hand, verbal
ectoplasms on the other. In short, the powers and complexities of
the novel were in the shuffling and counterpointing of scenes rather
than in dramatic structure. It seemed a therapeutic novel, an elaborate working out of personal traumas in slice-of-life disguise. Finally, there was the balancing act of the Epilogue, at once an empty spin-off and a wrapping up of loose ends. By then, for me at
any rate, the law of diminshing returns had set in. Once I knew
what was going on and who everyone was, I lost interest. Suspended
literary space without dramatic progression, however it might pur-
port to reflect a static social structure, did not work for me. It all,
somehow, "came off" too neatly, in a collage of voices that led
nowhere, because any part was equal to the whole. Even the creative energies of language were limited by an acceptance of its rhetorical patterns. The demons turned out to be childhood story ghosts.
The predictable and rather dull human psychologies seemed mere
conventions.

When I heard of the book being banned and even burned in
Lima, I was surprised. To me it seemed to evolve in its own fantastic circle, quite detached from any political or social context,
as a sort of black fairy tale, much closer, even in its violence, to
romance than to the kind of documentary "realism" implied in its
Naturalistic premises. I found the author, in a sense, like his work:
driven but at the same time coolly organized in a world of tastes
and opinions that buttressed him in his obsessions. His fanciful
theory of the rise of the novel from the garbage of history (and
the novelist as carrion eater feeding on the corpse of decaying society); his love of chivalric romance and distrust of humor (I remember his disapproval when I ventured the opinion that Dostoy-
evsky was a humorist); his melodramatic (and mechanistic) conception of human behavior, all disconcerted me so much that I forgot
to turn on the tape recorder while he talked and had to ask for another session in which, according to my notes, he went over exactly the same ground, in a surprising repetition of opinions as neatly
articulated—and uttered in the same dramatic whispers—the second time as the first.

Since then, of course, times have changed; masks have fallen. I
realize my bias is a form of resistance to the impact of works that,

within their more or less tortuous "realism," are much better than
they ought to be. The mistake, in the sixties, was thinking of Vargas
Llosa as a "total novelist" in the Tolstoyan sense. Certainly, by
that measure—with its implied scope and depth—he falls short.
There are no rounded characters; the range of emotions—urges
and instincts would perhaps be more accurate terms—is pretty basic. Oddly enough, the elaborately "subjective" techniques—interior monologues, streams of consciousness—create atmosphere, not
character. Even social types are often barely distinct in manner or
details of speech or behavior that a reader can perceive. When Don
Anselmo, for instance, toward the end of *La Casa Verde*, is revealed
as a jungle man, the piece fits into the poetic scheme (one might
almost say the color scheme) but does not reflect back on an understanding of the character or add to his specific weight. The fact
that identities are constantly in flux tends to efface them. There is
a play of surfaces rather than people, of textures rather than actions. The "total novel," it soon appears, is not a teeming social
canvas but a verbal substance of obsessive force, turning on itself.
Out of this substance the characters are born as variations on a
single theme of shadow being and loss of self in the metaphorical
tide of the poem that grinds them to dust. The Vargas Llosan process is self-consuming. A single page, endlessly multiplied by syntactical devices, as in a series of exponential mirrors, could stand
for each of his crowded volumes. The tapeworm he has spoken of
grows fat on its own hunger and—as the characters, fulfilled only
in their bloated dreams as they prey on the corpse of their defeat—
dies of its own bloom.

In 1966—the year of *La Casa Verde*—Vargas Llosa was in Buenos Aires as a member of a literary jury. I worked for the magazine
(*Primera plana*) that was cosponsoring the contest (with the Editorial Sudamericana), and we met again, briefly. The "boom" was
now official; a high priest, Rodríguez Monegal, was there to con-
secrate it. As the youngest member of the "boom," Vargas Llosa
seemed its walking symbol. I remember Cuba was in the air—and
Carpentier, who was declared a reactionary novelist because of his
historical fatalism (however forward-looking he might be in his
political ideology). There was also José Bianco, another member
of the jury (and one of the writers "revived" by the "boom"),
who had just been run off the editorial board of *Sur* by Victoria
Ocampo for his Fidelista sympathies. In this atmosphere it was
perhaps inevitable that the "Premio *Primera Plana*"—through Vargas
Llosa's insistence, some said, and possibly, according to others, because he was the only one to have read all the manuscripts—be given
to an obscure Paraguayan novelist (Gabriel Casaccia), for his craft

and social conscience. I thought it was one of those bleak moments
in which everyone was afraid to seem strange or eccentric. There
was a party in the Alvear Palace Hotel, where Leopoldo Marechal,
another survivor of political wars (he had been an unfashionable
Peronista in the forties and fifties) managed to look very much
like Borges (his deadly enemy). Among the books presented to the
contest was Néstor Sánchez's *Nosotros dos*, whose literary terrorism went unsung.

By then I knew *La Casa Verde*; in fact, Vargas Llosa had been
kind enough to show it to me in manuscript in Paris; and its Naturalist aura deceived me. In a sense, I suppose it was a jungle novel
with the usual themes and characters (the "green hell's" familiar
outlaws), but transfused with myth and a poetry of movement and
literary reminiscence (Flaubert, Conrad) that enriched its central
metaphor. I found its "straight" passages—Don Anselmo and the
founding of the Green House—rather dreary, and others (the rape
of Antonia) bloated and sentimental. But the jungle fantasy (Fushía's island dream, Aquilino's friendship, the tidal movement of
shadowy figures up and down the river of life and death) was incandescent. At the time I didn't know of the brothel with the
green shutters in *L'Education sentimentale* (where there is also
a blind harpist, on a river boat), or of the famous seventeenth-cen-
tury Tokyo brothel with 2,500 courtesans (the same that later inspired Utamaro) and also called the Green House, and it was these
mysterious coincidences that eventually—and perhaps not totally
irrelevantly—brought the book to life for me. The Naturalist saga,
it turned out, was a fantastic romance of love ravished and friendship betrayed. The machista gang code of the Unconquerables
(pimping filibusters blowing their brains out at Russian roulette)
had its counterpart, or Romantic undertow, in the limpid and tender friendship of Fushía and Aquilino. The jungle ethic, in a sort
of inverted metaphor—the aesthetics of the gang code raised to
poetry—turned out to be a gentle bard's song of lost paradise.

A year went by; then there was *Los cachorros*, which I thought
a noisy contrivance (another bloated horror story); and, somewhere in those years of constant Cuban crisis, the Rómulo Gallegos prize, which was noteworthy (according to the joke current at
the time) for the confusion that ensued when the aging Gallegos
thought he was to be the recipient rather than the honored deliv-
erer of the prize, and for Vargas Llosa's controversial acceptance
speech in which he managed to bite the hand that fed him. I forget his exact words, but they reflected the kind of maneuvering
for position that went on in those days when writers thought they
were social critics (in Argentina the left would soon be coming

around to backing Perón as a transitional figure on the road to the
Socialist utopia). The story had a gossipy footnote: it was said that
Vargas Llosa had invested the money of the prize in a Lima apart-
ment house that soon burned to the ground. The flame (if it existed) seemed symbolic of the writer's burning bridges, in his struggle to remain independent of every "system." There was dignity—
a dignity not always shared by other writers—and no little courage
in Vargas Llosa's defense, during those "Cuban" years, of the writer's vocation, against all political odds. It was, of course, a defense
of inner life, of the private self in exile from the demands of history (as defined by narrow ideologues). The writer, he said in various ways, was Camus's rebel, always on the fringes—sometimes the
lunatic fringes —of the social order, a freeshooter in the shadows of
the collective imagination. In his famous polemic with Angel Ra-
ma, for instance, during which much ink was wasted on both sides,
he wore the dark cape of the carrion eater in an almost Baudelair-
ian vindication of his "satanic Romanticism" over the "historical
terrorism" of the neo-Marxist commissars of literature. The psy-
chobiography of García Márquez that he developed in *Historia de
un deicidio* was a portrait of the demon artist (in knight-errant
dress) stalking the back alleys of the mind. The "autonomy" of
the artist's "verbal world"—a system in its own right—had the ob-
sessional quality of private fantasy.

Still, one must consider Vargas Llosa a "social novelist," if only
because of the vast public screen on which he projects his fantasies,
but also because of his highly "socialized" scale of values. In a
sense, he is the least radical of Spanish American writers. He uses
words as he hears them (there is none of the poet's distrust of language) and "plunders" reality as he sees it. His work is in shuffling
the bits of the puzzle to heighten their effect, not in reordering
perception. There is something institutionalized, even a bit bureau-
cratic, in the way he maps out his territory. The moralist is never
far from the surface, not so much judging the situation or the behavior of the characters as imposing certain "realistic" priorities.
It seems people behave in certain ways and clash on certain issues,
and there can be no deviance from the basic pattern. Even deviance within the pattern (such as homosexuality in *Conversación
en La Catedral*) is highly conventionalized. The result is that whole
areas of experience, when not reduced to some behavioral formula,
are blocked out. And yet, as I say this, I realize how unjust I am
being in constantly falling back on my first impressions of Vargas
Llosa, carried over from my reading of his early works. No doubt
over the years he has opened himself to unexpected searches and
seizures. *La ciudad y los perros* was, at least in underlying philos-

ophy, an almost totally behavioral novel. Its mechanics seemed a clear reflection of social and historical determinism (in what one might call the Sartrean variant of Faulknerian techniques). But, just as clearly, *La Casa Verde* breaks into areas of "nonhistorical" myth and metaphor. The "break" occurs, as it should, at the limits of perception, as we suddenly see through the phenomenological veil into the strangeness of mythical landscape. Oddly enough, the estrangement occurs not in the rather laborious "mythical" passages involving Don Anselmo and the Green House (which reduce myth to popular fantasy), but in the flowing mental scenery that carries us up and down the river with Aquilino and Fushía. The harpist, in a sense, belabors the Orphic theme; he "socializes" (or conventionalizes) it by making it too obvious (and thus losing much of his demonic stature). But in Fushía and Aquilino we hear a more shadowy music. They seem like mutants in the behavioral scheme, floating dream figures from some darker world. Even more surprising (to me at least) was the humor of *Pantaleón y las visitadoras.* A "situational" humor, to be sure, but one that nevertheless efficiently breaks down the Naturalist framework. It wasn't so long ago that Vargas Llosa used to say he was immune to humor in literature. Just as he claimed man was totally conditioned by his historical and social environment. So, obviously, there are aleatory factors at work.

A certain distance can be measured, I think, between two of Vargas Llosa's articles written about ten years apart. The first is his introduction to the 1967 Chilean edition of José María Arguedas's *Los ríos profundos*; the second, a recent note (in *Inti, Revista de literatura hispánica*, no. 4, Autumn 1976) on Camus. In the first, Vargas Llosa is very much the city boy. I mean, an instinctively urban writer, with all the prejudices that implies. The city—whether Paris, Barcelona, or Piura—means time, history, social conflict. Escape from the laws of the concrete jungle is difficult. Private corners, inner visions, seem to lead outside history and its appearance of ultimate "reality." For the Romantic Satanist this poses the constant danger—known to poets, madmen, and criminals—of spinning off into private fantasy. The Surrealist dream of a borderless community of being soon turns into a nightmare or an artificial paradise. Against these dark forces—the monsters engendered by the sleep of reason—the city stands fast. Compared to the mad bombings of poets, its conflicts, however violent, seem "real" and even —socially, historically—rational. And precisely the blind spot we find in Vargas Llosa at this time is his obsessive rationalism. Beyond the city, he senses, lie uncharted areas: the sexual jungle of the Green House; the "irrational" world of talking plants of the nature poet. Ernesto, the protagonist of *Los ríos profundos*, in Arguedas's conception, is a boy torn from the natural order (as reflected in the communal life of the *ayllu*). He lives in his thoughts and memories, a misfit in white and mestizo society, listening to the voices of dead gods. Rivers, trees, mountains, and the music of a spinning top (and wandering harpists) speak to him with animistic fervor. Ernesto's communion with the natural order is part of an ethos, not mere poetic ornament. But for Vargas Llosa, this "exaggerated enthusiasm for nature," which "verges on mystic rapture," turns the boy into a sort of freak. Animism is clearly equated with alienation, not just from the surrounding society (which is Arguedas's point), but from some sort of rational scheme that Vargas Llosa subscribes to as fully as do the boy's tormentors. Thus, he dismisses Ernesto's "pagan idealization" of plants, objects, and animals, his "fatalistic irrationalism" and "disguised fetishism"—which he calls absurdist and superstitious—as "a sort of inheritance of his Indian spiritual half." On the whole, the short article damns Arguedas with faint praise and raises questions about Vargas Llosa's ability to cope with certain perceptions that might appear to shake the stability of our factual world of habit and prejudice, a world that relegates much that we know to unreality. But in the more recent article, Arguedas appears reincarnated—and rehabilitated—in Camus, the country boy for whom nature was the "primordial presence," bursting through the walls of cement and asphalt. "History does not explain the natural universe," Vargas Llosa quotes Camus, who opposed the "natural man" to his blighted city cousin. "It was perhaps this conviction," says Vargas Llosa, "that separated Camus from the intellectuals of his generation" who "all, Marxists or Catholics, liberals or existentialists, had something in common: the idolatry of history." Vargas Llosa might be speaking of himself in the sixties when he defines these intellectuals, with whom he identified in his early rejection of Camus, as all coinciding on one point: that "man is an eminently social being, and understanding his miseries and sufferings, as well as proposing solutions to his problems, is something that can only be undertaken within the framework of history." Camus, he goes on to say, rejected the "modern commandment" that reduces man's fate to historical imperatives. He blamed the city, with its concentration of political, economic, and ideological power, for the "historical absolutism" that had cut man off from his roots in other times and places. There is a man, Vargas Llosa suggests (as Camus did before him), outside history, capable of other forms of individual and communal life. In Camus-Arguedas—joined, as Vargas Llosa sees them, in their "mystical identification with the elements"

–this man was a nature worshiper. But he could also—in some future explosion of awareness on the part of an author who has yet to burst his last barriers—be one of the city's mad bombers.

West Virginia University
Morgantown

Malva E. Filer

Vargas Llosa, the Novelist as a Critic

The dedication of Vargas Llosa to the task of literary criticism
has resulted, to date, in a book on García Márquez, two essays on
Tirant lo Blanc,[1] a book on Flaubert and *Madame Bovary* entitled
La orgía perpetua, plus several book reviews and short articles in
newspapers and literary magazines. The current bibliography on
Vargas Llosa[2] does not yet give enough attention to these works
of literary criticism. I believe these to be worthy of independent
study, since they allow us to share the creative experience of a
very perceptive novelist-reader. Also, in giving expression to his
most carefully considered ideas about these authors, Vargas Llosa
is clarifying to himself, and for our benefit, the process of his own
formation and the principles that have guided him as a writer. No
doubt, Vargas Llosa's essay on *Madame Bovary*, for which he has
used excellent selective bibliographical sources, is both the most
serious study on the subject written in Spanish and the occasion
for an analysis of the Peruvian novelist's artistic credo. Our focus
here is on Vargas Llosa's perception of his indebtedness to the
French writer and on how this influence may have contributed
to his own brand of literary realism.

Vargas Llosa approaches the novel from three points of view, all
of which —he says—are always used by critics, no matter what school
of literary criticism they might subscribe to. They take into account the impact the work has on its readers, what the novel is in
itself, and its place and importance in the history of literature. The
first part of the essay deals, therefore, with Vargas Llosa's enthusiasm for Flaubert's works—*Madame Bovary* in particular—and his
affinity with the French novelist's attitude toward writing. He explains his predilection for *Madame Bovary* by saying that he prefers works built with rigorous order and symmetry, that have a beginning and an end, and impress us as being self-sufficient, closed,
and finished. He favors this type of novel over the open novel that
deliberately suggests vagueness or conveys the picture of an unfinished process. What he likes to find in books is not a reflection

of the flux and indeterminate quality of life but, on the contrary, totalities, arbitrary but convincing structures that seem to be a synthesis of reality, a summary of life (pp. 18–19).

This preference, stated by Vargas Llosa in order to account for his enduring devotion to Flaubert's novel, may also have prompted his choice of García Márquez as a subject for a book. He also finds in this Colombian writer a will to unify, to build a closed reality, an autonomous world (*García Márquez*, p. 87). For Vargas Llosa, *Cien años de soledad* marks the culmination of the process by which García Márquez has built a fictitious reality. It is a "total novel" and that implies, in his view, the writer's usurping the Divine creative powers, taking the place of God.[3] The novelist, he thinks, works toward a description of a "total reality" and confronts "real reality" with an image that is both its expression and its negation (*García Márquez*, p. 480).

Vargas Llosa's concept of realism is, to be sure, not the simple-minded realism of those who would want the literary work to faithfully reproduce reality (as if this goal was indeed attainable). For him a novel is always an invention of reality. However, he prefers those novels that feign the real rather than the unreal, for unreality is extremely "boring" to him (*La orgía*, p. 44). Within this context of realism, he openly expresses his attraction to those novels that include violence, sex, and melodrama. He feels that Flaubert's mastery is evident in the measuring and distribution of the erotic in *Madame Bovary* (*La orgía*, p. 44).

If Flaubert's novels evoked in Vargas Llosa such an enthusiastic response, Flaubert's letters, which he started to read in 1962, were a source of inspiration and encouragement for his own literary efforts. He recommends them as a guide for the literary education of young writers. His careful reading of the *Correspondance* helped him to avoid the distortion of seeing Flaubert as a "formalist" for whom the essential was to describe, and not to narrate.[4] Quoting from his letters, Vargas Llosa shows how Flaubert was aware of the function and importance of anecdote and expresses his pleasure at being able to prove that the great master's idea of the novel coincides with his own. Another point of affinity that he discovered in the *Correspondance* is Flaubert's enthusiasm for the novels of chivalry.

In his "Carta de batalla por *Tirant lo Blanc*,"[5] Vargas Llosa calls Martorell the first in that lineage of God's supplanters that are, for him, the creators of the "total novel." According to him, Flaubert perfected and modernized a concept of fiction that was already present in the chivalresque novels, particularly in *Tirant lo Blanc*: fiction as self-sufficient reality, with the elimination of the narrator from the narrative. Flaubert was the first to elaborate on the need to abolish the author, so that the work of fiction would seem to depend only on itself and would convey to the reader the perfect illusion of life. However, notes Vargas Llosa, four centuries before Martorell already had the intuition that autonomy was the necessary condition for the existence of fiction, that he had to banish himself, or at least hide, so that the world he had built could live for the reader.[6] Also, in *Tirant lo Blanc*, he detects an awareness of the need to keep a distance from the described reality in order to render it vividly. Vargas Llosa finds in Martorell's novel not only the totalizing ambition of "God's supplanters," but also techniques and methods of organization that already announce the strategy of the modern novel.[7] He traces to *Tirant lo Blanc*, what he calls in Bretonian language, the principle of the "vases communicants," which has been extensively used ever since Flaubert made it famous in his chapter on the "Comices Agricoles" in *Madame Bovary*. Enriching the role of the "vases communicants" is one of the major contributions made by Vargas Llosa to literary technique in the Spanish American novel. His expanded versions of that device are called by J. M. Oviedo "telescopic procedures."[8] They are narratives that intertwine two dialogues—one present, the other evoked and made present by the first—happening in two different moments of time and space. *La Casa Verde* offers a rich variety of these procedures:

> "And did you get away with much money, Fushía?" Aquilino asked.
> "Five thousand *soles*, Don Julio," Don Fabio said. "And my passport and some silverware. I'm terribly upset, Señor Reátegui. I know what you must think of me. But I'll make it up to you, I swear, with the sweat of my brow, Don Julio, down to the last cent."
> "Haven't you ever felt sorry, Fushía?" Aquilino said. "I've been asking you that question for quite a few years now."
> "For robbing that bastard Reátegui?" Fushía asked. "That guy is rich because he stole more than me, old man. But he had something to begin with and I didn't have anything. That was always my bad luck, I always had to start from scratch."
> "And what's your head for, then?" Julio Reátegui asked. "How come it didn't ever occur to you to ask to see his papers, Don Fabio?"   (p. 41)

Vargas Llosa makes reference to the circumstances of the conception of *Madame Bovary* and to the long and painful process of writing that the self-demanding Flaubert imposed on himself. He follows the French novelist in his search for a new method of writing, for a way to avoid the pitfalls on which he blamed the failure of his first *Tentation de Saint Antoine*. Flaubert's theory of impersonality was mentioned in the letter to Louise Colet of 1 February 1852, in which he says: "Je tâche d'être boutonné et de suivre une ligne droite géométrique: nul lyrisme, pas de réflexions, la personalité de l'auteur absente."[9] Later on, he was to reaffirm this principle in his letter to Mlle de Chantepie (18 March 1857), in which he states that "l'artiste doit être dans son oevre comme Dieu dans la Création, invisible et toutpuissant, qu'on le sente partout, mais qu'on ne le voie pas."[10] He strongly believes that the novelist should take pains not to make value judgments, for truth is in everything.

Flaubert's ambition of objectivity, his effort to find a technique that would erase any traces left by the author, may imply, to some extent, a concept of the novel as a scientific product. The French writer was elaborating his ideas in the time of Comte and Claude Bernard, during the development of positivism and the enthronement of the experimental sciences as the model for all human knowledge. Nevertheless, he finds a receptive reader in Vargas Llosa who, one century later, says: "No escribo para demostrar nada" ("I don't write to prove anything").[11] If Flaubert has been said to describe with the impassivity of a physician, Vargas Llosa's objective view of reality is, most of the time, behavioristic in nature; what counts for him is manifested behavior, which he describes with a language of absolute neutrality.

A major aspect of Flaubert's method was the conscious pillage of "real reality" in order to build fictitious reality. But it is a complex of different experiences that provide the raw material that the writer transforms into fictitious reality. Vargas Llosa showed, in *Historia secreta de una novela*, how this type of process had developed when writing *La Casa Verde*. He interprets Flaubert's famous phrase "Madame Bovary c'est moi" as meaning that the novelist can invent stories stemming only from his own personal history. He documents Flaubert's method of converting personal experiences into literature, and his attitude, assumed early in life, of seeing people and events as literary material. "Je voudrais écrire tout ce que je vois, non tel qu'il est, mais transfiguré," Flaubert wrote to Louise Colet on 26 August 1853.[12] It is the novelist's addition to reality that makes for the literary work's originality and autonomy. If the concept of realism can be expanded to include the "added element," and is not conceived, therefore, as an attempt to produce by means of literature a mere duplication of the real, then and only then can Flaubert be called a realist—and Vargas Llosa be willing to accept this label for himself.

The conjugation of opposites, reality and illusion or—in Flaubert's words—the "lyric" and the "vulgar," constitutes a binary system on which fictitious reality is built. These dialectic aspects do not merge in a superior synthesis as in the Hegelian model but, on the contrary, coexist as different although mutually dependent elements. They require each other to achieve full reality (*La orgía*, p. 172). The association of opposites is, in Vargas Llosa's view, part of the "totalizing design." In fictitious reality, this ambition is expressed through the binary system, in which each object, event, or person is both itself and its contrary. Flaubert did not separate the virtuous from the villainous; he understood that kindness and wickedness could be attributed to the same person, and he presented the complexity of life with its ambiguities and contradictions (*La orgía*, p. 174). In Vargas Llosa, the desire to give literary expression to those moral considerations and ambiguities that he found in life no doubt played a major part in the writing of his first novel. *La ciudad y los perros* opens with the following quotation from Sartre (another decisive and acknowledged influence in his intellectual formation): "On joue les héros parce qu'on est lâche et les saints parce qu'on est méchant. . . ."[13]

Flaubert's free indirect style permits the narrator and the character to be so close that the reader sometimes has the impression of being addressed by the character himself. His cautious switches from omniscient-narrator to character-narrator are a far cry from the liberty and flexibility sanctioned by modern novelists. Vargas Llosa believes, however, that the importance of Flaubert's discovery for the development of contemporary narrative can hardly be overstressed, and that Flaubert's technique paved the way for Joyce's stream of consciousness. The switching of the point of view, used by most contemporary Spanish American novelists— Cortázar, Carlos Fuentes, Donoso, and others—is an important technique in the novels of Vargas Llosa. In *La ciudad y los perros*, for instance, not only does each character speak with his own voice but he is also viewed—like the Artemio Cruz of Carlos Fuentes—from both outside and inside. The whole narrative depends on these constant switches:

> "I could go and tell him I've got to have twenty *soles*, but I
> know what'd happen, he'd get all weepy and he'd give me
> forty or fifty, but that'd be just like telling him I forgive you
> for what you've done to my mother . . . Alberto's lips were
> moving silently under the wool muffler his mother had given

him a few months before. His jacket and his military cap, which he had pulled down to his ears, protected him against the cold. He was so used to the weight of the rifle that he hardly felt it. I could go and tell him there's no half way, not even if he sends us a check every month. . . . The regulations said that the cadet guards had to patrol the patios in front of their own barracks. . . ." (p. 14)

At the beginning of *Los cachorros*, Vargas Llosa makes switches, not unlike the ones he points out in *Madame Bovary*, but far more abrupt and extreme in form since they destroy normal syntax:

"They were still wearing short pants that year, we didn't smoke yet, among all sports they preferred football and we were learning to chase after the sea waves. . . . That year, when Cuéllar entered the Champagnat school. . . ."
(p. 13)

Vargas Llosa has continued to explore and enrich the technique of narration through *Conversación en La Catedral* and *Pantaleón y las visitadoras*. It should be observed, however, that for him technique is not an end in itself. When commenting on Flaubert's initial breakthrough into the rigid separation of omniscient-narrator and character-narrator, he points to the literary advantages derived from it. He thinks that this technique brings dynamism and condensation to the narrative and, at the same time, allows a phrase or a paragraph to reproduce a totality, a short text being able to narrate an event simultaneously from two perspectives: that of an impartial observer and that of the actors themselves (*La orgía*, p. 233). In *La Casa Verde*, for instance, the display of techniques—pluridimensional narration, "telescopic dialogues," juxtaposition of time levels, etc.—builds that total world that is his avowed ambition. Vargas Llosa strives to express objective and subjective reality simultaneously; his aim is a narrative where the individual points of view are dissolved into a collective narrator.

Madame Bovary brings into literature the world of the antihero. It breaks with romanticism by starting the kind of novel where mediocrity systematically submerges the characters, depriving them of moral, historical, or psychological greatness (*La orgía*, p. 248). "Pas de monstres et pas de héros,'" Flaubert wrote to George Sand in December 1875. The mediocre, however, is handled by Flaubert according to his view that the novelist must be, above all, an artist. The selection of a "realistic" subject does not exonerate a narrator from this responsibility, for whatever the subject—he thinks—the life of his book will depend on its form (*La orgía*, p. 255).

Critics have questioned the wisdom of Flaubert's selecting undistinguished characters such as Emma Bovary, Frédéric Moreau, Bouvard, and Pécuchet for his ambitious and self-demanding projects.[14] Even Sainte-Beuve's moderately positive review of *Madame Bovary* lamented the absence, in the novel, of "quelque figure à sentiments doux, purs, profonds et contenus, également vraie."[15] Another critic of that time, writing on *L'Education sentimentale*, complained of what he describes as Flaubert's "rage d'abaisser ce qui s'élève, d'éteindre ce qui brille, la science, le talent, le patriotisme. . . . les grandes vertus comme les petites."[16] Vargas Llosa, in a way quite similar to that of the French writer, has also populated his novels with mediocre, ignoble, and generally antiheroic characters. His people, unlike the tortured intellectual protagonists of Cortázar or the psychologically complex characters of Fuentes and Donoso, are, with few exceptions, simple, mostly ignorant, and incapable of greatness. Like Flaubert, but taking advantage of resources accumulated by a century of literary experience, Vargas Llosa builds a careful and complicated structure, innovating and developing sophisticated narrative techniques, in order to account for his world of prostitutes, rogues, exploited Indians, corrupt merchants, and lower-rank soldiers. His conscious and determined effort to be the architect of a total world, a world in which talent, heroism, and nobility are conspicuously absent, links Vargas Llosa, perhaps more than any other aspect, to the French master whom he admires so much.

When discussing the autobiographical elements that went into the composition of *La Casa Verde*, he mentions reading *L'Education sentimentale* while he was working on his novel and discovering, with emotion, the reference to "la maison de la Turque," a brothel to which Vargas Llosa's memory attributes, mistakenly, green painted shutters.[17] Actually, Flaubert's text does not include this feature,[18] much to the chagrin of those who would have loved the coincidence. Nevertheless, finding his own recollection of a "green house" in Piura so closely resembling the memory evoked by Frédéric and Deslauriers at the end of that novel added, no doubt, to his already strong feeling of empathy with Flaubert. There is, however, a deeper level at which this affinity becomes evident. *L'Education sentimentale* is hopelessly pessimistic with respect to human nature and society. Flaubert expressed his pessimism often in his letters, and his characters are a vivid illustration of the futility and failure of all human enterprises. *L'Education sentimentale* may have appealed to Vargas Llosa because it so completely embraces a decadent world, with characters that are inexorably bound to fail. Enid Starkie, in her book *Flaubert the Master*, points at failure as a recurrent aspect in Flaubert's life and novels. "There was failure of romantic love in *Madame Bovary*, failure of a whole generation in *L'Education sentimentale*, of religion in *La Tentation de Saint Antoine*, and of knowledge in *Bouvard et Pécuchet*."[19] The important point is, though, that their failure does not elevate the characters to the dignity of tragic heroes, for there is no dignity or greatness in them. The same is true of Vargas Llosa's novels. *La ciudad y los perros* deals a fatal blow to the myth of the young hero, and, from then on, his novels show life as a grinding machine that cancels all distinctions, kills any rebellious impulses, and leaves the living characters at the end as bare survivors, all initiative and strength gone. The quotation that opens the Epilogue of *La ciudad y los perros* could serve as an epigraph to all of Vargas Llosa's novels: ". . . in each lineage / deterioration exercises its dominion."

Wolfgang A. Luchting, in his essay on "Los fracasos de Vargas Llosa,"[20] points out this recurrent aspect in Vargas Llosa's fiction and relates it to the frustrated and frustrating life of the artist, particularly in Latin America. There is no question that the geographical and human context that forms the primitive and brutal world of Vargas Llosa's novels makes us see as civilized, refined, and comparatively mild Flaubert's picture of life through the upheavals of 1848, the failure of the Republic, and the triumph of the Second Empire. Latin American reality produces its own brand of frustrations, highly justified by a complex of negative social, economic, and political factors. And yet the destiny of Vargas Llosa's characters who—unlike Artemio Cruz or Aureliano Buendía—pass so obscurely through life cannot be accounted for solely on the basis of the above-mentioned factors. It is more likely to result from the writer's individual perspective that, in this case, has compounded the failure or futility of action with the general obscurity and baseness of his protagonists. Ricardo, Alberto, Jaguar (*La ciudad y los perros*), Anselmo, Bonifacia, Lituma (*La Casa Verde*), Ambrosio, Bermúdez, Amalia (*Conversación en La Catedral*), to name some, fit into the above description. The few educated characters—such as Fontana, the victimized French teacher of *La ciudad y los perros*, or Santiago Zavala, a University dropout turned mediocre journalist (*Conversación en La Catedral*)—are as impotent and frustrated as the others.[21]

Vargas Llosa's negative view, manifested in the description of his own country's social realities, obviously has a critical value. He would not want to be confused with those who make of literature an ideological tool. However, his novels may be interpreted as social criticism, rather than as expressing a view of man that would preclude the possibility of change. If this is correct, then the concept of critical realism[22] could very well apply to them. This point of view is especially encouraged by Vargas Llosa's statements in "La literatura es fuego,"[23] where he speaks of literature as a permanent form of insurrection. Literature's mission, he says, is to agitate, to keep men dissatisfied with themselves; its function is to stimulate change and improvement. It is interesting to note that Flaubert is, precisely, an example of a writer who had given up any hope or illusion with respect to the bourgeois society of his time. His novels can be placed and interpreted within the evolution of European critical realism.

Vargas Llosa's familiarity with Flaubert's novels and letters and his great admiration for the French writer—whom he has cultivated, he tells us, since 1959, and whom he has often mentioned as one of his models—have resulted in the extensive and serious essay on *Madame Bovary*, the subject of our study. His affinity with the nineteenth-century novelist, and frequent reading and thinking about his works and ideas, has had a strong and long lasting influence that can be traced in his own fiction. The similarities with Flaubert's principles, attitudes, and techniques, as manifested in Vargas Llosa's novels—technically complex while realistic in purpose and implacably negative in outlook—are some of the aspects pointed out in the preceding pages. The study of Vargas Llosa's works of literary criticism leads to a better understanding of his own novelistic production and enhances the image of this major contemporary figure in the world of Spanish American literature.

Brooklyn College
The City University of New York

Notes

1. Mario Vargas Llosa, "Carta de batalla por *Tirant lo Blanc*," prologue to Joanot Martorell, *Tirant lo Blanc* (Madrid: Alianza Editorial, 1969); Martín de Riquer and Mario Vargas Llosa, *El combate imaginario* (Barcelona: Barral Editores, 1972).

2. José Miguel Oviedo's *Mario Vargas Llosa: La invención de una realidad* (Barcelona: Barral Editores, 1970) was published prior to the publication of these critical works. We do not know whether a second recent edition, not yet available in this country, has made any additions on the subject. Rosa Boldori de Baldussi does not deal with it in *Vargas Llosa: un narrador y sus demonios* (Buenos Aires: F. G. Cambeiro, 1974). The same is true of the es-

says collected in *Homenaje a Vargas Llosa*, ed. Helmy F. Giacoman (New York: Las Americas,1971).

3. Vargas Llosa often uses the concept of deicide to describe the novelist's creation, even though the word, etymologically and traditionally, means the killing of God, and not the usurpation of God's powers.

4. *La orgía*, p. 50. Vargas Llosa criticizes Nathalie Sarraute for having taken out of context a fragment of Flaubert's letter to Louise Colet ("Ce qui me semble beau, ce que je voudrais faire, c'est un livre sur rien . . .") and having built on it a theory according to which Flaubert would have wanted to write novels without subject, characters, anecdote, or plot. He thinks that nothing could be further removed from the truth than this characterization of Flaubert's way of writing.

5. "Carta de batalla," p. 10.

6. Ibid., p. 23.

7. Ibid., p. 28.

8. Oviedo, p. 114.

9. Gustave Flaubert, *Oeuvres Complètes* (Paris: Louis Conard, 1902), III, 90.

10. Ibid., IV, 113.

11. Quoted by Oviedo in the epigraph to the third part of his book (see note 2).

12. Flaubert, *Oeuvres Complètes*, III, 347.

13. Alexandre Dumas, *Kean*, adapted by Jean-Paul Sartre (Paris: Gallimard, 1954), p. 81.

14. "Why did Flaubert choose, as special conduits of the life he proposed to depict, such inferior and in the case of Frédéric such abject human specimens," wondered Henry James in *The Art of Fiction* (New York: Oxford Univ. Press, 1948), p. 135.

15. Quoted by Maurice Nadeau in *Gustave Flaubert écrivain* (Paris: Ed. Denoël, 1969), p. 153.

16. Ibid., p. 213.

17. Mario Vargas Llosa, *Historia secreta de una novela* (Barcelona: Tusquets Editor, 1971), p. 59.

18. Gustave Flaubert, *L'Education sentimentale, Oeuvres*, II (Paris: "Bibliothèque de la Pléiade," Gallimard, 1948), p. 456. In its English version, Flaubert's text reads: "It was during the holidays of 1837 that they visited the Turkish woman. This name had been given to a lady who was really called Zoraïde Turc; and many people thought she actually was a Mohammedan from Turkey. This added to the romance of her establishment, which was situated on the river bank, behind the ramparts. Even in high summer there was shade round her house, which could be recognized by a bowl of goldfish and a pot of mignonette on the window ledge" (*Sentimental Education*, trans. A. Goldsmith [New York: Dutton, 1961], p. 396). Vargas Llosa's memory, after a few years, has probably merged the two images and lent, inadvertently, the green color of his own "house" to Flaubert's text. The statement in question first originated as an answer to Emir Rodríguez Monegal in "Madurez de Vargas Llosa," *Mundo Nuevo*, 3 (1966), reprinted in *Homenaje a Vargas Llosa*, p. 57.

19. Enid Starkie, *Flaubert the Master* (New York: Atheneum, 1971), p. 349.

20. Wolfgang A. Luchting, "Los fracasos de Vargas Llosa," *Mundo Nuevo*, 51–52 (September–October 1970), reprinted as "El fracaso como tema en Mario Vargas Llosa" in *Homenaje a Vargas Llosa*, p. 223.

21. In his last novel, *Pantaleón y las visitadoras*, Vargas Llosa adds another dimension to this overwhelming picture of failure. For Pantaleón's failure is, ironically, a result of his success. To some extent, the trajectory of Anselmo, the founder of the first, legendary Green House, had also been one of failure provoked by success. In *Pantaleón y las visitadoras*, this subject is conveyed by the use of techniques that are new to Vargas Llosa: humor, satire, and the direct presentation of letters, official documents, and dialogues. The kind of reality, though, remains the same, and Pantaleón's simpleminded devotion to his duty is punished in a way not unlike that of Lt. Gamboa of *La ciudad y los perros*.

22. I am using Georg Lukács's definition of critical realism, as explained in his book, *The Meaning of Contemporary Realism* (London: Merlin Press, 1962).

23. *Homenaje a Vargas Llosa*, pp. 17-21.

Robert Brody

Mario Vargas Llosa and the Totalization Impulse

Western literature is not a single entity but rather a whole whose
parts exist in relationship to each other, Octavio Paz reminds us,
"and the great works in our tradition [have been] consequences—
sometimes imitations—of other works."[1] To all except perhaps
Third World literature zealots, this seems reasonable enough. Why
then, one wonders, has contemporary fiction in Latin America
stimulated frequently outlandish critical attention regarding its
newness, its break with the past, its literary revolution, its boom?
Is it really lacking in ties to a tradition—and therefore devoid of
greatness, as one may infer from Paz's postulate—or has critical
enthusiasm accentuated the new without sufficiently exploring
the traditional bases that pervade many of Latin America's best
contemporary novels? In my view, the latter is true, just as it is
true that the Latin American novel since the 1940s has been of
high quality. Whether or not any individual novel is great still remains, however, to be seen.

Mario Vargas Llosa, perhaps because of his accessibility as inter-
viewee, critic, lecturer, and teacher, has made quite clear his debt
to literary tradition; that is, he is consciously aware of the relationship of his own work to earlier forms of fiction.[2] The first such relationship that strikes a reader, even after a cursory examination
of Vargas Llosa's work, is that he writes in the tradition of Realism. His Realism or Neo-Realism may be traced to a specific ante-
cedent. Virtually all the critics who discuss influences, including
Vargas Llosa himself, point out the presence of Flaubert in his
work. And his recent critical study, *La orgía perpetua. Flaubert
y Madame Bovary* (Barcelona: Seix Barral, 1975), testifies to the
pervasiveness of his relationship to one of the greatest nineteenth-
century novelists. The Flaubertian lesson, for Vargas Llosa, consists of the writer's objectivity and impartiality toward his work.
He sees this apparent authorial autonomy as having reached its apex
with Flaubert. The Peruvian novelist regards this aspect as Flaubert's
main contribution to the history of the novel, a contribution that
he consciously seeks to emulate in his own work.

The second main area of influence in Vargas Llosa's work involves a relationship even further back in time: the Medieval romance of chivalry, specifically *Tirant lo Blanc* by the Catalonian writer Joanot Martorell. In a 1966 lecture at the University of Montevideo, Vargas Llosa speculated that the true beginnings of what we know as the novel did not originate in ancient cultures but rather in the High Middle Ages with the appearance of novels of chivalry, which were both disinterested and subversive. They were disinterested in that they did not serve any pedagogical, exemplary, or didactic function. And they were truly subversive in that they and their frequently anonymous authors were accused of being "foolish, absurd, and—above all—of diverting men's attention from God toward worldly things."[3]

These are, then, the main literary relationships to be found in Vargas Llosa's major novels—*La ciudad y los perros, La Casa Verde,* and *Conversación en La Catedral*—which may indeed be seen as consequences of these relationships, according to Paz's statement.[4] My goal, however, is not only to indicate the ties to the past in Vargas Llosa's novels, but also to suggest the nature of his involvement in the making of a new tradition in the Latin American novel. This tradition, still in the process of formulation, has yet to be adequately studied, and to attempt to do so in this space would cloud my focus on Vargas Llosa, rather than sharpen it. Suffice it to say that efforts to define the essence of Latin American narrative fiction since the 1940s—that is, since the pioneering work of Borges, Asturias, and Carpentier—have resulted in the delineation of at least two fundamental forms, which are not necessarily mutually exclusive. One encompasses texts that portray fantasy, "magical realism," and "marvelous reality."[5] The other is a "totalization impulse," that now-famous effort to achieve the "total novel," or a novel embracing "total reality," which was first characterized by the appearance of fusive and integrative tendencies in the post-World War II novel. The Neo-Realist, regionalistic literature of the twenties and thirties had emphasized description of nature while it documented customs and social conflict. Novelists of the forties and fifties, such as Asturias in *El señor Presidente* and Rulfo in *Pedro Páramo*, did not reject these documentary themes and concerns but rather fused into them a type of subjectivity—in the form of imagination and dreams—previously unknown in Latin American fiction. More specifically, what Vargas Llosa refers to as the maturity of contemporary fiction comes about as the result of a shift of focus from external nature to the inner life of man. He comments on this change: "Man's problems, his nightmares, and his ambitions are the essential themes of this fiction, rather than the pampas, the plateaus, or the cane fields, as was the case in the primitive novel."[6] This, then, may be said to have been the first stage of the totalization impulse.

In the novels of the sixties there was not only a continuation of these tendencies but even an intensification, a veritable explosion of them in such books as Cortázar's *Rayuela*, García Márquez's *Cien años de soledad*, and Lezama Lima's *Paradiso*, to name a few. In addition to the already mentioned objective/subjective approximation, other forms of fusion and integration became visible, such as myth with history in García Márquez's work (which had also appeared in the novels of Asturias and Carpentier), and criticism with creation in Cortázar's. The Peruvian critic Julio Ortega, writing on contemporary Latin American fiction in his book, *La contemplación y la fiesta*, comments on an "integrative will" and a consequent self-critical feature as being the essential characteristics of this fiction: "Current Latin American fiction reveals an integrative will, which is its problem-generating nucleus, its insertion also into a more universal aesthetic; and this integrative impulse demands a self-critical perspective insofar as the genre itself is discussed in the writing."[7]

Novels displaying this "integrative will" have been referred to as "total novels." Luis Harss wrote of the current tendency toward the complete novel as being related to Leopoldo Marechal's *Adán Buenosayres* (1949), but did not elaborate as to the nature of this completeness.[8] More recently, in his excellent study of Carpentier's fiction, Roberto González Echevarría writes of *Cien años de soledad* and Fuentes's *La muerte de Artemio Cruz* as "the two most notorious exponents of what came to be known in the sixties as the 'total novel.'" He defines it as a Hegelian "relentless attempt to synthesize history and the self in a form of Latin American writing" and shows how this attempt characterizes at least one significant phase of Carpentier's literary trajectory.[9] Vargas Llosa himself has written most eloquently on the subject. It is certainly true, he states, that integration of the subjective dimension into the Latin American novel—either in the form of fantasy, myth, or oneiric experience—constitutes one of the essential characteristics of the "total novel." He also says, though, that the European and North American novel had undergone the very same process earlier in the century. The difference between the contemporary Latin American novel and its counterpart in Europe and North America may be indicated on a strictly literary basis but ultimately, Vargas Llosa theorizes, must be explained as a consequence of historical evolution. The basis of his theory is not new; societies in crisis generate superior novels. The novelist is a modern Janus with one face directed toward creation and the other toward destruction: "Rescuer and verbal gravedigger of an epoch, the great novelist is a kind of vulture: the putrid flesh of history is his favorite nourishment and has served to inspire him to his most audacious undertakings."[10]

With the societies of Latin American countries experiencing rapid decay, the entire continent is dying, says Vargas Llosa. This is the fundamental stimulus for today's novel, then, and the basis of its difference from narrative fiction being written elsewhere. Whether or not one agrees with this apocalyptic vision is not crucial to the present discussion. It is enough that we understand Vargas Llosa's vision of reality and how he uses it to explain the "total novel" as a pervasive, conspicuous fictional form in contemporary Latin America: "The historical reality, the framework of experiences within which the Latin American novelist writes, is a reality threatened with extinction. This perspective is traditionally the one which has nurtured the illusion—naive, demented, but nevertheless formidable—of wishing to recapture with words the total image of a world, of seeking to write novels that express this total reality not only qualitatively, but also quantitatively."[11] Today's novel, then, is at once an expression of the novelist's total rejection of reality and his attempt to replace it—totally.

The fact that Vargas Llosa sees the first appearance of this "total" fiction in the novels of chivalry would suggest the notion of the contemporary novel as a direct avatar of the earliest novels written. According to this scheme, the same could not be said about the contemporary novel in Europe and North America. This situation would necessitate expanding somewhat Paz's "imitation" and "consequence" idea to include historical circumstance as a significant variable. Be that as it may, Vargas Llosa has made perfectly clear his admiration for the "total novel," the progenitor of which is the Medieval novel of chivalry, and has related the richness of the contemporary Latin American novel to this totalization impulse. The question to be answered now deals with the shape this impulse assumes in his own work.

There is no doubt that the spatial-temporal juxtapositions, the montage effects, the narrative-dialogical mixtures, and the multiple perspective—to name some of the main techniques in Vargas Llosa's novels[12] —may be characterized as fusive and integrative. This does not mean, however, that all his major novels substantially exemplify his theoretical statements about the "total novel." As already suggested above, we may represent as an objective-subjective fusion the attempt to express reality in all its complexity and on all possible levels. The subjective dimension would encompass levels of experience to be found in fantasy, dreams, myth, magic, and mystery.

In *La ciudad y los perros*, the objective dimension predominates. Though there are areas of mystery, they are—for the most part—revealed at the end: Teresa's role as sweetheart to the Slave, Alberto, and Jaguar, for example. Another mystery revealed at the end is the identity of Jaguar as one of the novel's narrative voices. Also, the reader sees in this first novel an example of what Wolfgang Luchting calls "narrative relativization."[13] Vargas Llosa purposely has Jaguar both confess and deny his guilt in the murder of the Slave, thereby placing in doubt and ultimately abolishing objective information about the matter. The deliberately imposed subjectivity here deals with but one episode, however, and cannot be said to "totalize" the novel.

Rodríguez Monegal's statement that the whole of *La Casa Verde* is based on hidden identities is true enough but may also apply to all the major novels under consideration.[14] We have just seen how *La ciudad y los perros* functions in this respect. Let us temporarily postpone discussion of *La Casa Verde* to consider *Conversación en La Catedral*. The dynamic structure of the entire novel is based on hidden identities. Luchting's phrase, "narrative relativization," may be applied to Hortensia's murder but only until the novelist reveals the objective information, that is, the identification of Ambrosio as her murderer. The same holds true concerning Don Fermín's identity as a pederast and his relationship with Ambrosio. Though these disclosures objectify identities and relationships that had been purposely ambiguous, the objectification process is not complete. Ambrosio's motives for killing Hortensia remain ambiguous (subjective).[15] Again, as in the case of *La ciudad y los perros*, the subjective dimension appears in connection with a murder. In *Conversación*, we know the identity of the murderer but remain in doubt regarding his precise motives. This lack of objective information, however, certainly does not "totalize" this novel either, since it is limited, restricted to this one episode.

There is no doubt that, of the three major novels, *La Casa Verde* explores the subjective dimension to the most significant degree. Much has been written about the mythic aspect of this adventure novel,[16] but the specific term to indicate what Vargas Llosa does in *La Casa Verde* (whether he creates and utilizes myth, mythlike stories, legends, or fables) is not as important as a clear understanding of what he actually does, how he does it, and what it means. To be sure, the technique of hidden identities referred to above is at least as relevant a part of this novel as of the others, perhaps even more so. The striking series of transformations involved in

Bonifacia's change to La Selvática testifies to this. But her identity is revealed finally, just as is Jaguar's in *La ciudad* and Ambrosio's (as murderer) and Fermín's (as pederast) in *Conversación*.
There are other identities, however, that not only remain undis-
closed from an objective point of view, but are purposely made
contradictory and ambiguous.

One of these involves the existence or nonexistence of the first
Casa Verde, said to have been founded by Anselmo, and its subsequent destruction by fire. Early in the novel we learn of the mysterious stranger (Anselmo) who arrives in Piura and establishes
the brothel known as the Casa Verde. The perspective here is all-
important, since later in the novel the very existence of the first
Casa Verde is placed in doubt. Anselmo, in fact, now a musician
in the "second" Casa Verde, denies categorically that the first ever
existed. This, in turn, leads us to a reexamination of the foundation story and to the conclusion that the point of view from which
the story was told was not in fact a reliably omniscient one, but
rather a collective narrator constituted by the inhabitants of Piura
who were merely transmitting what they themselves had heard or
had been told by others.[17] There is no doubt about the existence
of the "second" Casa Verde in which Anselmo works as a musician.
There is sufficient doubt about the reality of the first, however,
though it definitely exists in the myths, legends, and fables of the
Piurans. The nature of this doubt provides an omnipresent subjective dimension to all the chapters dealing with Piura and thereby
enriches the reality represented in the novel.[18]

The most interesting hidden identity in *La Casa Verde*, then, is
the narrative voice of the people of Piura. It is interesting in that,
once revealed, it does not provide the reader with objective information, such as in the case of the disclosure of the Jaguar's narrative perspective in *La ciudad*. The hidden identity characteristic in
La ciudad and *Conversación* is akin to the technique known as
suspension of meaning, practiced by some of the best twentieth-
century novelists, notably Faulkner. Carefully hidden information
that is revealed gradually generates interest and produces tension,
which is resolved only when all the information is finally revealed.
No such resolution occurs in *La Casa Verde*. In fact, the process is
almost reversed. We accept the foundation story about the first
Casa Verde before realizing that we cannot count on the reliability
of its narrator for an objective account of reality. We finish the
novel without knowing for certain whether there ever was in fact
an original Casa Verde founded by Anselmo.

This purposeful ambiguity most certainly exemplifies the totalization impulse in Vargas Llosa's work.[19] But we may not conclude

that he has written the "total novel." Perhaps the conception of such a novel—one in which there would be a perfect balance of the subjective and objective portrayals of reality—is "naive" and "demented," according to the novelist's own words. And it is certainly easy to agree that any attempt to totally represent reality is doomed to failure from the outset. What is unequivocally present, though, in the work of Vargas Llosa, is the attempt, the impulse to do it. This impulse is stronger in *La Casa Verde* than in any other of his novels.[20]

The University of Texas at Austin

Notes

1. Octavio Paz, "A Literature without Criticism," *Times Literary Supplement*, 6 August 1976, p. 979.
2. For literary influences in the work of Vargas Llosa, see José Miguel Oviedo, *Mario Vargas Llosa: La invención de una realidad* (Barcelona: Barral Editores, 1970), pp. 45–61. In addition to an excellent discussion of major influences, Oviedo situates Vargas Llosa within the context of Peruvian narrative fiction.
3. Mario Vargas Llosa, *Mario Vargas Llosa: La novela. José María Arguedas: La novela* (Buenos Aires: América Nueva, 1974), p. 31.
4. The exclusion of *Pantaleón y las visitadoras* from consideration as a major novel is admittedly an opinion, not an established fact. This is not to suggest that *Pantaleón* is not inventive, entertaining, and skillfully written. It is. However, Oviedo (p. 185) writes of Vargas Llosa confessing privately that he had contributed as much complexity as he was able to *Conversación* and that from then on he wished to devote himself to a more humble literary project. *Pantaleón* seems to exemplify that wish.
5. The critical literature on this subject is relatively extensive and polemical. For an excellent introduction and overview, see Lorraine Elena Ben-Ur, "El realismo mágico en la crítica hispanoamericana," *Journal of Spanish Studies: Twentieth Century*, 4 (1976), 149–63.
6. Mario Vargas Llosa, "The Latin American Novel Today," trans. Nick Mills, *Books Abroad*, 44 (1970), 8.
7. Julio Ortega, "La narrativa latinoamericana actual," in *La contemplación y la fiesta* (Caracas: Monte Avila Editores, 1969), p. 8.
8. Luis Harss and Barbara Dohmann, *Into the Mainstream* (New York: Harper and Row, 1967), pp. 17–22.
9. Roberto González Echevarría, *Alejo Carpentier: The Pilgrim at Home* (Ithaca: Cornell Univ. Press, 1977), p. 273.
10. Vargas Llosa, "The Latin American Novel Today," p. 12.
11. Ibid., p. 16.
12. For an examination of techniques utilized in individual novels, see Oviedo. For a detailed, comprehensive study of how specific techniques function in the context of all the novels, see José Luis Martín, *La narrativa de Vargas Llosa: acercamiento estilístico* (Madrid: Editorial Gredos, 1974), pp. 153–257.

13. Wolfgang Luchting, "Los mitos y lo mitizante en *La Casa Verde*," *Mundo Nuevo*, 43 (January 1970), 57.

14. Rodríguez Monegal, "Madurez de Vargas Llosa," in *Narradoras de esta América: II* (Buenos Aires: Editorial Alfa Argentina, 1974), p. 416; this article originally appeared in *Mundo Nuevo*, 3 (September 1966), 62-72.

15. See Oviedo's discussion of *Conversación*, pp. 183-238.

16. See Luchting; Oviedo, pp. 121-66; and Vargas Llosa, *Historia secreta de una novela* (Barcelona: Tusquets Editor, 1971).

17. This collective narrator is neither immediately apparent nor even easily discernible after a first reading. See Oviedo's discussion of *La Casa Verde*, pp. 121-66; and Vargas Llosa, *Historia secreta*, p. 53 et passim.

18. A similar doubt exists with regard to the story of Anselmo and Toñita. Their story unfolds from basically the same collective-narrator point of view, and the reader is unable to decide whether to despise Anselmo for having taken advantage of the helpless Toñita or to admire him for the tenderness and love he devotes to her.

19. See Carlos Fuentes, "El afán totalizante de Vargas Llosa," in *La nueva novela hispanoamericana* (México: Editorial Joaquín Mortiz, 1969), pp. 35-48.

20. I wish to gratefully acknowledge support for this study from the Institute of Latin American Studies, the University of Texas at Austin.

Joseph A. Feustle, Jr.

Mario Vargas Llosa: A Labyrinth of Solitude

Thoroughly modern from the point of view of structure, style, and technique, Mario Vargas Llosa's works are also a tour de force on the more traditional themes of Latin American literature. From his first short stories, *Los jefes* (1959), through his most recent novel, *Pantaleón y las visitadoras* (1973), Vargas Llosa touches on themes such as violence, oppression, dictatorship, civilization versus barbarism, and solitude. As a literary theme, solitude is a constant in Latin American literature from Domingo Faustino Sarmiento's *Facundo, Civilization and Barbarism* of 1845 to Gabriel García Márquez's masterful *One Hundred Years of Solitude* of 1967. A manifestation of the barbarism of the *pampa*, solitude in Sarmiento's *Facundo* is geographic isolation: lack of roads, of railways, of the telegraph, in short, a lack of communication due to the vast size of the *pampas*. As the Latin American novel gradually turned away from its preoccupation with the land and the rural setting and more toward man himself in the twentieth-century urban setting, the theme of solitude ceased to be a simple problem of rivers, mountains, and plains and, by the 1950s, had become a chronic sociological and psychological problem seen as having its roots in the period of Conquest and as still exerting its influence today. The purpose of this study is to elucidate the form and meaning of solitude in the works of Mario Vargas Llosa, and, toward this end, I have chosen two traditional masters of this theme, the Argentinean essayist Ezequiel Martínez Estrada and the Mexican poet-essayist Octavio Paz, to provide the theory and background of solitude in Latin American literature.

To use the terminology of Martínez Estrada, the period of Conquest and Colonization of Latin America is the *mold* in which all the forces that control contemporary Latin America were formed.[1] The Wars of Independence changed nothing, leaving the colonial system intact: Spanish political control was replaced by foreign economic control; individual political freedoms suppressed by the Spaniards continued to be suppressed by the dictators who followed; and, above all, the original violence of the Conquest was perpetuated through the Wars of Independence into the many civil wars that followed. Little freedom was gained, and the essentially closed, violent colonial system is still visible in Latin America today.

The pre-Colonial period is Paradise Lost; the Colonial period is the mold and the moment of Original Sin. According to Martínez Estrada, the Original Sin of Latin America was the sin of rape—the rape of the native civilizations and of the native women by the conquerors. The Spaniard arrived alone. His first objective was the destruction of the native civilizations and confiscation of their riches; his first desire, concubines. Holding no love for his new lands, the conqueror conceived the future only through the eyes of avarice and lust (*Radiografía*, p. 106). In the words of the Mexican novelist Carlos Fuentes, this was the period of "original violation," of "founding illegitimacy," a period that was a "big rip-off" that populated the continent with bastards and sons of bitches.[2] Fuentes, in his most recent novel, *Terra Nostra*, has the New World colonized by the power-mad Guzmán and populated by Don Juan, two incarnations of avarice and lust whose drives cannot be tempered by Friar Julián.[3] Octavio Paz, in his *Labyrinth of Solitude*, finds in the Colonial Period, in the figures of Hernán Cortés and his Indian concubine Malinche, the roots of a psychosociological problem that he calls "children of the *Chingada*."[4] The fictional characters of Vargas Llosa's works are the descendents of the "founding illegitimacy," of the "big rip-off," and are presented as trapped in the closed labyrinth of appearances and expectations that is the Latin American concept of *hombría* (manliness).

Paz observes that the ideal of manliness for other people is that of an "open and aggressive fondness for combat" (p. 31). The Mexican, however, emphasizes "defensiveness, the readiness to repel any attack." The real man, *hombre, macho*, however, "is a hermetic being, closed up in himself, capable of guarding both himself and whatever has been confided to him." Even his language shows how closed and defensive the real man is: "the ideal of manliness is never to 'crack,' never to back down. Those who 'open themselves' up are cowards. Unlike other people, we believe that opening oneself up is a weakness or a betrayal" (pp. 29–30). The *hombre* is an essentially closed being, a component part of a society whose closed structure is characterized by impassivity, distrust, irony, suspicion, and love of form: "Form surrounds and sets bounds to our privacy, limiting its excesses, curbing its explosions, isolating and preserving it" (pp. 31–32), a love of form that is inherited from both the Spanish and Indian sides.

As far as women are concerned, Martínez Estrada points out

their traditional position as pleasure objects: women served the white invader as a nocturnal delight after a lazy day (*Radiografía*, p. 29). For Paz, woman is the essence of openness by the very nature of her sex. She is the victim of Fuentes's Don Juan, she is the *Chingada*: the mythical Mother, the female, passive, inert and open, defenseless against the exterior world (p. 77). The relationship between the *macho* and the *chingada* is violent and "is determined by the cynical power of the first and the impotence of the second." The essence of this relationship is found in the verb *chingar* ("to fuck"). Associated with alcohol, failure, disappointment, being made a fool of, the essence of *chingar* is violence: "*Chingar*, then, is to do violence to another. The verb is masculine, active, cruel: it stings, wounds, gashes, stains. And it provokes a bitter resentful satisfaction." A man may *chingar* a woman yet never possess her.

In Mario Vargas Llosa's works, the adjective *closed*, in the meaning that Octavio Paz has given to it, characterizes both society in general and the relationships between men and women within the code of *hombría*.

The characteristically closed structure of society is most visible in Vargas Llosa's presentation of caste and class relationships. The lines that divide one social group from another are well defined. The young men of the Leoncio Prado military academy in Vargas Llosa's first novel, *La ciudad y los perros*, arrive for their first year of study already well versed in the distinctions of class and caste: Alberto Fernández, the Poet, one of the principal characters in this novel, finds in his black schoolmate Vallano a characteristic synthesis of all blacks: they are untrustworthy and cowardly. Boa, another schoolmate, characterizes *serranos* (uplanders) as traitors, cowards, and of twisted souls. Whites, in Boa's words, are people with men's faces and women's souls. These same whites are the Zavalas of *Conversación en La Catedral*: a class of shallow people, preoccupied with appearances and material possessions and, to a great extent, degenerate. They are more worried that their son Santiago will associate with *cholos* (half-breeds) if he attends San Marcos University than with the quality of education that he will receive there. *Cholos*, as characterized by Santiago's brother Sparky, are shoeless, dirty, and infested with fleas. Cayo Bermúdez, the principal political figure in this same novel, ascends to Minister in the Odría Government but remains, success to the contrary, a mere *cholo* for the white, well-to-do Senator Fermín Zavala. *Cholo*, *zambo*, *negro*, and *serrano* are pejoratives that are used not only to characterize a particular class of people but also to drive a wedge between them, to keep them at the proper distance and in their proper place. Fictional characters in Vargas Llosa's works are first isolated in a particular caste or class, by color or geographic origin, and second, within their caste, by the mask of *hombría* that each is expected to wear.

As Ariel Dorfman has noted, there is no such thing as a code of honor in Vargas Llosa's works, only the code of *hombría*.[5] In *La ciudad y los perros*, the Leoncio Prado military academy serves as much as a correctional institute as an educational institution. The Army makes men out of boys. It instills in them the value system of *hombría*. This particular system of values places a premium on dominance of others through force and aggressive activity. The process itself is Darwinian, and the rules of the game are simple. Jaguar, the prototype of male aggression, expresses it this way: everybody is out to "screw" the other guy, and he who lets himself be "screwed" is ruined. As Jaguar says: "If they didn't fuck around with me it's because I'm more of a man. It's not my fault" (p. 293). Jaguar is "more of a man" because he never "cracks"; he remains closed and is always the one who "opens," never leaving himself "open." Opposite to Jaguar is the "Slave," Ricardo Arana, the one student who is "open" and who pays for it with his life. Sent to the Leoncio Prado to become a "man," Arana informs on his classmate Cava who has stolen an examination for the benefit of the dominant group of students who form the "Circle" that Jaguar heads. Arana breaks the mafia-like code of silence with which his classmates had responded to inquiries into the theft because he has fallen in love with Teresa, a girl he hardly knows. Love causes Arana to "crack" and also to open a "crack" in the closed structure of the group. His nickname, the "Slave," is indicative of his position in his peer-group structure. Unable to defend himself against Jaguar's superior ability as a fighter, Arana has earlier commited the sin of falling to his knees and begging to be left alone. At that moment Arana became a disgusting creature, a person without dignity, in Jaguar's words, a "Slave."

Alberto Fernández is a character situated between the extremes that Jaguar and the "Slave" represent. Cowards make him sick, and his advice to Arana is that one has to punch other people from time to time just to keep one's self-respect. After all, as he says, the important thing in the Army is to show that one is a real *macho*, that one has "balls," and can beat others to the punch and not be beaten. Alberto is neither completely "open" nor completely "closed." Like Arana, Alberto is a poor fighter, but he is able to survive because he is a master of appearances and words. He is able to build a wall of words and fake his way along. Like others, he too takes advantage of the "Slave," but, at the time of Arana's death, Alberto "opens" enough to denounce Jaguar as Arana's

killer. In this regard, Alberto is a fictional incarnation of the ambiguity that characterizes Vargas Llosa's works. Like Boa and Jaguar, he is able to give the impression of having had sex with the
prostitute Pies Dorados. Yet as the reader discovers, Alberto, in
bed with Pies Dorados, is incapable of intercourse, settling in the
end for manual stimulation. This is the chink in the wall of words
that Alberto uses to build the image of *macho* around himself.
Even before entering the Leoncio Prado, he is seen in the less than
macho position of having declared himself to Helena five times
and of having been dumped as many. Yet, at the end of the novel
we find Alberto planning his life in imitation of his father's: he
will go to the United States to study engineering, return and marry
his new girlfriend Marcela, and, like his father, be a "don Juan."
Like his father, Alberto is incapable of relating to a woman as an
equal on the "open" basis of love. He will be able to survive marriage to Marcela, who is indeed stronger than he, only with the
support of that society's double standard—one set of rules for the
male and quite a different one for the female. Alberto's life and
expectations raise the question of the meaning of women and love
within the closed structure of *hombría*.

Paz observes that women are thought of as inferior beings because, when they give themselves to a man in love, they "open"
themselves: "their inferiority is constitutional and resides in their
sex, their submissiveness, which is a wound that never heals" (*Labyrinth*, p. 30). Paz feels that the normal thing in love is for a man
also to open himself; however, the Mexican male conceives of love
as a conquest, a fight not so much to penetrate the other reality as
to violate it (p. 42). The "good" woman is passive, she is the *chingada*. The "bad" woman is always conceived as active, "hard and
impious and independent like the *macho*" (p. 38).

Discussing Arana's love for Teresa, the young girl that Alberto
also claims to love and the one who eventually marries Jaguar, Alberto mouths the opinion expected of the *hombre*: he likes women
only to go to bed with them. Jaguar, when he tells his friend Higueras that he is in love with a girl, Teresa, is told that love is the
worst thing that can befall a man, that he forgets about himself,
does strange things, and can "screw himself up" for life in a minute. Higueras has a remedy for love: a trip to the brothel. Love,
then, is one thing and sex another. Love is "open"; sex is "closed."
Love is dangerous because it makes the *macho* open himself. Sex
is an expression of this very *machismo*, a violation of the "other."

Eroticism is commonplace in the works of Vargas Llosa and is
presented in the most graphic and realistic of terms. In such sexual
episodes José Miguel Oviedo sees a liberating impulse, a savage pro-

test against the hypocrisy that infests the surroundings, a formula
of expression for those who cannot express themselves.[6] Regarding these same themes, José Luis Martín finds in them a manifestation of "uglyism," a characteristic actually more in line, in
our opinion, with the generally neo-baroque style of most Latin
American novels, than of what Martín has chosen to call "novels
of structural realism."[7] The opinions of Oviedo and Martín to the
contrary, I believe with Paz that modern eroticism, Vargas Llosa's
included, is mostly a rhetoric that reveals a society that stimulates
crime and condemns love (*Labyrinth*, p. 200).

In *La ciudad y los perros*, the Leoncio Prado is the location for
all manner of sexual activity—bestiality (a chicken and a dog), homosexual rape of a younger and weaker student, group masturba-
tion. These episodes are too polished to be a mere exercise in *V-
effekt*, a stage long since past in the Latin American novel. Each
of these episodes has, in my opinion, a common denominator:
they are expressions of *hombría*. Through these acts, the *macho*
shows his peers that he is indeed capable of sex with animals, of
imposing himself on another male, or of ejaculating first. He is
macho because he is capable of *violating* another body.

In *Conversación en La Catedral*, Vargas Llosa places a *voyeur*,
the aforementioned *cholo* Bermúdez, in opposition to a passive
pederast, the white Senator Zavala. In his analysis of the erotic
element in this novel, José Miguel Oviedo finds a lesson that becomes a commonplace: sex does not exculpate but rather serves
to sharpen the complexes of social inferiority, containing "a dose
of humiliation for the one" and leaving the other with a "clear
conscience" (p. 219). Oviedo perhaps uses the term "humiliation"
in the case of Fermín Zavala because Zavala is a *passive* pederast;
he takes the place of the woman and allows himself to be "opened"
by his pratman Ambrosio. There is no "humiliation" for Ambrosio
because he is the active agent; he penetrates, violates the other.
What leaves Cayo Bermúdez with a "clear conscience" is that,
although mostly passive and with a stoicism that borders on ata-
raxy, while not violating, he is not violated, he remains "closed."
Likewise, there is no humiliation for the young men of the Leoncio Prado who have intercourse with animals and other cadets for
the same reason: through these acts they are violating, expressing
their *hombría*. As Paz notes, in a homosexual relationship only the
passive partner is considered humiliated and abject (*Labyrinth*, p.
40). Nor is there any humiliation to be found in the homosexual
activity of Hortensia and Queta: they are, as Martínez Estrada
stated, traditional pleasure objects first, and women second. A
quick survey of the lexicon of sex in Vargas Llosa's works will pro-

vide additional insights into the interrelated concepts of humiliation and *hombría*.

Among the multiple synonyms for sexual intercourse in the works of Mario Vargas Llosa, a definite pattern is discernible, that of violence combined with sex. For example, in *La ciudad y los perros*, the verb *tirar* (to throw) also means "to lay" and is used in relation to animals, other males, and women. In *La Casa Verde*, the washerwomen returning from the river and the maids of the Buenos Aires district on their way to the market are frequently raped by the soldiers of the Grau Barracks: the victim is called an *atropellada* (from *atropellar*, "to trample" or "knock down"); the operation itself is a *fusilico* (from *fusil*: the penis is a rifle); and the children born from these violations are called "son of the *atropellada*," *fusiliquito* (little *fusilico*), or *siete leches* ("seven milks": "seven" for the number of possible fathers and "milks" for the similarity in color between semen and milk). In *Conversación en La Catedral*, one finds *correrse* (from *correr*, "to run"), *trabajar* ("to work"), *mojar* ("to wet"), and, the Hispanic standard, *joder* (Lat. *futuere*). Like the Mexican *chingar*, Vargas Llosa's use of *joder* is also associated with failure, the opening lines of the novel where Santiago asks himself at what moment Peru had "fucked" itself up and at what point in his own life had he "fucked" himself up, and with being made a fool of, as in Santiago's going home to his wife when Norwin wants him to stay in the bar: Santiago is afraid of his wife, he is "fucked up." Cuéllar, the principal character in *Los cachorros*, castrated by a dog while taking a shower at school, is better known by his nickname *Pichulita* (diminutive of *pichula*, synonym for the penis) than by his real name. *Los cachorros* narrates, then, the tragic life of Pichulita Cuéllar, a youth who, in a society that gives so much emphasis to *hombría*, has lost what Julio Ortega calls "the social symbol of integration" in his society.[8]

Obscenity in the works of Vargas Llosa is also more sexual than fecal. The worst and most violent obscenity, *Conchesumadre* ("motherfucker"), like any off-color reference to the Mother, is taboo. Like Paz's *Chingada*, the taboo lies in a reference to maternity, the Mother who has suffered the violent and corrosive action that the web implies. Thus, insulting the Mother leads to the violent episode that is found in *La Casa Verde*, which begins with this taboo and ends in a test of *hombría*—the game of Russian roulette that results in the death of Seminario and is the beginning of Lituma's downfall.

The code of *hombría* sets the standards for male behavior in the works of Vargas Llosa. It establishes the bounds and limits, and it creates a hermetic individual, closed off from others, defensive and violent. It differentiates between love and sex, between the female and the male, between what Paz calls the "open" and the "closed." Although there may be a danger in analyzing a Peruvian author with the critical tools borrowed from a Mexican and an Argentinian, a sufficient number of common denominators support my thesis that the code of *hombría* is both the form and the meaning of solitude in the works of Mario Vargas Llosa.

The University of Toledo
Toledo, Ohio

Notes

1. Ezequiel Martínez Estrada, *Radiografía de la pampa (X-Ray of The Pampa)*, 5th ed. (Buenos Aires: Editorial Losada, 1961), p. 340; hereafter cited in the text as *Radiografía*. See, also, Martínez Estrada's *Diferencias y semejanzas entre los países de la América Latina* (México: Universidad Nacional Autónoma de México, 1962), p. 147. Hereafter cited in the text as *Radiografía*.
2. Carlos Fuentes, *La nueva novela latinoamericana* (México: Joaquín Mortiz, 1969), pp. 45–46.
3. Carlos Fuentes, *Terra Nostra* (México: Joaquín Mortiz, 1975); English translation by Margaret Sayers Peden (New York: Farrar, Straus, Giroux, 1976).
4. Octavio Paz, *El laberinto de la soledad*, 4th ed. (México: Fondo de Cultura Económica, 1964); English translation by Lysander Kemp, *The Labyrinth of Solitude* (New York: Grove Press, 1961), pp. 75–80. This edition hereafter cited as *Labyrinth*.
5. Ariel Dorfman, "José María Arguedas y Mario Vargas Llosa: dos visiones de una sola América," *Homenaje a Mario Vargas Llosa*, ed. Helmy F. Giacomán and José Miguel Oviedo (New York: Las Américas, 1971), p. 150.
6. José Miguel Oviedo, *Mario Vargas Llosa: la invención de una realidad* (Barcelona: Barral Editores, 1970), p. 111; hereafter cited in the text by page number.
7. José Luis Martín, *La narrativa de Vargas Llosa* (Madrid: Editorial Gredos, 1974), p. 30.
8. Julio Ortega, "Sobre *Los cachorros*," *Homenaje a Mario Vargas Llosa*, p. 273.

Mary Davis

Mario Vargas Llosa: The Necessary Scapegoat

Since 1963, Mario Vargas Llosa has elaborated an intricate web
of novels whose style has enticed readers to hazard another, more
dangerous step into his labyrinth. Although the now hopelessly
bewitched reader may realize that he is entering the heart of darkness, his fears are somewhat allayed by both the ambiguity and the
deliberate melodrama that characterize the fictional rings of the
web. As the reader progresses from the outer fringes of *La ciudad
y los perros* to the darker, more insidiously evil circles of *Conversación en La Catedral*, he suffers crises of terror and of inevitable
self-identification with the obscure drama of the characters. Finally,
in *Pantaleón y las visitadoras*, the entrapped reader comes face to
face with the spider in the center of the web. In spite of the fes-
tive humor and the cliché plot, he must confront the diligent spider whose face, he discovers, horrified, reflects his own.

To unravel the puzzle created by Vargas Llosa's bizarre blend of
chivalry and Sartre, critical focus must shift from the dazzling surface of the text to the deep structures underlying it. Critics have
always sensed that aspects of the ambiguity of the Peruvian's texts
arise from the combination of realistic elements of style with something else. Finding a term adequate to designate the other aspect
has led to a minor polemic over whether or not the term "mythic"
should be employed with Vargas Llosa's peculiar verbal world.
Rodríguez Monegal explicates *La ciudad y los perros* as an "allegory of honor,"[1] while Mario Benedetti prefers the term "legendary" to characterize *La Casa Verde*: "the novel's atmosphere is
legendary (after all, what is the old bordello if not a legend that is
reborn, what the harpist Anselmo but a kind of rhapsodist?)."[2]
Commenting on the absence of free will that Vargas Llosa's characters must endure, Jorge Lafforgue describes "A world of isolated
souls, of predetermined destinies. Characters who slide over the
Earth like those of Greek tragedy—the suspense barely distracts
us from their inexorable end known from the beginning."[3] If the
action of Vargas Llosa's plots recalls the world of Greek tragedy,

it would seem appropriate to characterize at least one aspect of his style as mythic.

The mythic context of Vargas Llosa's fiction becomes apparent if we concentrate on the figures (to borrow a term from Julio Cortázar) or patterns woven by the interaction of the characters. An analysis of all the novels reveals the Dance of Death so beloved of Hispanic writers since the Middle Ages. The significance with which Vargas Llosa endows the Dance illuminates both the meaning of his novels and his concept of the role of the artist. Alfredo Matilla Rivas, summarizing the effect of *Conversación en La Catedral*, isolates death as the fundamental event in the intricate plots of Vargas Llosa: "Death can be physical or spiritual (it is always present, centrally, in his works), but nothing remains except the structure itself of the novel."[4] Death for Vargas Llosa never becomes gratuitous; it must assume a deeper meaning than that presented on the surface of his novels. Although it may take on an infinity of forms and degrees, death will provoke the self-confrontation that always results from the plot.

Vargas Llosa's characters exemplify conflicting levels of society, and the signal events in their often mundane lives hold a significance for society as a whole. The novelist, functioning as Calderón's "marvelous magician," reveals the alternating levels of reality necessary for a city or society to understand itself as a whole. The manner in which Vargas Llosa achieves this understanding hides itself behind the apparently realistic, Flaubertian aspect of his prose:

> Vargas Llosa does not resort to magic as does García Márquez in *One Hundred Years of Solitude*. But his sleights of hand are somewhat like substitutes for that magic. Suddenly we turn a page, like one who discovers an inextricable mystery, and Bonifacia is converted into Jungle Lady, the Sergeant into Lituma, and all the Piuran narration is retroactively enriched by becoming connected with the scene of possession. . . . Vargas Llosa seems to be saying that if we reshuffle the data of reality, or if we simply withhold some cards from the stack, the probable is transformed into the magical, the regular into the surprising, and the ordinary becomes fabulous.[5]

Vargas Llosa, by transforming the ordinary into the fabulous, makes human life once again a ritual. The time and space which he so tightly welds together with the acts and consciousness of his characters become the interior stage for a drama as old as man's attempt to give meaning to the universe. Early in Vargas Llosa's career, the Mexican novelist and critic Carlos Fuentes maintained that "The world of *The Time of the Hero* is ritual, in the deep meaning that Lévi-Strauss attributes to this term: the rite as a great biological and social game between the living and the dead, between the young and the old, between the animate and the inanimate, between the masters and the slaves."[6]

Although he weaves together several mythic patterns in his novels, Vargas Llosa reiterates most obsessively the search for paradise and the sacrifice of the scapegoat. The first of these appears in many critical appraisals of Vargas Llosa, perhaps most succinctly in an analysis by Ariel Dorfman: "in *The Green House* . . . just as in the *Odyssey*, the theme is the search for a home, the search for a woman as the axis around which the family nucleus can be created, something that would be a fixed island in the temporal whirlwind that scourges and exhausts the characters."[7] The constant failure that frustrates the search finds its significance in the image of the *pharmakos*.

The judgment and subsequent condemnation of some levels of reality configured in his novels have attached the term "moral" to Vargas Llosa's concept of fiction. The reader, therefore, is hardly surprised to find Vargas Llosa recasting religious patterns to mirror a distinctly secular universe, nor is he amazed when Lima or Piura or Iquitos becomes the significant precinct that Dublin was for Joyce or Macondo for García Márquez. For the historian of religions Mircea Eliade, religious sensibility differs from profane in that its abode must be at the center of the world: "*If the world is to be lived in*, it must be *founded* —and no world can come to birth in the chaos of the homogeneity and relativity of profane space. The discovery or projection of a fixed point—the center—is equivalent to the creation of the world."[8] Although modern society would appear to be more profane than sacred, "a profane existence is never found in a pure state. To whatever degree he may have desacralized the world, the man who has made his choice in favor of a profane life never succeeds in completely doing away with religious behavior" (Eliade, p. 23). Vargas Llosa, by his use of mythic patterning in the deep structure of his novels, adds thereby another level of reality, one to be rescued and celebrated, if only through a momentary flash of consciousness.

Before the select characters in each novel can come to know themselves, the scapegoat must die. In order to understand the function of the *pharmakos'* death, we first should retrace the historical development of the ritual figure. The *pharmakos* was sacrificed amidst elaborate ceremony, whose object was "to effect a

total clearance of all the ills that have been infesting a people."[9]
The ceremony ultimately connected the person offering the sacrifice, the animal sacrificed, and the god whose acceptance of the
gift restored the temporarily lost sense of wholeness to the universe. As offerings to restore the oneness of a whole society, the
ceremonies of sacrifice often coincided with the arrival of the New
Year or the changing seasons. The animal scapegoat could be a sub-
stitute for the king, as Géza Róheim explains: "In Babylonian
texts we find the king doing penance for the people. The king who
was killed for famine or drought may be called a scapegoat himself
and in some cases . . . we find a regular scapegoat ceremony as a
mitigation or equivalent of regicide."[10]

The Hebrew nation, during the ceremony connected with the
Day of Atonement, used two scapegoats: one, called Azazel's goat,
took away the nation's sins to the desert, and the other was sacrificed to Jehovah. The expulsion of the scapegoat was also a feature
of the ceremonial Thargelia in Athens. Two *pharmakoi* were expelled from the city, and firstfruits were then dedicated to Apollo,
the god of expiation and atonement.

> The human scapegoats of this festival are called pharmakoi,
> that is, "sorcerers." It is a universal feature of primitive life
> in all countries and periods that disease, deaths, blight of
> crops and in general, calamities of every kind are attributed
> to the activity of the magician, and we might therefore regard
> the ritual as an attempt to get rid of evil by expelling the au-
> thor of evil.   (Róheim, p. 345)

Whereas the Hebrews demanded a perfect animal for their scapegoat, the Athenians preferred "a monstrous, idiotic or misshaped
person as these were generally regarded as sorcerers, as embodi-
ments of black magic" (Róheim, p. 345). Remnants of the long-
past connection between sacrificing the scapegoat and fertility
rites can still be discerned in the strings of figs (white around the
neck of the male and black around the neck of the female) hung
on the *pharmakoi* before they were marched around the city and
stoned (Róheim, p. 345). The scapegoat, then, may represent a
king, a city, a god, or a single person, but his "sacrifice always implies a consecration; in every sacrifice an object passes from the
common into the religious domain."[11] The ceremony itself was
made elaborate to protect the person or society sacrificing the
pharmakos from the terrifying power unleashed by the death and
acceptance of the sacrifice; successfully completed, "sacrifice is
a religious act which, through the consecration of the victim, mod-

ifies the condition of the moral person who accomplishes it" (Hubert and Mauss, p. 13).

The *pharmakos'* death within a sacred precinct or his expulsion from the city consecrated the society and restored the sacred nature of time and the seasons. His death was like that of the phoenix: his function and beauty could only be reached through the painful corridor of death. When a person or society had been regenerated, a change of name sometimes signified a new status. The scapegoat, taking upon himself the sins, illnesses, and despair of society, provided a means of communication between the sacred and the profane.

Vargas Llosa employs only those aspects of the sacrifice that suit his purpose. He frustrates the basic purpose of sacrifice; that is, the death of the *pharmakos* does not achieve the purification of society. It serves, instead, to emphasize the lack of morality within modern society. Neither society nor the sacrificer of the scapegoat is regenerated, but the sacrificial death instigates a crisis of conscience and ultimately reveals heretofore unknown reality to the remaining characters. The *pharmakos* once again becomes the sorcerer, uniting and unveiling realities to the participants in a completely secular ceremony.

Although Vargas Llosa's novels do not always present a protagonist, they inevitably contain a *pharmakos*. All except *Los cachorros* follow the Hebrew and Greek ceremonies and utilize two or more *pharmakoi*. At the conclusion of the plot, one is dead and the other expelled from his society into a desert of additional suffering. As Vargas Llosa's style becomes more complex, an increasing ambiguity develops between the *pharmakos* and his sacrificer, and their Dance of Death will create the structure of the plot. The tempo of the Dance may retard or accelerate, but during its progress some characters will accept themselves, reject their society, and be rewarded with a flash of recognition by at least one other character.

The ambiguity and omnipresence of the scapegoat can be more clearly seen if we think of Vargas Llosa's novels cumulatively, as each of them appeared in his canon. *La ciudad y los perros* (1963) presents the figure of the "Esclavo" ("Slave"), Ricardo Arana, a weak cadet sacrificed to maintain the superficial code of honor at the Leoncio Prado military school. The death of the Esclavo initiates a crisis of conscience within his only friend, the "poet" Alberto, as well as within Gamboa, the perfect military man, and within his self-confessed assassin, Jaguar. Vargas Llosa presents the Esclavo's life with Sartrean precision. The Esclavo lives almost completely in the bitter present; the flashbacks that have to do

with his past customarily begin with some form of "forgetting."
His solitude both within and without the military school is radical:
"He could bear the loneliness and the humiliation that he had
known since he was a child and that only wounded his spirit. What
was horrible was this imprisonment, this vast exterior solitude that
he had not chosen, that had been imposed on him like a strait jacket" (p. 136). Liberty hardly exists in the tortured world of the
Esclavo; he could, however, choose how to invest his solitude.
"Freedom was the only thing he wanted now, to handle his loneliness in his own way" (p. 137). The Esclavo reaches his limit when
his section is denied weekend leave. To escape this intolerable situation, he reveals the identity of the cadet who snatched the chemistry test and thereby incurs his fate.

The versions of how the Esclavo was shot—that he shot himself,
that Jaguar shot him, that some unknown person shot him from
behind—are left unresolved by Vargas Llosa. The significance of his
death revolves around the fact that everyone in the Leoncio Prado
is implicated in communal guilt. Because he is the only innocent
being in the school, the Esclavo is killed to maintain the cult of
the strong. Although his death affects everyone, the significance of
his sacrifice is best illustrated in the lives of Jaguar and Gamboa.
Jaguar, the complete opposite of the Esclavo, after he has been accused of murdering Arana, experiences a total change of consciousness as a result of his section's reaction to the Esclavo's death. He,
too, becomes a solitary cadet without friends, and he confesses to
Gamboa: "It's just that I understand the Slave better now. To him,
we weren't his friends, we were his enemies. Haven't I told you I
didn't know what it was like to have everybody against you?" (p.
386). At this point, Vargas Llosa effects a change of roles; Jaguar
assumes that of the dead Esclavo: "At this point, the two histories
come together: the adolescent's features have hardened, but Jaguar
has become a solitary child again. In his solitude, he touches the
cold hand of the Slave."[12]

The Esclavo serves as an intermediary between two realities,
and he is killed on the battleground between them, during the
field games which toughen the cadets into military reality. His almost lifeless body is carried from the field by his double, Gamboa,
the *pharmakos* who will continue to live, but who will suffer exile
from the Leoncio Prado. The school's reaction to the Esclavo's
death forces Gamboa to understand the hollowness of military
form, and he realizes that his beloved code of justice is only as
strong as the moral nature of the human beings within the system.
As Gamboa experiences the fall into ambiguous reality, he begins
to yearn for that paradise of idealism so recently lost:

Until a few weeks ago, he had never remembered the past,
spending his off hours in making plans for the future. Thus
far he had realized his objectives, and no one had taken away
the post he obtained when he graduated from the Military
School. Why was it, he wondered, that ever since these recent problems arose, he thought constantly, and with a certain bitterness, of his youth?   (pp. 371-72)

The disillusionment produced by the lack of honor within the military system forces Gamboa to submit to his exile. Now he has become another man, and he advises Jaguar, after the humbled cadet
confesses that he killed the Esclavo, to return to school, "and from
now on try to see that the death of Cadet Arana serves some use"
(p. 387).

   Through his technique of supressing the identity of the murderer
and by implicating everyone within the walls of the Leoncio Prado
in a shared guilt, Vargas Llosa makes society itself responsible for the
death of the *pharmakos*. Alberto fears that Jaguar will not be pros-
ecuted, "because the colonel, the captain, everybody here, they're
all like you, they're your accomplices, they're just a gang of bastards"
(p. 359). Vargas Llosa compares the military society to a family, and,
by implication, he asserts that the iron system is the only real family the cadets possess. Frustrated paternity, the search or desperate
desire of the cadets for a father, and the configuration of a home as an
ideal reiterate the mythic infrastructure of *La ciudad y los perros*.

   In his first novel, then, Vargas Llosa sets the Faulknerian pattern
for his later usages of the scapegoat. First, an ironic relationship
develops between the sacrificer and the sacrificed. A double will
then mirror the role of the *pharmakos*, and he will be forced to
suffer an ambiguous fate within a distinctly nonparadisiacal reality.
Both *pharmakoi* serve as mirrors to the society that both produced
and subsequently destroys them.

   La Casa Verde presents five intertwined plots, one of which
parodies the romance of chivalry. The love affair between the
founder of the original Casa Verde, Don Anselmo, and a young
orphan, Antonia, is narrated in reverse, and both the incredible aspects of the affair and the magical site of its consummation—Don
Anselmo's private isolated tower in the bordello—recall that world
parodied by Cervantes. Mario Benedetti maintains that "Vargas
Llosa is writing a twentieth century novel of chivalry, and perhaps
it is worth remembering that the elusive system is a normal expedi-
ent of the epic fantasy, as well as the fabulous changes of fortune,
the magical transformations that constitute the flavor of that remote genre" (*Homenaje*, p. 256).

As he creates the legend of Anselmo, Vargas Llosa reveals more of the past of Antonia than he does of the founder. When Antonia's adopted family is massacred, she is left mute and blind, and the neighborhood "witches" insinuate that she lived because an iguana licked her wounds. Witchcraft is connected with Anselmo's career when, after the Casa Verde has been built, a series of natural disasters strikes Piura. To attract the favor of the gods once again, "Witch doctors from neighboring settlements sprinkled the planted fields with the blood of young goats, they rolled about in the furrows, they made spells to attract the water and chase away the insects" (p. 88). The subtle correlating of the actions of witches with the lives of Anselmo and Antonia recalls the ancient Greek connection between the sacrifice of the scapegoat and removing from society those members most actively in contact with evil.

After Anselmo kidnaps Antonia and carries her away to his tower, she dies in childbirth, and her death becomes the excuse for the women of Piura to burn the Casa Verde. Anselmo's life changes completely; he becomes even more lonely than during his brief paradise with Antonia. As Antonia's daughter rebuilds the Casa Verde, a degraded phoenix, she hires her father as the harpist, and Anselmo finishes his life as a reincarnation of Orpheus, creating music to console himself for the loss of the one person who had made his universe a habitable place. As he approaches death, his filtered monologues revolve around the significance of Antonia's death.

> And one last time ask yourself if it was better or worse, whether life should be like that, and what would have happened if she no, if you and she, if it was a dream or if things are always different from dreams, and one more final effort, and ask yourself if you ever became resigned, and if it's because she died or because you're old that you accept the idea of dying yourself.   (p. 331)

Antonia's death reveals at once the splendor and the misery of her love for Anselmo. Vargas Llosa has reiterated the use of the house of prostitution as a metaphor for the difficulty of attaining love in the society of his novels. Although Antonia and Anselmo inhabit a magical precinct within the Casa Verde, their love is inevitably compromised by the love bought and sold in the surrounding milieu. The death of Antonia functions as a scapegoat's in that it absolves and epiphanizes her love for Anselmo; she dies because she has loved in a manner and a place unacceptable to society. Anselmo's death later reveals his role as a scapegoat; in the reactions of other characters to it, his sacrificial death restores at least a partial sense of wholeness to society. Wolfgang Luchting observes that "Father García experiences the true meaning of his vocation; Don Anselmo is instrumental in this experience of the priest, but only through means of his own death."[13] In the interrelationship between the two *pharmakoi*, as well as between them and society, Vargas Llosa manifests the sense of community possible in the Mangachería. Although he criticizes, at the same time, many of the manifestations of reality within that society, he does show a form of individual redemption made possible within the close-knit interaction of the community and its scapegoats.

Los cachorros elevates the *pharmakos* to protagonist. More obviously than before, Vargas Llosa reveals in the *novella* the differences between the scapegoat and the society that he ironically represents. He adjusts the mode of narration to ensure that Pichula Cuéllar always reflects the opinions and desires of his peers, but he reflects them in a fractured mirror. After comparing Cuéllar's mutilation to that of the Fisher King, Frank Dauster reveals that "there is a clear suggestion that Pichula Cuéllar, with his flaunting nickname and his distinctive mutilation, is very close to being a scapegoat. He may well be the victim, that one who is best among his people, through whose sacrifice the mediocrity of those people may go on recapitulating itself without the example of a whole, living king to shame them."[14]

Cuéllar initially distinguishes himself from his peers by his application to academic success and to prowess in athletics. After the school dog, Judas, emasculates him, he begins to differentiate himself emotionally from the other "cachorros" ("cubs"), but the change within reveals itself only through his bizarre actions. He gradually becomes accustomed to his scandalous nickname, one that projects the center of Cuéllar's emotional turmoil and recalls the ancient connection between the sacrifice of the scapegoat and puberty rites. Hubert and Mauss, explicating modes of regeneration through personal sacrifice, explain that "often a change of name marks this re-creation of the individual. In some cases this change is restricted to the addition of an epithet" (p. 63).

Protecting himself behind the mask of the horrible name "Pichula," Cuéllar gradually exaggerates all the characteristics of the "cachorros," and at the same time he develops exactly those tendencies which his society would repress. By the time of his hopeless enfatuation with Teresa, Cuéllar has become a person quite beyond and distinct from his peers, who withdraw from his life yet continue to influence it. Benedetti states that "the dog's bites terminated his virility, certainly, before it was born; but the bites of his peers terminated his life" (*Homenaje*, p. 260).

As the reader understands the changes from "we" to "they" and back within the narration, he sees the process whereby the group separates from itself the *pharmakos*. In this case, the process is doubly insidious, because Cuéllar is forced to sacrifice himself; the group does not actually kill him, as the "perros" ("dogs") did the Esclavo. Vargas Llosa takes another step with this technique; he forces the reader also into the collective narration, "a way to install his reader within the tribal guilt, to make him somehow feel like the scourge of his fellows" (*Homenaje*, p. 261). The last impression the group gives the reader of Cuéllar reveals the *pharmakos*' active participation in his own fate: "he had already killed himself, going to the North, how?, in a wreck, where?, on the treacherous curves of Pasamayo, poor thing, we said at the burial, how he suffered, what a life he had, but his end was an event for which he had searched" (p. 102). The reader can no longer comfort himself by thinking that Vargas Llosa writes only about Peru and Peruvians. Now he realizes that the interior stage in Vargas Llosa's fiction is peopled by actors representing different aspects of his own consciousness.

Conversación en La Catedral reveals the intensification and elaboration of all the characteristic elements of Vargas Llosa's style. No longer do the separations of city and jungle, desert and towns that enliven it matter; everything exists simultaneously. Vargas Llosa does not separate a protagonist, but he prefers to interweave an infinity of ritual lives absorbed in useless ceremonies. Although it is difficult to extricate scapegoats from the tapestry of characters, the actions of the ambiguous double executioners Cayo Bermúdez (familiarly known as Cayo Mierda) and Fermín Zavala (Bola de Oro) ultimately are responsible for the physical or spiritual deaths of Hortensia (La Musa) and Don Fermín's son, Santiago. As we have observed in *La ciudad y los perros* and *La Casa Verde*, the death of one *pharmakos* initiates both a shift in the intensity of the narration and a crisis of conscience within the *pharmakos*' double.

Through the course of the extensive plot, Santiago must continually meditate on the question of who he is, and, like Oedipus, in order to answer the question he must discover who his father is. Before he can believe that his father, the paradigm of the comfortable bourgeois, is Bola de Oro, La Musa (The Muse) must die and Santiago must descend to the dark underworld of Lima. The deliberate refusal of society to reveal the killer of La Musa, the symbolic participation in her murder, and the clumsy efforts to hide the significance of her death force Santiago to realize that everyone is guilty.

He thinks: that no one demanded anything, insisted, that no one made a move on your behalf. Forget about it or did they really forget you, he thinks, bury the matter, or did they really bury it on their own? Did the same people kill you again, Muse, or did all Peru kill you this second time?

(p. 370)

Like his prototype Gamboa, Santiago will spend the rest of his life sunk in a mediocrity he has chosen as a defense, expiating through his anguished conscience the sins of his father: "'In prep school, at home, in the neighborhood, in the study group, in the Party, at *La Crónica*,' Santiago says. 'My whole life spent doing things without believing, my whole life spent pretending.'" (p. 101). At the end of the excruciating novel, Santiago has solved the sphinx's riddle, but Vargas Llosa leaves him in The Cathedral, a bar rather than a church, faced by the murderer of La Musa. The scapegoat and the murderer would seem to exhaust the roles available to the inhabitants of the debased reality of this bleak novel.

Pantaleón y las visitadoras delights in the fabulous adventures of a world in between the comic strip and the Western. Its constant humor and irony mitigate the serious patterns employed more obviously than in Vargas Llosa's earlier novels. Pantaleón Pantoja is a more humanized version of Gamboa, the paradigmatic military man who believes that the military system functions efficiently. Pantaleón must go to Iquitos, a city in the jungle, endure a series of trials (in the old sense of *hazañas* or "epic deeds"), and, finally, suffer the same fate as Gamboa—exile to an insignificant post. The counterpoint narration intertwines the history of the Hermano Francisco and introduces the theme of crucifixion, an act that spreads through the jungle around Iquitos, eventually touching Pantaleón's own family. Like Cuéllar, Pantaleón suffers a change of name; from the correct officer Pantoja, he metamorphosizes into Pan-Pan, "that Creole Farouk" (p. 189), ruler of a complex system whereby prostitutes are supplied to the army personnel stationed at remote jungle outposts. He is a double of Fushía and Anselmo in *La Casa Verde* in that his kingdom, Pantilandia, becomes "a paradise of women" (p. 134), and that his fall from paradise is swift and absolute.

The Hermano Francisco and his fanatical followers bring to the surface of the text the apocalyptic tone subtly hidden in the conflagrations, murders, and sudden fallings from power in earlier novels. Before a new world can be imagined, the old one must die, hence the repeated figure of the *pharmakos* who seeks his own death. Meditating on Vargas Llosa's inversion of the classic structure of myths, Luchting suggests: "Evidently Vargas Llosa tends to convert the *regressus ad origines* or *ad illud tempus* into something like a *regressus ad illud tempus futurum*. It is a way of evoking an earthly eschatology."[15] Francisco, then, signals the inevitable futility of Pantaleón's grand enterprise, and his actions parallel Pantoja's from the initial page of the novel, as Pantaleón's wife reads in the newspaper of "a fellow who was crucified in order to announce the end of the world" (p. 11).

As Pantaleón founds his Casa Verde, he chooses a place taken over from the followers of Francisco. Before Francisco used the site for ritual crucifixions of animals, it was the home of "a witch or healer" (p. 41). Vargas Llosa thus connects the two *pharmakoi* with withcraft, as he had insinuated earlier its connection with the life of Anselmo. The sacrifice of animals is not uncommon among primitive tribes; Sir James Frazier describes one such ceremony:

> The animal chosen has a rope fastened around its neck and is led to the outskirts of the village, killed, then crucified on bamboos set up on the ground. Here the crucified rat or ape is the public scapegoat, which by its vicarious sufferings and death relieves the people from all sickness and mishap in the coming year.   (p. 569)

The series of animal and human crucifixions that threads the novel reiterates the sacrifice of Francisco and Pantaleón. The ritual death of the "boy-martyr" provides the excuse for selling "boy-bread" in Iquitos, recalling the ancient ceremonies culminating in the eating of the actual body of the scapegoat. Finally, Francisco is crucified by his followers, and his death parallels the catastrophe awaiting Pantaleón's Amazonian paradise.

Pantaleón's life is considerably more complex than that of his double. He enters the "inferno" of Iquitos as an innocent; he is forced to adopt a disguise in order to carry out his clandestine activities, and his family is prohibited from enjoying the privileges of the military compound. The erotic paradise he sets in operation ultimately comes between Pantaleón and his family, an event forecast by his wife's dream: "You and I were crucified on the same cross, one on each side" (p. 138). The double life Panta is forced to lead sinks him deeper into the solitude he had endured all his life. Vargas Llosa employs the leitmotif "wake up" to indicate the gradual process of Panta's "dark odyssey" (p. 205). Like Anselmo, Pantaleón falls into a new reality because of a scandalous love affair. His delirious passion for the irresistible prostitute La Brasileña causes the indiscretion that terminates his brief season in paradise.

La Brasileña, like Antonia, dies for love, but La Brasileña is cruci-fied on a magical tree and later becomes a saint celebrated by med-als much like those commemorating Francisco's "boy-martyr."

Vargas Llosa shows once again that the society in which love can be trafficked for money must continue to sacrifice useless scapegoats. Although Vargas Llosa finally reunites Pantaleón with his family, Pantaleón himself has become another man. The awak-ened sleeper is no longer a "boy-martyr," but an adult *pharmakos* who must be exiled to expiate the mistakes of his commanding of-ficers, his own fiery passion, and the secret sins of Iquitos. At the end of the plot, Vargas Llosa has symbolically destroyed the reality he has configured: "Pantoja moved away, the prophet dead, the visiting ladies evaporated, the Arc dissolving itself" (p. 304). Pan-taleón, whose self-image has suffered the most radical metamor-phosis, remains to hold his broken mirror to society.

Vargas Llosa has celebrated in each of his novels a significant cluster of "feats," and through the Dance of Death he has given a deeper level of meaning to the actions of his doomed characters. As Julio Ortega observes, the characters' actions directly influence reality itself:

> His basic interest in observing the individual in the spatial action of the adventure has to do, doubtless, with his reiter-ated admiration for the novel of chivalry: the adventures of the knight have the resonance of a myth because they com-promise all reality through their fantasy, just as in Vargas Llosa the world is compromised by the action of his charac-ters.   (*Homenaje*, p. 266)

The frustration of the sacrifice of the scapegoat comments indi-rectly on the incomplete, nonsacred nature of modern society. The destruction of several layers of reality gives the reader the im-pression that not only are the *pharmakoi* being sacrificed futilely, but that society itself is moribund. Although Vargas Llosa's fic-tional universe seems particularly violent, violence itself has always been the ground of sacrifice.

> Through this act of destruction the essential action of the sacrifice was accomplished. The victim was separated defi-nitively from the profane world; it was consecrated, it was sacrificed, in the etymological sense of the word, and various languages gave the name sanctification to the act that brought that condition about. Its death was like that of the phoenix: it was reborn sacred.   (Hubert and Mauss, p. 35)

Vargas Llosa's pessimism concerning the possibility of redeeming his society, and his stubborn refusal to abandon that same society at a time when it may be self-destroyed in order to rise again, create the ambiguous tension within his texts. Steadily refining the narrative technique whereby he implicates the reader in the communal guilt that pervades his vision of society, he also allows the reader to share in those triumphs of consciousness that the second *pharmakos* experiences. The complementary interacion between the *pharmakoi* and their milieu always inserts another, mythic degree of significance to the frequently banal actions of his characters. His choice of sacrifice itself reveals the intense seriousness with which Vargas Llosa approaches his craft. Gradually the reader senses the importance of these sacrifices, which can reveal themselves in a multiplicity of forms:

> . . . beneath the diverse forms it takes, it always consists in one same procedure, which may be used for the most widely differing purpose. This procedure consists in establishing a means of communication between the sacred and the profane worlds through the mediation of the victim, that it, of a thing that in the course of the ceremony is destroyed.
> (Hubert and Mauss, p. 97)

Through the ritual form underlying his use of the *pharmakos*, Vargas Llosa unites the realities of society as it exists and society as it might become, and he thereby functions as did the ancient sorcerer, the dark double of the scapegoat. Because he unites these diverse realities, Vargas Llosa becomes the vehicle of sacrifice, and the insidious appeal to his reader to share the transformation of consciousness of the second *pharmakos* creates yet another set of double *pharmakoi* reflected in his shifting mirrors, perhaps the most significant scapegoats of all, the reader and Vargas Llosa.

University of Oklahoma
Norman

Notes

1. Emir Rodríquez Monegal, "Madurez de Vargas Llosa," collected in *Homenaje a Mario Vargas Llosa*, ed. Hemly F. Giacomán and José Miguel Oviedo (New York: Las Américas, 1971), p. 51. Subsequent citations from this volume of essays will follow the abbreviation *Homenaje*.
2. Mario Benedetti, "Vargas Llosa y su fértil escándalo," *Homenaje*, p. 256.

3. Jorge Lafforgue, "*La ciudad y los perros*, novela moral," *Homenaje*, p. 120.

4. Alfredo Matilla Rivas, "*Conversación en La Catedral*: estructura y estrategias," *Homenaje*, p. 86.

5. Mario Benedetti, *Homenaje*, p. 256.

6. Carlos Fuentes, "El afán totalizante de Vargas Llosa," *Homenaje*, p. 166.

7. Ariel Dorfman, "José María Arguedas y Mario Vargas Llosa: dos visiones de una sola América," *Homenaje*, p. 139.

8. Mircea Eliade, *The Sacred and the Profane* (New York: Harcourt, Brace and World, 1959), p. 22.

9. Sir James George Frazier, *The Golden Bough* (New York: Macmillan, 1922), p. 575.

10. Géza Róheim, *Animism, Magic, and the Divine King* (London: Kegan Paul, Trench, Trubner, 1930), p. 311.

11. Henri Hubert and Marcel Mauss, *Sacrifice: Its Nature and Function* (Chicago: Univ. of Chicago Press, 1964), p. 9.

12. Lafforgue, *Homenaje*, pp. 111–12.

13. Wolfgang A. Luchting, "El fracaso como tema en Mario Vargas Llosa," *Homenaje*, p. 243.

14. Frank Dauster, "Vargas Llosa y el fin de la hidalguía," *Homenaje*, p. 201.

15. Wolfgang A. Luchting, "Los mitos y lo mitizante en *La Casa Verde*," *Mundo Nuevo*, no. 43 (January 1970), 60.

*The following is a bilingual presentation
of an interview with Mario Vargas Llosa,
conducted by José Miguel Oviedo.*

José Miguel Oviedo

Conversación con Mario Vargas Llosa sobre
La tía Julia y el escribidor

A mediados de marzo de 1977, la Universidad de Oklahoma y la revista *World Literature Today* (antes *Books Abroad*) organizaron una Conferencia dedicada a Mario Vargas Llosa, para la que invitaron especialmente al escritor peruano y a un grupo de críticos y estudiosos de su obra narrativa. Esta Conferencia se realizó como parte del ciclo establecido por los auspiciadores para honrar a importantes escritores del mundo hispánico, y en él se han presentado, entre otros, Borges, Octavio Paz y Julio Cortázar.

Durante las dos semanas previas a esa reunión, el autor habló en seminarios y conferencias sobre su propia obra, su experiencia de escritor y otros problemas vinculados a su situación de novelista hispanoamericano. Aprovechando su presencia y el hecho de que había traído consigo el original de su nueva novela, para darle los últimos toques antes de su publicación en Barcelona posiblemente este mismo año, el autor accedió a grabar un fragmento de la obra para el Archivo de Literatura Hispánica, de la Biblioteca del Congreso. Mientras él hacía su lectura en los estudios de la Universidad, surgió la idea de que esa grabación se complementase con una entrevista, conducida por mí, sobre su nueva novela. Éste es el origen del texto que se lee a continuación y que se publica con autorización del escritor y de la mencionada Biblioteca, gracias a la gestión de la señora Georgette Dorn, a quien expreso mi reconocimiento.

Vargas Llosa debe haber concedido centenares de reportajes, sobre los temas más variados, y seguirá concediéndolos. Si algo justifica la publicación de éste, es que contiene una exposición muy completa y detallada de la génesis, desarrollo y resultado final de su último trabajo novelístico. El lector podrá luego comparar estas declaraciones con la novela misma y sacar sus propias conclusiones.

José Miguel Oviedo

A Conversation with Mario Vargas Llosa about
La tía Julia y el escribidor

About the middle of March 1977, the University of Oklahoma and *World Literature Today* (formerly *Books Abroad*) organized a Symposium dedicated to the work of Mario Vargas Llosa, to which the Peruvian writer as well as a group of critics and students of his work were invited. This conference was one of the series of conferences established by the University of Oklahoma and *World Literature Today* to honor prominent writers of the Spanish-speaking world, conferences that have previously featured Borges, Octavio Paz, and Julio Cortázar, among others.

During the two weeks previous to the conference, Mario Vargas Llosa lectured and conducted seminars about his work, about his experiences as a writer, and about his situation as an Hispanic-American writer. Due to his presence and to the fact that he had brought along the manuscript of his new novel, which he was revising for publication in Barcelona later this year, Vargas Llosa agreed to tape a reading of a fragment of his novel for the Hispanic Literature Archives of the Library of Congress. While he taped his reading at the University recording studio, the idea arose to complement the tape with an interview, to be conducted by me, about his new novel. This is the origin of the following text,[1] which is reproduced here with the permission of the Library of Congress, thanks to the assistance of Mrs. Georgette Dorn, to whom I express my gratitude.

Vargas Llosa must have been interviewed hundreds of times, about a variety of subjects. But if one needs a justification for publishing this interview, let it be the fact that it contains a detailed account of the genesis, development, and final results of his latest novelistic achievement. The reader will later be able to compare these comments with the novel itself, and to draw his own conclusions.

JMO: Bien, Mario, ahora que tienes tu novela muy avanzada y en proceso final de revisión, me gustaría que echases una mirada hacia atrás y me contases cómo surgió en tí la idea de escribir este libro. ¿Cómo se definió, cómo fue tomando forma la historia que contiene? ¿Y cuándo comenzaste a escribirla?

MVLl: Bueno, nació como casi todo lo que he escrito, a base de ciertos recuerdos. En este caso, recuerdos del año que pasé trabajando en Radio Panamericana en Lima, o sea el año 1953 o 54. Yo recordaba siempre esta época vinculada a un personaje que trabajaba, no exactamente en Radio Panamericana donde yo me ocupaba de los servicios de noticias, de los boletines, sino en una radio contigua, Radio Central, que era además del mismo propietario de Panamericana. Y ése era un personaje muy pintoresco que escribía todos los radioteatros que eran el plato fuerte de Radio Central. Era un boliviano que había sido importado por los dueños de la radio, los hermanos Delgado Parker, porque habían descubierto que este hombre era un "as" en Bolivia de todo lo que fuera radioteatros e incluso teatro melodramático. Entonces se ocupaba en Lima de todos los radioteatros de esa emisora, que no solamente escribía sino también dirigía e interpretaba como galán. Y era un personaje realmente muy pintoresco que trabajaba como un galeote, que tenía una extraordinaria conciencia profesional y estaba muy imbuído de su papel de escritor, de artista, pero al mismo tiempo, juzgado desde un punto de vista literario, digamos, era un especie de parodia o de caricatura, de versión pedestre, deformada, un poco patética, de lo que podía ser un escritor. Y tenía realmente mucha popularidad. Entiendo que sus radioteatros eran un éxito en Radio Central. A mí me divertía mucho, hasta me fascinaba, porque era justamente una época en la que yo sentía cada vez más fuerte la vocación de la literatura. En la que realmente creía que lo que más me gustaba ser en la vida, era ser un escritor. Y creo que el único escritor que yo conocía en esos años, que realmente podía merecer ese nombre por el tiempo consagrado a su oficio, por el público que seguía y apoyaba su trabajo, era esta caricatura de la literatura, el autor de radioteatro boliviano, Raúl Salmón. Bueno, le ocurrió una historia entre jocosa y trágica a Raúl Salmón: se volvió loco. Pero la forma como se descubrió que estaba loco fue realmente regocijante porque fue a través de los oyentes de su radioteatro. Un día Radio Central comenzó a recibir cartas, llamadas y protestas de oyentes que descubrían gruesas incongruencias, incoherencias en sus radioteatros. Personajes que cambiaban de profesión o cambiaban de nombre, o que incluso saltaban de un radioteatro a otro. En fin, empeza-

JMO: Well, Mario, now that your novel is practically completed
and in fact undergoing final revision, I'd like you to look back
and tell me how the idea of writing this book came to you.
How did its story take shape? And when did you start writing
it?

MVLl: Well, it took shape, like almost everything I've written,
from my old memories. In this case, memories of the year that
I worked for Radio Panamericana in Lima, that is, 1953, or '54.
I've always remembered this period as linked to a man who used
to work, not for Radio Panamericana where I was in charge of
the news bulletins, but for a neighboring radio station, Radio
Central, which was also owned by the owners of Radio Panamericana. This fellow was quite a colorful person who wrote all the
scripts for the soap operas which were the highlight of Radio
Central programming. He was Bolivian, and had been brought
to Lima by the proprietors of the radio station, the Delgado
Parker brothers, because in Bolivia he was an "ace" in all that
concerned radio soap operas. He was in charge of all the soap
operas of that radio station, not only writing the scripts but
also directing and acting the male leads. He was truly a picturesque character who worked like the devil, who had an extraordinary sense of professional responsibility, and who was very
absorbed by his role as writer and performer. But at the same
time, judging him from a literary perspective, let's say, he was
a sort of parody or caricature, a pedestrian version, twisted and
somewhat pathetic, of a "writer." Still, the man was quite popular. I understand that his soap operas were a real success on
Radio Central. He greatly amused me, even fascinated me, because it was precisely at this time that I was feeling a stronger
and stronger urge to become a writer myself; I was thinking
that what I wanted most in my life was to be a writer. And I
think that the only writer I knew at that time—who could be
really called a "writer" because of the amount of time dedicated
to writing, and because of the public which followed and appreciated his work—was this literary caricature, the writer of the
Bolivian soap operas, Raúl Salmón. Well, something happened
to Raúl Salmón, something between the comic and the tragic:
he went insane. But the way in which his insanity was revealed
was rather amusing, because it was through his listeners. One
day, Radio Central began to receive letters, telephone calls, and
all sorts of protests from listeners of the soap operas who were
discovering gross incongruities and incoherences in the scripts:
suddenly, the soap opera characters would change names or professions or would even skip around from one soap opera to an-

ban a contarse extravagancias y disparates descomunales en los
radioteatros de Raúl Salmón, y así, los dueños de la radio descu-
brieron que este señor sufría una crisis. Hablaron con él. Entonces, él, muy nervioso, comenzó a introducir toda clase de catás-
trofes en sus radioteatro para liquidar a sus personajes y poder
comenzar de nuevo las historias que se le habían empezado a
confundir. Al final, la cosa no tuvo solución: Raúl Salmón tuvo
que irse a descansar a un hospital. Siempre me quedó dando
vueltas en la cabeza la historia de Raúl Salmón y siempre pensé
en escribir alguna vez algo que se relacionara con esto. . . . En
realidad ése es el origen más remoto de esta novela. Por supuesto, en mi libro toda esta historia está muy transformada, se puede reconocer de ella sólo una especie de embrión. Además, he
añadido a la historia de este personaje, otra que hace una especie de contrapunto, que es como un lastre, terreno, verosímil,
a ese mundo de pura imaginación, de pura fantasía, de locura,
que es el mundo de los radioteatros del protagonista.

JMO: Muy bien. ¿Y cómo has trabajado ese contraste entre el
mundo totalmente imaginario, delirante, del personaje y el mundo más lastrado por la realidad? ¿De qué manera has estructu-
rado narrativamente esto?

MVLl: Después de mucho pensar—porque ésta historia la tuve como
proyecto, como te decía, durante bastante tiempo—cuando em-
pecé más o menos a tratar de darle una estructura, una forma de
materialización a esa historia, se me ocurrió que para que no
fuera excesivamente abstracta, para que no ocurriera en un mundo puramente de juego mental, de delirio fantástico, podría ser
contrapesada por una historia real, es decir, por una historia más
terrestre, más directa; una historia más vivida que fantaseada o
imaginada. Entonces se me ocurrió lo siguiente: ¿por qué esa
historia de Raúl Salmón no se entreveraba con una historia personal? La época en que ocurrió la historia de Raúl Salmón, fue
un tiempo bastante importante para mí, en primer lugar, porque
como ya te dije, corresponde más o menos a los años en que se
definió una vocación que venía pugnando desde años atrás, pero
que yo hasta entonces no me había atrevido a asumir del todo.
En segundo lugar, es la época en que me casé por primera vez
y ese matrimonio fue en cierta forma un acto sumamente te-
merario, porque yo tenía 18 años y además porque me trajo
muchos problemas en la vida práctica e incluso muchos problemas familiares. Y entonces se me ocurrió que las historias deli-
rantes del protagonista que escribe radioteatros y que tiene una
imaginación perturbada, quizás podía mezclarse con una historia que fuera exactamente lo contrario, algo absolutamente ob-
jetivo y absolutamente cierto. Una historia en la que yo con-

other. And so, because enormously bizarre and extravagant things began to happen in Raúl Salmón's scripts, the owners of the radio station discovered that he was undergoing some crisis. They spoke with him about it. As a result, Salmón nervously started to conjure up in his scripts a series of catastrophes designed to kill off those characters who were becoming confused even in his own mind, so that he could begin anew with a clean slate. But in the end, there was no solution: Raúl Salmón had to go off to a hospital to recuperate. His story always stuck with me and I kept thinking that I would some day write something related to it. . . . Actually, that story is the most remote origin of this novel. Naturally, all this is quite transformed in my book, and one can see only vestiges of that story. Furthermore, I have added to the story of Raúl Salmón another story that serves as a kind of counterpoint, that anchors in the tangible, verifiable world the purely imaginary, purely fantastic, mad world of the protagonist and his soap operas.

JMO: How have you achieved this contrast between the totally imaginary, delirious world of the protagonist and the more real world? How did you handle this within the narrative structure?

MVLl: After giving it a lot of thought—because this novel has been a project of mine, like I said, for a long time—when I began to try to shape it, to give form to this story, it occurred to me that in order for it not to be excessively abstract, for it not to take place in a realm of purely mental games, of delirious fantasy, it should be balanced by a realistic story, that is, by a more ordinary, more direct one;—a story more of lived experience than of fantasy or imagination. Then I thought of this: why couldn't the story of Raúl Salmón be intermingled with personal experience? The Raúl Salmón story happened during a very important time in my life because, in the first place, it was at that time that after feeling the urge for years, my vocation was decided, although until then I had not dared to pursue it totally. Secondly, it was then that I got married for the first time, and that marriage was in certain ways a very daring act, because I was only 18, and also because it caused me many practical problems and even family problems. Then it occurred to me that the delirious stories of the protagonist who writes the melodramas and who has a disturbed imagination could perhaps be intertwined with a story which was precisely the opposite, something absolutely objective and absolutely true. I would narrate

taría exactamente unos episodios de mi vida a lo largo de unos meses: el tiempo que trabajé en Radio Panamericana, cómo conocí a la que fue mi mujer, lo que fue mi matrimonio y todo lo que eso significó en mi experiencia personal, etc. Intercalar esas dos historias era un poco como presentar el reverso y el anverso de una realidad, una parte objectiva y una parte subjectiva, una cara verídica y otra inventada. Traté de hacer esto en la novela. Alternar un capítulo, digamos, de imaginación pura o casi pura, con un capítulo de historia personal auténtica, documental. Lo que pasó es que también en este caso, como a mí me ocurre siempre, el proyecto empezó a desbaratarse a la hora de llevarse a la práctica. Es decir, los episodios en los que yo quería no ser sino veraz y contar solamente cosas que estaba absolutamente seguro que habían ocurrido así, eran completamente imposibles, porque la memoria es engañosa, y se contamina de fantasía y porque en el momento mismo de escribir ese elemento imaginario se filtra, se instala y se incorpora irremediablemente a lo que uno escribe. Y al mismo tiempo, en los capítulos que son supuestamente o síntesis o paráfrasis de los radioteatros del protagonista, la pura invención tampoco existe. Hay también unos ingredientes intrusos, diríamos, que proceden de la realidad objetiva, que se van infiltrando poco a poco. De tal manera que yo creo que la versión final de la novela es algo bastante distinto de lo que había planeado, aunque en realidad fue construída sobre esta idea básica.

JMO: Me gustaría preguntarte ahora si el personaje principal de esta novela, entra en relación estrecha con un conjunto de personajes muy crecido, o si es una novela que se concentra en un protagonista, digamos como en *Pantaleón*. ¿Dejas que los personajes vayan tejiendo historias muy complejas? ¿Es una novela dónde te reduces a márgenes narrativos estrechos, o más bien, corresponde a ese tipo de novelas de ejecución más ambiciosa e intención plenaria, como *La Casa Verde*?

MVLl: No es el caso de *Pantaleón*, en el sentido de que no hay un único protagonista, sino varios. Hay varios que pueden ser considerados centrales. Ahora, lo que pasa es que hay personajes de dos categorías. Hay personajes que, diríamos, corresponden a ese nivel "real," donde está el narrador de la historia, en este caso yo mismo, donde está el autor mismo de los radioteatros y donde está todo el mundo de las radios, el de la universidad, el de la familia del narrador. Y luego están los personajes que forman parte de ese otro nivel de realidad, la realidad imaginaria o inventada. Y esos personajes son, por supuesto, mucho más numerosos y además son de otra naturaleza. A medida que avanza

accurately some episodes of my own life, covering several months: the time during which I worked for Radio Panamericana, how I met my wife, how my marriage was, and all that the whole thing meant in my personal experience, etc. To alternate between these two stories was a little like presenting the front and back of reality, an objective part and a subjective part, a real face and a made-up one. I tried to do this in the novel, to alternate a chapter totally or almost totally imagined, with a chapter of personal history, authentic, documented. What happened was that, again in this case, as happens with me always, my project began disintegrating when put into practice. That is, it was totally impossible to write the chapters in which I wanted to be absolutely truthful and tell only of things which I was absolutely sure had happened precisely so, because memory is tricky and gets contaminated with fantasy, and because even as one is writing, an element of imagination seeps in, takes hold and inevitably becomes part of what one is writing. And at the same time, in the chapters that are supposedly syntheses or paraphrases of the soap operas of the protagonist, there is no "pure invention." There, too, there are foreign ingredients which come from objective reality, which infiltrate little by little. So, I think that the final version of the novel is quite different from what I had originally planned, even though it was built on that basic idea.

JMO: I'd like to ask you if the main character of this novel comes into close relationship with a good number of characters, or if the novel is concentrated on a single protagonist, as in, say, *Pantaleón*. Do you allow the characters to weave very complex stories? Is it a novel in which you have narrow narrative margins, or is it instead a type of novel of more ambitious design and broader scope, like *La Casa Verde*?

MVLl: It is not like *Pantaleón* in the sense that there is no single protagonist, but, rather, several. There are several characters that can be considered "central." Now, what happens is that there are two categories of characters: there are characters that belong to that "real" dimension, where the narrator is, in this case myself, where the author of the soap operas is, and where everybody from the radio stations, the university, and the narrator's family belong. And then there are the characters that make up that other level of reality, the imaginary or invented "reality," who are, of course, much more numerous, and of a different nature. As the novel develops, the mental disturbance

la novela, se profundiza y agrava la perturbación del escritor; simultáneamente, los personajes van perdiendo su individualidad, se van confundiendo entre sí. Cambian no solamente de nombre sino de funciones. Van borrándose las fronteras que los separan. Mi idea era mostrar a través de este tipo de episodios y de fenómenos, un tratamiento cada vez más irrespetuoso, diríamos, del tiempo y del espacio narrativos. Esto fue haciendo más precisa la historia narrada en el otro nivel de realidad.

JMO: El elemento melodramático en tu obra está muy presente desde sus comienzos. En *Pantaleón* pareces haber llegado a una especie de apoteosis, pero aquí parece que todavía vas a exceder ese límite. ¿Es correcta la impresión que tengo por el capítulo que acabas de leer?

MVLl: Yo creo que sí. Ese elemento efectivamente debe haber estado siempre presente en mi obra, porque siempre fui muy sensible a él. Durante mucho tiempo procuré disimularlo o encubrirlo. Pero cada vez menos en los últimos libros. Pero yo creo que éste es el primero dónde realmente constituye la materia profunda del relato. No solamente porque el mundo del radioteatro, el mundo de esa subliteratura que produce al protagonista así lo exige, sino porque la novela misma trata de mostrar cómo todo ese mundo no es sino la magnificación o la selección de una suma de experiencias, que son profundamente melodramáticas y sensibleras en los personajes de la vida real.

JMO: ¿Inclusive el personaje que inicialmente iba ser el que encarnaba experiencias personales tuyas?

MVLl: Bueno, la idea, más que eso, el resultado del libro, es descubrir también en esa vida real, en esa versión de una vida corriente, el melodrama del radioteatro. El melodrama existe allí tan profunda, tan vívidamente como en el mundo de la imaginación y la fantasía.

JMO: El tono de la novela, por el pasaje que he escuchado, resulta también interesante de comparar con lo que has logrado anteriormente. Es decir, en este caso parece que tu estilo se ha vuelto más parecido al lenguaje, de carácter dominantemente oral, que tú habías ensayado en *Pantaleón*. No sé si estoy equivocado en esto.

MVLl: Mira, en los capítulos que llamo "objectivos," hay un lenguaje sumamente informativo, escueto. . . .

JMO: ¿Como los "partes" de *Pantaleón*, por ejemplo?

MVLl: No, porque allí hay un elemento paródico, que en este texto no debería aparecer de ninguna manera. No, son capítulos en los que realmente de una manera muy "factual," como se diría en inglés, se va desarrollando la acción. En cambio, en los otros

of the protagonist deepens and becomes aggravated; simultaneously, his characters begin to lose their individuality, becoming
confused with one another. They change not only in name, but
also in function. The boundaries that separate them begin to
vanish. My idea was to show through this type of episode and
phenomenon, an increasingly irreverent treatment, let us say,
of narrative time and space. This brought into better focus the
story narrated in the other level of reality.

JMO: The melodramatic element in your work is there from the
very beginning. With *Pantaleón* you seemed to have achieved
a certain apotheosis, but it looks as though here you'll go even
beyond that. Is my impression of the chapter that you've just
read an accurate one?

MVLl: I think so. That element must have indeed always been in
my work, because I've always been very sensitive to it. For a
long time I tried to hide it or cover it up. But less and less in the
last few books. But I think that this is the first one in which it
constitutes the deep core of the narrative. Not only because the
soap opera world, the world of that subliterature which produces
the protagonist, demands it, but because the novel itself tries
to show how all that world is nothing but a magnification or a
selection of a sum of experiences, which are profoundly melodramatic and sentimental in the real-life characters.

JMO: Including the character who originally was to be the one to
portray your own personal experiences?

MVLl: Well, the idea, or more than that, the *result* of the book,
is to discover in that real life, in that version of ordinary life,
the melodrama of a soap opera. The melodrama exists there just
as deeply, just as vividly as in the world of imagination and fantasy.

JMO: The tone of the novel, according to the passage I've just
heard, is also interesting to compare with what you've achieved
before. That is, in this case it looks like your style has become
more like spoken language, something which you had already
tried out in *Pantaleón*. I don't know if I'm wrong in this.

MVLl: Look, in the chapters I call "objective," there is an extremely informative, stark language. . . .

JMO: Like *Pantaleón*'s official reports, for instance?

MVLl: No, because there is parody there, which should not appear
anywhere in this text. No, they are chapters in which in a very
"factual" manner (as one would say in English) the action develops. On the other hand, in the other chapters, there is an ele-

capítulos, había un elemento de "huachafería," como se diría en limeño. Es decir, un elemento paródico y risueño, que aparecería de una manera muy disimulada al principio y que luego se iría acentuando, hasta llegar a ser agresivo, casi insolente en las últimas historias. Este fragmento de capítulo que acabo de leer es una de las historias en las que ya hay una especie de desmelenamiento, en la exageración y la confusión de personajes. La mayoría de los personajes provienen de capítulos anteriores, pero con nombres, oficios y sexos cambiados. Lo que quería era que hubiera una especie de crescendo en ésto. No sé si al final en la novela resultará así o si todo es más homogéneo que al principio; de eso no logro darme cuenta todavía.

JMO: Esa tendencia de la novela a cruzar las líneas de lo real y lo imaginario, debe tener un significado ulterior. Me gustaría saber cuál es el diseño que la novela propone al final. ¿Cuál es la imagen que puede descubrir el lector? ¿Qué es lo que da sentido y unidad a esos dos niveles por los cuales conduces la acción de la novela?

MVLl: Bueno—como tú sabes, a mí no me gustan las novelas con moraleja—en todo caso jamás he procurado dar una moraleja. . . .

JMO: Hombre, no pregunté por ninguna moraleja, sino por el sentido total de la historia. . . .

MVLl: Pues no sé cuales podrían ser las conclusiones, digamos, interpretativas que se puede sacar de toda esa historia. Eso ni siquiera me lo he planteado. Mi intención era contar esta historia simultáneamente en dos niveles y mostrar cómo estos dos niveles, que al principio parecen tan rígidamente independientes uno de otro, en realidad están visceralmente comunicados. En las historias del protagonista uno lo va descubriendo poco a poco; lo que parece a primera vista totalmente imaginativo, producto de la fantasía, está en realidad enraizado en menudos acontecimientos de su vida, en sórdidos episodios cotidianos. Lo mismo ocurre en esa experiencia que tú puedes llamar diminuta y trivial del otro narrador que cuenta sus peripecias privadas a lo largo de ese año. Hay elementos allí que son tan extravagantes, distorsionados y excesivos, sobre todo a nivel del sentimiento, como en el mundo de los radioteatros. O sea que esos dos mundos en realidad no están tan diferenciados; constituyen sólo distintos grados de una misma realidad, de una misma experiencia. Pero la historia misma concluye más o menos como lo había pensado al principio. Porque me olvidé de decirte, al contestar tu primera pregunta, que yo volví a ver a este personaje años después de haber dejado la radio y salido del Perú, en uno de los cortos viajes que hice de regreso a Lima. No recuerdo bien,

ment of bad taste or "huachafería," as one would say in Lima. By that I mean an element both parodic and playful, which would initially be well hidden, but would gain impetus until it became aggressive, almost insolent, in the last stories. This fragment of a chapter that I've just read is one of the stories in which there's already a sort of complete chaos in the exaggeration and confusion of the characters. Most of the characters come from previous chapters, but with changed names, changed professions, even changed genders. What I wanted was a sort of crescendo effect in this. I don't know if that will be so at the end of the novel, or if everything will be more homogeneous than at the beginning; I can't quite see that as yet.

JMO: That tendency of the novel to cross over boundaries between the real and the imaginary must have an ulterior significance. I'd like to know what is the final design. What image can the reader discern? What gives meaning and unity to those two levels on which you direct the action of the novel?

MVLl: Well, as you know, I don't like novels with a moral—I've never tried to give a moral. . . .

JMO: Now, wait. I'm not asking about a moral, but about the ultimate meaning of the story. . . .

MVLl: Well, I don't know what interpretative conclusions might be drawn from this whole story. I haven't even posed that question to myself. My intention was to tell this story simultaneously on two levels and to show how these two levels, which at first seem so rigidly independent from one another, are actually viscerally connected. One begins to discover the protagonist, step by step, through his own stories; what looks at first sight totally imaginative, the product of fantasy, is actually rooted in minute daily occurrences in his own life, in sordid, daily episodes. The same thing happens with the seemingly trivial and insignificant experiences of the other narrator telling his private experiences during that year. There are in it extravagant, twisted, and sentimental elements, as much as in the world of soap operas. Which means that those two worlds are actually not so different; they are actually different levels of the same reality, of the same experience. But the story itself ends more or less the way I had planned from the beginning. Because I forgot to tell you, when I answered your first question, that I saw this person again, years after I had left the radio station and travelled abroad, in one of my short visits back to Lima. I don't remember too well, but I think it was in the 1960s. I met this man, the author of the soap operas, who had left the hospital, cured, but had never returned

pero creo que fue en los 60. Me encontré con este autor de radio-teatros que ya había salido del hospital, se había curado, pero que no había vuelto al mundo de la radio. En esos momentos estaba trabajando en una revista de Lima, una publicación sensacionalista y además de política turbia que se llamaba *Extra*, financiada en parte por la gente de Odría. Mi personaje trabajaba allí en un puesto modestísimo. Era "datero" policial, ni siquiera redactor. Traía los datos de las comisarías para que los redactara alguien en la revista. A mí me impresionó mucho verlo. Él había sido dentro del mundo de la radio un personaje realmente muy importante, muy famoso en Lima, y ahora pues estaba realmente convertido en la última pieza en el mecanismo de una revista, pero curiosamente lo que hacía, estaba también íntimamente vinculado con lo que había hecho o imaginado antes: el mundo grotesco y exagerado de los hechos policiales. O sea que siempre tuve el final de la historia desde un comienzo.

JMO: ¿Está tu novela situada en algún período reconocible de la vida peruana? Te lo pregunto porque justamente tú dices que hay una gran base de realidad y muchos personajes y experiencias concretas. Me gustaría saber si alude a circunstancias de algún tipo, políticas o sociales, o si, tal vez está desconectada de toda referencia histórica.

MVLl: No, no, está muy precisamente fechada en los años 50, a mediados de esa década.

JMO: Que es la de costumbre para tí. . . .

MVLl: Sí, como de costumbre. Y hay algunas alusiones, por supuesto, al momento político, y también a algunas modas, a la música de esa época, lo que contribuye a situarla en el tiempo. Y tiene un final o epílogo que ocurre unos diez o doce años después.

JMO: Una última pregunta. ¿Cómo se llama tu novela?

MVLl: Bueno, como ya me ocurrió otra vez, también esta novela me ha dado muchos dolores de cabeza con el título. He dudado muchas veces. Había pensado en un momento ponerle uno que después deseché porque me parecía demasiado jocoso y distorsionador de la historia. Era *La tía Julia y el escribidor*,[1] pero la descarté y al final creo que me voy a quedar con un título que es más . . . de novela picaresca: *Vida y milagros de Pedro Camacho*.

JMO: Bueno, creo que eso es todo. Gracias, Mario.

Indiana University, Bloomington

Nota

1. Julia es el nombre de la primera esposa del autor.

to radio. He was then working for a magazine in Lima, a sensa-
tionalist publication of murky politics called *Extra*, which was
partly financed by Odría's partisans. Salmón worked there, in
a very humble position. He was not even a reporter himself, but
gathered facts for police stories. He would bring the information from the precincts for someone else to write the reports. It
shocked me terribly to see him. He had been quite an important
character within the world of radio, very famous in Lima, and
now he had become the smallest cog in the mechanism of a magazine. But strangely enough, what he was doing now was inti-
mately connected with what he'd done or imagined before: the
grotesque and exaggerated world of police reports. Which means
that I always had the epilogue, from the very beginning.

JMO: Is your novel set in some recognizable period in Peruvian
life? I ask you because you say that it has a broad basis in reality and many concrete characters and experiences. I'd like to
know if there are allusions to specific political or social circumstances or if it is completely devoid of historical references.

MVLl: No, no, it is very precisely dated in the '50s, in that decade.

JMO: Which is the usual one for you.
MVLl: Yes, the usual one. And there are some allusions, of course,
to the political moment, and also to some trends, to the music
of that time, all of which contribute to placing it in a certain
time. And it has an epilogue which takes place about ten to
twelve years later.
JMO: One last question: what's the name of your novel?
MVLl: Well, like once before, I've had headaches over the title of
this novel. I've had so many doubts. I had thought at first of a
title that I later dismissed because it seemed much too jocular
and distorting of the story. It was *La tía Julia y el escribidor*,[2]
but I discarded it and finally I think I will retain a title which
is more . . . that of a picaresque novel: *Vida y milagros de Pedro
Camacho*.

JMO: Well, I think that is all. Thanks, Mario.

Indiana University, Bloomington

Notes

1. Interview translated by Marcela Loiseau de Rossman
2. Julia is the name of Vargas Llosa's first wife. After this interview was
made, the writer changed his mind and published the novel under this title.

José Miguel Oviedo

La tía Julia y el escribidor,
or the Coded Self-Portrait

At the beginning of his *Historia secreta de una novela*, Vargas Llosa declares:

> Writing a novel is a ritual like a strip tease. Very much like the girl who, under bold spotlights, sheds her garments and bares one by one her secret charms, the novelist, too, reveals his intimate self through his novels. But, of course, there are differences. What the novelist reveals of himself are not his secret charms, like the stripper, but rather the demons that torment and obsess him, the ugliest parts of himself: his nostalgia, his rancor, his regrets. Another difference is that a stripper starts out dressed and ends up naked, while the opposite is true in the case of the novelist: he starts out bare and ends up covered. The personal experiences (those lived, dreamed, heard, read) which were the initial stimuli for the writing of the story become so maliciously disguised during the creative process that when the novel is finished no one, often not even the novelist himself, can easily hear the autobiographical heartbeat that inevitably pulses in all fiction. To write a novel is to engage in a reverse strip tease, and all novelists are discreet exhibitionists. (pp. 7–8)

Even though this ritual strip tease, this passion to narrate himself away as he narrates his fiction, is present in all of his work, it has never been as intense, as rigorously intimate, as in *La tía Julia y el escribidor*, Vargas Llosa's fifth novel. And this is so, not only because half of the novel is a retelling of an episode from the writer's early adulthood (his first marriage, evoked in minute detail, including proper names and indiscreet revelations), but also because the other half of the story, the one which presumably would take place on the unreal and exaggerated soap opera level, the exact opposite of the autobiographical, is also an oblique fragment of that life, of personal obsessions and perversions that seep into and saturate the novel, making it, as a whole, the first of Vargas Llosa's narratives whose subterranean thread is that of the writer in the process of writing—writing about the fiction in his life, writing himself a life through his fiction.

As the title implies, the structural constant in *La ciudad y los perros* and *Pantaleón y las visitadoras* is found here again: the story is a double story, a game of contrasts, parallelisms, and sudden "vasos comunicantes." The novel is an alternating sequence of episodes which we will call autobiographical (the chapters with odd numbers) and episodes which we will call imaginary (those chapters with even numbers, except for chapter XX, which is like an epilogue to the first series of episodes). The autobiographical episodes are noted for the lack of the most basic norms of novelistic discretion. Not the slightest attempt is made to veil the sharp focus on the private affairs of actual people; there are no (apparently) rhetorical disguises or even name changes. As never before in his previous novels, the protagonist, the narrator, and the author coincide perfectly and without the least ambiguity: the narrator-protagonist is unequivocally called Varguitas or Marito, his relatives and his parents (whose presence is important in the novel) maintain their proper names, and, above all, the most intense and beautiful character in the novel, the tía Julia of the title, is simply Julia, Vargas Llosa's first wife. (The dedication of the book makes it clear for those who don't know or remember this biographical fact: "For Julia, to whom I and this novel are deeply indebted.")

This decision to incorporate into the story, rather than created characters, real and verifiable people such as himself and Julia creates an effect that seems to belong more to the autobiographical genre than to that of a novel; we feel that there is a first person protagonist who remembers, rather than imagines. Of course things are not that simple: at the end, as we shall see, the memory which tries to remember is inevitably the memory which invents; it is not a real individual who tells his story or a fragment of it but a novelist inventing (also) his life, a writer writing fiction which looks like life. The epigraph which Vargas Llosa chose for his book comes from Salvador Elizondo and alludes, ironically, to this process, this perversion of writing which is one of the great themes of the novel: "I write. I write that I write. Mentally I see myself writing and I can also see myself watching me write. I remember myself writing and also watching me write," etc. But there's no doubt that, initially, what Vargas Llosa tried to do was to reclaim a piece of his past as faithfully as possible, down to the minutest details. That strong desire to accomplish not only verisimilitude but also accuracy and objectivity surfaces at the very beginning of the novel:

> In those days, I was very young and lived with my grand-
> parents in a big house with white walls on Ocharan Street, in
> Miraflores. I was attending the University of San Marcos,
> studying law I believe, resigned to earning my living later by
> means of a liberal profession, even if, deep down, I would
> have much rather become a writer. I also had a job with a
> pompous title, a modest salary, some opportunities for mild
> intellectual thefts, and an elastic schedule: I was Information
> Director for Radio Panamericana.[1]

Whether or not the reader knows that these facts of Vargas
Llosa's life are accurate (a knowledge that is immaterial to the en-
joyment of the novel), it is necessary to see in the above lines
three elements essential for the making of the biographical docu-
ment: the all-encompassing familial world to which tía Julia herself belongs ("La tía Julia" is the way she is identified before and
after the marriage with the narrator Vargas Llosa); the grim world
of the radio station (which connects the narrator with the character Pedro Camacho, on the other level of the book); and the fascinating world of literature, which will, in turn, obscurely connect
with the first two. Of those three versions—the family member,
the newscaster, and the writer—which Vargas Llosa gives of himself, the one which seems to dominate from the start is the first
one, and doubtless the reader will prefer it with eagerness and curiosity: its central episode is the marriage adventure of the author
and tía Julia. The autobiographical half of the book is aggressively
indiscreet, like the strip tease, but the marriage episode is perhaps
scandalously so: its goal is to take the most intimate and decisive
events and bring them under the most implacable spotlight, to relive them, examine them, and watch the transformations they endure as they are fitted into the structure of the novel.

The marriage venture is a folly destined to failure because it
challenges all conventional norms: he is an eighteen-year-old student, without a steady job to support a family and with a somewhat romantic idea about his own future; she is a thirty-two-year-
old woman, a foreigner, divorced, unable to have children, and,
besides, related by marriage to his immediate family. In one fell
swoop, the protagonist wants to accomplish two contradictory
goals: to break away from family ties by establishing new ones,
this time through his own free marriage decision; that is, he wants
to form his own family, establishing his independence, by snatch-

ing away for his wife a member of his family, since Julia "was the sister of my uncle Lucho's wife" (p. 16). The mismatched marriage and the circumstances surrounding it became a novel not merely out of a brash and provocative impulse but because that episode is part of his intellectual history and gives an account of his most stubborn obsessions. It is a gesture of total rebellion, the test of fire that marks the beginning of adulthood, an irrevocable and passionate choice. Like literature, this marriage is a rupture and perhaps a radical dissent. One could go on, performing the psychoanalysis that this novel seems to invite, to note that, by getting married, the protagonist violates the existing mores which prescribe certain compatible ages, certain rites, certain reasonable prerequisites. The fact that, even if tía Julia is not directly related to him, she is nevertheless a member of his family is not the only reason that this union borders on incest: it is quite evident that this "aunt-wife" functions, symbolically, in the role of mother, the distant and difficult mother for whom the Vargas Llosa of this story searches, under the masks of certain characters from previous novels.

Julia herself realizes this: "I must seem to you like your mother, and that is why you feel like confiding in me. . . . So Dorita's son turned out a bohemian, how about that. The trouble is that you will starve to death, sonny" (p. 109). And she alludes to the age difference between them as "just right for you to have been my son" (p. 110). But there is still more; the marriage plan is constantly tied (as in the first passage cited) to the classic image of a life wholly dedicated to literature, in the hypothetical Parisian garret: "I told [Julia] about my whole life, not what I had lived already, but the one I'd live when I was in Paris and had become a writer. I told her that I had wanted to write ever since the first time I read Alexander Dumas and that, since then, I had dreamed of traveling to France and living in a garret, in the artists' quarter, totally immersed in literature, the most fabulous of all things" (pp. 108–109). Such plans demand sacrifices and special circumstances, one of which seems granted by Julia's infertility: "If I ever marry, I'd never have children—I warned her—; children and literature are incompatible" (p. 110). Paradoxically, biological infertility seems to guarantee creative fecundity, which might be a clue to the strange passion they share: he himself will be the son Julia cannot have and, at the same time, the father of the literary works he will write at her side.

All these implications do not prevent the marriage adventure from being a romance with all the ingredients of melodrama and the paraphernalia of forbidden love: tender scenes, fights, reconciliations, tears, jealousies, secret meeting places, duels, coconspirators and confidants, providential friends, a hazardous flight, an elopement, a temporary separation, and a happy reunion, after which they start their life together, which will last eight years an(which the narrator sums up in only one page at the beginning of the last chapter. His story, then, is not of his married life but of his challenge of matrimony, the exciting part of the novel. The story is told with remarkable balance between the most detailed objectivity and a tone of intimacy, between an outright aloofness in the recording of accurate circumstances and the undeniable emotion (even passion) evoked by the image of Julia. This is enough to transform her into one of the most interesting feminine characters in the author's gallery—which brings back the conflict that runs through the book between the real and the imaginary. Intense, consistent, authentic in her moments of tenderness and irony, in spite of the fact that she must have seen the inevitable outcome of her adventure, Julia is a credible human figure with whom we can sympathize. Her ability to accept failure as part of the risky game of life gives added dimension to the character (and authentic interest to the narrative), besides giving her a certain aura of the tragic heroine; after eight years of marriage, she is alone again, but the narrator has already realized himself, "thanks to my persistence and to her help and enthusiasm" (p. 429). This novel is, simultaneously, the testimony that the narrator is, to some extent, her own creation and the late but mature homage that she receives from the adolescent he once was.

There are two somewhat incidental details that, from the beginning, tie these autobiographical episodes to the other part of the novel, that of the absurd stories projected by the imagination of Pedro Camacho: both Julia and Camacho are Bolivian, two foreigners trying to adjust to new surroundings; and the "character" Vargas Llosa is a radio journalist, a colleague of script writer Camacho who works in a neighboring station. The genuine interest that the young man develops in Camacho is somewhat like that which the arrival of Julia generated: a fascination not without wonder and curiosity; both are, in different ways, anomalous beings. There is something absurd even if ultimately respectable in Pedro Camacho, whose first appearance is recorded thus:

> He was small and dainty, right on the borderline between a short man and a dwarf, with a big nose and extraordinarily vivacious eyes with a strange restless gleam in them. He was wearing a worn-out and threadbare black suit, and his shirt and little bow tie were stained, but nevertheless there was an

air of tidiness and order about him, of stiffness like that of
old-fashioned gentlemen in old photographs who look
trapped in their starched coats and snug top hats. He could
have been anywhere between thirty and fifty years old and
his long, slick black hair reached down to his shoulders. His
posture, his gestures, his expression seemed the very contradiction of spontaneity and naturalness and reminded one of
a marionette, of puppet strings. (pp. 23–24)

Camacho arrives in Lima under contract to a radio station to organize and produce, all by himself, all the several soap operas
which the radio station transmits. He has a specific job to fulfill
and he does it with enormous dedication. His nature is clearly
"Pantaleonic" to the point of having his great zeal distort the mission at hand: Pantaleón's visiting ladies' corps and Camacho's soap
operas are expressions of *methodical excess*, of fanatic and limit-
less devotion. The narrator insistently emphasizes this "intellectual" rigor: "His concentration was absolute, he wouldn't notice me
standing right by him. He would be staring bug-eyed at the paper,
typing with two fingers, biting his tongue" (p. 55). Since his works
"grasp reality like the bark to the tree" (p. 64), he invents a blue-
print system to work on his stories according to the physical surroundings in which they were taking place, and thus with the aid
of a city map "he had classified the areas of Lima according to
their social importance" and had invented a code system on the
map. His religious zeal toward his work infects his actors and col-
laborators because, as an actress remarks, they are all convinced
that Camacho "sanctifies the artists' profession." He works like a
galley slave but, wisely, tries not to write "more than sixty min-
utes on one story but rather go from one to another" (p. 162), lin-
ing up the stories not by their affinities but by their contrasts: the
"total change of climate, place, plot, and characters would strength-
en the sensation of change" (ibid.). And finally we discover that
his secretmost mania is to disguise himself as his own characters,
becoming a little like them: "Why wouldn't I have the right to
share the substance of my own characters, to be like them? Who
would forbid me to wear, while I write, my character's noses, hair,
and frock coats?—he'd say, exchanging a bishop's hat for a pipe,
the pipe for an apron, the apron for a crutch . . . " (p. 164).
Glancing back at Vargas Llosa's previous work, one can find isolated but symptomatic individual characters whose activity is to
write, even if they couldn't be called *writers*. Roland Barthes (in
his *Essais Critiques*) has drawn a distinction between the *écrivain*
and the *écrivant*, between the *writer* and the *"scribbler"* (a word

that Barthes prefers to the word *intellectual*, to designate those who use the written word for ends other than literature). Barthes distinguishes them thus: "The 'écrivain' fulfills a function, the 'écrivant,' an action";[2] "the écrivain' is to the priest what the 'écrivant' is to the altar boy" (p. 182). The "écrivain" is "one who absorbs radically the *why* of the world in the question 'how to write'" (p. 179). As soon as he uses the written word not as a means but as an end, "he loses all right to truth, because language is precisely that structure whose end . . . is to neutralize truth and falseness" (p. 180). The "scribblers," on the other hand, are "transitive" men, who use words as tools: "Words are a means *for* something, they are not that something" (p. 182). Their "nature is that of an instrument which moves toward the end for which it is a means" (p. 183). The "scribblers" in the works of Vargas Llosa are typical: the poet in *La ciudad y los perros*, writing his pornographic tales; Zavalita, La Crónica's "cacógrafo," resigned to the journalistic garbage of his editorials against hydrophobic dogs, and to the crime reports; Pantaleón with the official reports which he writes, unwittingly, in the truest *Kitsch* style, invoking nationalism, institutional spirit, and respect for hierarchies; and now this Pedro Camacho, who conceives his strident soap operas with "scientific" pulchritude and earnestness.

The most irritating trait of the "scribbler" is precisely that lack of proportion between the pompous (and even grandiose) display of his methods and the trivial quality of his subject: his attitude is entirely professional, his writing goal is to produce a cheap subproduct, sneered at even by its consumers. For him, however, his endeavors enjoy the quality and the justification of art: paraphrasing Barthes, one could say that Camacho is an "altar boy" who fancies himself a "priest," a *"scribbler"* who considers himself a *writer*. Camacho always refers to the administrators of the radio station as "the merchants" (p. 115) and, when the narrator asks him if he really means what the poster in his miserable office says ("The artist is working! Respect him!"), he answers: "I mean it seriously. . . . My time is gold and I can't spend it on foolish things" (pp. 114–115). The foolishness is the merchants' concern, and "it is clear that art and profit are mortal enemies, like pigs and daisies" (p. 115). Through Camacho, Vargas Llosa has intended to parody literary production. But in comparing Camacho with himself, as protagonist and writer of generally bad stories, Vargas Llosa has gone farther yet: he has written a *critique* of literature and has shown how all literature (especially that which claims to be most realistic) is a betrayal of reality.

Nine chapters of the book present the stories invented by Pedro

Camacho; not one reaches a culmination (the stories are interrupted by a series of rhetorical questions meant to create suspense about the possible outcome: "Would she do it? Would she obey? Would a shot be fired?" [p. 102]). All the stories are basically autonomous and differ totally from each other in the type of characters, location, and plot, and they all exaggerate and twist reality in a most bizarre manner, trying to move radically away from Camacho's human experience. The first issue to examine is the identity of the narrator of the stories. There is some ambiguity because, even if it is evident that these are Camacho's stories, they cannot be said to be the same ones broadcast on the radio; more than melodramas and the typical popular love stories, they seem deformations, rewritten versions coming from the increasingly delirious consciousness of Camacho. They are not *texts* like those objectively presented in *Pantaleón y las visitadoras*. They are chaotic and dispersed fragments of Camacho's imagination, which actually give shape to a *history of his mind*. This is a fundamental issue because of the relationship of the actual experiences with their literary illustration. Like no one else in the novels of Vargas Llosa, Camacho is the embodiment of Vargas Llosa's theory about the writer and his "demons."

The "scribbler's" fantasies are so annoyingly superficial that the language itself in those parts of the novel acquires a tone of triviality. In some stories (especially those of chapters IV, XIV, and XVIII) the prevailing flavor and tone are those of "criollo" satire, with plenty of local color and picturesque characters and a dangerous tendency to superficiality. Certainly, it is imperative that one understands the parody and realizes that it is not Vargas Llosa who writes, but the "scribbler" Camacho, and that the former is nothing but a faithful vehicle of Camacho's style. In any case, the reader may find some of these passages to be annoying examples of Camacho's graphomania and, as such, real narrative *impasses*, obstructions to the fascinating tales of tía Julia. It is curious that the fantasies of a soap opera script writer are not real melodramas, typical sentimental love stories, but rather a type of "Grand Guignol" built up through violent expression of the most heinous sentiments of the human heart, full of morbid and frightful situations. There is no way in which to believe in Camacho's imaginary world or to sympathize with him. It is scrupulously *unreal* and *perverse*. His mind is incapable of conceiving of a romantic, familial, or friendly relationship without inevitably dashing it to spectacular disaster: he's interested in *catastrophes*, the more devastating the better. Let us see how his imagination works: during a formal, upper-class wedding, a forbidden passion and an incestuous pregnancy are discovered (chapter II); a religious preacher, accused of rape, threatens to castrate himself to prove his innocence (chapter VI), a man driven insane by his phobia of rodents and by an obsession with imposing moral discipline on his daughters ends up as a rat would, beaten to death by his wife and daughters (chapter VIII), a medical supply salesman suffering from "herodism," that is, the compulsion to abuse children, insults and strikes any child he sees following the orders of his doctor to treat a previous trauma (chapter X); an aristocrat from the provinces has an invalid wife who is sexually assaulted by a traveling salesman, after which the family sinks into ignominious decadence (chapter XII); a priest in a slum sector preaches advocating onanism for men and prostitution for women (chapter XIV); the heir of a wealthy family becomes a soccer referee and is killed in a riot at a sports event (chapter XVI); a folk singer falls deeply in love with a nun and disappears inside a convent, victim of an earthquake (chapter XVIII); etc.

We have, then, a catalog of horrors, not syrupy or romantic versions of everyday life. The subliterature of the "scribbler" consists of a series of perverse variations of his own life, itself very limited and mediocre. What happens to him happens only in the realm of his own imagination, and that allows us to know him better than through his appearances in the autobiographical tales of Vargas Llosa and tía Julia: Camacho's biography literally is in his "scripts," that is, he lives at a completely imaginary level. But it is not only his stories that show us that the internal world of Camacho is an inferno of psychopathic obsessions looking for a way to express themselves (anal fixations and incestuous, masturbatory, sadistic, pornographic, destructive compulsions are always part of them) but, also, his own relationship with his own created characters is morbid and neurotic. On the one hand, his characters depend upon him like slaves depend upon their master; they are disjointed, deformed marionettes whom he subjects to the worst abuse, with a ruthlessness reminiscent of the inexorable discipline of military hierarchies; each and every one zealously performs his duty in the name of unassailable principles. (Camacho's fantasies are also like pornographic writing in that the characters are slaves to the rituals imposed by the author. But, in both cases, this imposition involves a vengeance against the omnipotent creator: the ritual involves him also in its mechanism and makes him too a prisoner, condemned to reiterate for them the same scenes.) On the other hand, the characters engage in compulsive activities and fanatical endeavors which are part of a fixed pattern—someone discovers a truth or a myth, a religion or a hobby, and gives himself over to it completely—which is adhered to despite the obvious thematic or geographical differences of the plots. They are heroically given over to their vocation, to the point of insanity and death. They identify with their vocation to the point of being crushed and destroyed by it. Most of them are dogmatic militants: the crusader of the antirodent campaign, the unorthodox preacher from Mendocita, the uncompromising soccer referee, etc., are alike because, with the fixed stare of the possessed or the mystic, they all search for one objective, and they fail or die in their endeavor.

Thus, the free flow of Camacho's fantasies (drafts and sketches of soap operas that the public demands) is in reality a coded record of his perturbed mind. Camacho believes that he is imagining, that he is working with unreal and absurd material, that he is inventing and dreaming, but what he is actually doing, obliquely, is revealing himself. Perhaps that explains the ease and fecundity of the "scribbler"; the narrator is astounded to watch him at work:

> He couldn't believe what he saw: he'd never stop to look for a word or to complete an idea, there was never a shadow of a doubt in those fanatic bulging eyes of his. He appeared to be typing out a memorized text, or taking dictation. How could he, at the speed with which those tiny fingers hit the typewriter keys for nine or ten hours a day, how could he be *inventing* situations, anecdotes, dialogues of several different plots? But, nevertheless, he could: the scripts came out of that stubborn little head, and from those indefatigable hands, one after another, in the right measure, like strings of sausage in a sausage factory. When he finished a chapter, he never corrected it, he wouldn't even proofread it; he'd ask the secretary to make copies of it, and proceed on to the next one. Once I told him that to watch him work reminded me of the French surrealist theory about automatic writing, that which emanates directly from the unconscious, evading the censorship of reason. (p. 158)

Fanatic bulging eyes, stubborn little head, indefatigable hands, which produce the *right measure, evading the censorship of reason*: Camacho is the ludicrous portrait, the caricature, of Vargas Llosa's image of a writer—the stubborn man-at-the-typewriter, who works on real and immediate events and thus creates imaginary, autonomous worlds. As though guided by tenuous threads which soon become heavy lines insidiously crisscrossing the soap operas, we finally begin to see in his fantasies the commonplace horrors of his private life, even things that remain hidden from Camacho himself. For instance, the antirodent phobia of Federico Téllez Unzátegui, one of his characters, is clearly the projection of his own furor against the rodents which infest his boardinghouse room; sexual repressions, especially resulting from his strict misogyny, are reflected in his artistic morality which rejects the thought of having a wife and children: "Do you think I'd be able to do what I do if women soaked up my energy. . . ? Do you think that one can produce stories and children at the same time? That one can invent, imagine, if one lives under the threat of syphilis? Women and art are mutually exclusive, my friend. There is an artist buried in each vagina. To reproduce oneself, where is the challenge? Don't dogs and spiders and cats do it? One must be original, my friend" (p. 193). It is also possible that his neurotic sing-song about age fifty being "the prime of life" (pp. 167 passim) is a self-encouraging comment about his own age, a magic invocation against his mental and physical decadence. And certainly his comical scorn toward Argentines ("The bestial mores of the gauchos" [p. 160]), which abounds in his stories, is his vengeance for the conjugal tragedy he once suffered, about which we learn at the end: his wife was "an old and fat Argentine, with bleached and tinted hair," a dancer and tango singer in a slum bar, who abandoned him to "whore around" for awhile, until "she returned to him when he went insane" (p. 445).

The progress of his insanity is accurately recorded in the nine imaginary stories, especially in the last four. In chapter XI, a radio station administrator comments to the narrator that Camacho is beginning "to switch characters from different soap operas and to change their names, to confuse the listeners. . . . The priest from Mendocita and the Jehova Witness have the same name" (p. 242). In the story of chapter XII, we see what's happening: within the same story, Ezequiel Delfín, traveling salesman, absurdly becomes Lucho Abril Marroquín, medical supply salesman and protagonist of the story in chapter X. By chapter XIV, the confusions are frantic and unforgivable: the priest Seferino Huanca Leyva is not related to Sarita Huanca (chapter VI), Doctor Alberto de Quinteros (chapter II) suddenly becomes Reverend Father Quintero (p. 297), and the old country gentleman Sebastián Bergua (chapter XII) has become an evangelist preacher. Later there are characters like Lieutenant Jaime Concha, who drowns in one chapter even though "he had died in the Callao fire three days before" (p. 329). Chapters XIV and XVIII are pathetic proof of the mental chaos which Camacho suffers: there are foolish and illogical moments and absurd confusions, sometimes in nearly consecutive paragraphs, like the passage in which the tragedy set in a stadium ends up in a bullring (pp. 354–355). Camacho, after a brief taste of fleeting glory, ends up in a mental hospital and winds up his professional career, pathetically, as a crime reporter for a third-rate newspaper. The painful truth that he is not really a journalist, although almost a "writer," comes in a brutal remark by Camacho's boss: "He can't write. . . . He's tacky and ridiculous, uses words no one understands, the negation of journalism" (p. 446). The caricature could not be more cruel.

The image of Camacho is precisely contrary to that which Vargas Llosa offers of himself as an adolescent writer. One of the subtopics that go along with Julia's stories is that of the young narrator who tries to write and to publish. Unlike Camacho's, young Vargas Llosa's life is not methodically centered around his writing, and the results are meager or simply unsatisfactory. We have here, ironically, a "scribbler" who does write, who does nothing else but write, and a "writer" who can't write, who is distracted from his task, who spends his life on things other than literature. The stories of the narrator are always variations of actual experiences or stories that someone has told him. That is, he approaches his subject in much the same manner as Camacho, although the results are quite different. One of his first topics (pp. 54–55), that of the "pishtacos" (demons), is as frightful as Camacho's delirious nonsense, but he poses himself a question which never occurs to the "scribbler," that of form: "I was about to title my story 'The Qualitative Leap' and wanted it to be cold, intellectual, intense, and ironic like a story by Borges, whom I'd just discovered in those days" (p. 55). There is a difference also in the intensity of the effort: "I'd dedicate to my storytelling all the bits and pieces of time I had left after the news bulletins for Panamericana, the university and the coffee breaks at Bransa's, and I also wrote at my grandparents' house, at noon and at night. . . . I'd write and tear up pages, that is, I'd write just one phrase and it would seem horrible and I'd start over." When he wanted to write a story based on a humorous theatrical anecdote, he tried to prepare himself—as Camacho, who never reads even his own scripts, would never do—by reading the works of "all the humorous writers that came within my reach, from Mark Twain to Bernard Shaw to Jardiel Poncela and Fernandez Flores. But, as usual, I couldn't write, and Pascual and Gran Pablito would keep track of the sheets of paper in the waste basket" (p. 120). That theatrical anecdote, which tía Julia had told him, gives rise to a story called "The Humiliation of the Cross," the reading of which provokes her criticism:

—But it was not like that at all, you've got everything up-side down—she'd tell me, surprised and somewhat angered—but that was not what was said, but. . . .

I would stop, very distressed, to tell her that what she heard was not meant to be a verbatim account of the anecdote she had told me but, rather, *a story, a story*, and that what I had added or suppressed was a deliberate effort to get a certain effect:

—Comical effect—I emphasized, hoping she'd understand, and at least out of pity, I'd smile.

—Not at all—protested tía Julia, fierce and dauntless—your changes have taken all the humor out of it. . . . How is it funny now?

And, even though I had already made up my humiliated mind to send the story of Doroteo Marti to the waste paper basket, I remained caught in a passionate, painful defense of the rights of the literary imagination to transgress reality. . . . (pp. 151–152)

That combination or inevitable deformation that everyone ac-cepts in the language of the "scribbler" presents a problem for the young writer. If writing means narrating some event in the auth-or's reality, literature is a complete impossibility. When the author tells of a lived experience or a dreamed image, he masks and denies reality, makes it into something else, perhaps even its opposite. Maybe that is why later the young writer tries to leave the "real-istic" story for the "fantastic," like when he persists in writing about the levitationists at the airport (chapter IX). But it is actual-ly his everyday life that most stimulates his imagination. Com-menting on the romance with tía Julia and the anxiety it has pro-voked within the family, his friend Javier remarks accurately: "Deep down, you are eager to have a scandal so you have some-thing to write about" (p. 241). The proof of it is that, when that story remains unpublished, the narrator writes "*La tía Eliana*," "based on something which happened in my family" (p. 274). It is interesting to note that in this story, whose topic is the family's prejudice toward an unconventional marriage, the narrator is re-sponding, perhaps unwittingly, to the pressure of a real and im-mediate situation: in a coded fashion, he is writing about tía Julia and himself. The last story he writes is a free version of his experi-ences with capricious and unscrupulous civic authorities, which take place in one of the settings where he had to meet them and bribe them in order to marry tía Julia in secrecy (chapter XVII).

These intense contrasts, fusions, and parallels among the sub-literature of Camacho, the work of the young writer, and the lives of both make it clear that the dominant novelistic technique of the book is that of "vasos comunicantes," that narrative art of emptying one level of the story into another and conjugating them and contrasting them constantly—all done mainly in a humorous way. Even if unreal and unlikely, Camacho's world comes in contact with the private world of the narrator and his love affair with tía Julia, and there is a mutual effect: in both, reality generates the artificial and exaggerated mood of melodrama; in both, the humorous perspective redeems (almost always) the grossness of the subject matter. Julia herself comments on it, recognizing the similarity between their situation and those invented by Camacho:

> —The romance between a baby boy and an old lady who, besides, is sort of his aunt—Julia told me one night when we were walking across Parque Central.— Just perfect for a soap opera by Pedro Camacho.
> I reminded her that she was merely my uncle-in-law's sister and she told me that, in the three o'clock soap opera, a young man from San Isidro, handsome and a superb surfer, had an incestuous relationship with his sister, whom he had, good grief, made pregnant. (p. 112)

The narrator later admits that "unconsciously, Pedro Camacho became an ingredient in our romance" (p. 113). His own diction sometimes bears the imprint of his association with the "scribbler": "I am hopelessly love-sick, Camacho, my friend—I blurted out to him, startled at myself for using such soap opera expression; but I felt that talking like this I was able to keep some distance from my own predicament and, at the same time, unload my burden. —The woman I love is betraying me with another man" (p. 191). Some minor incidents provoke confusion between the two levels of the book: a fire in Callao (p. 322) and an incredible shipwreck (p. 329) are mentioned as if they were actual events, when they are only soap opera episodes. But the "vasos comunicantes" go farther and make some of the febrile episodes take place not only in Camacho's imagination but also in real life. The fight with the Argentine "churrasqueros" (pp. 243–246) and the hilarious episode with the Mexican couple (pp. 271–274), for example, seem to come straight out of Camacho's scripts, even if they are narrated by Vargas Llosa in the first person. Humor flows from the hallucinatory world of Camacho into the biographical fragment of Varguitas and into the inevitable imaginary world which emerges from his life: literature invades the space of concrete life. With undeniable good humor, the novel displays, in action, the internal process of the creative phenomenon.

The final effect is clear: life—that specific period in his life, with its sentimental and ridiculous scenes—becomes, as it is written about, something as disconcerting and enigmatic in its contact with reality as the absurd tales of the "scribbler." Camacho does not (cannot) produce literature, but perhaps he is writing his own life: yet the writer, whose fidelity to truth takes him to the superstitious extreme of keeping the actual names of the people involved, falsifies and changes his own story. The autobiography of a writer is possible only as a novel, and as such it matters not at all where it remains close to actual events and where imagination takes over. All is fiction, and both Camacho and Vargas Llosa know that it is impossible to be "realistic": all art is "unreal." That explains the admiration that the young narrator feels for Camacho; for him "he was the closest thing to a writer that I'd ever seen" (p. 236). That is why it is ironic that in the penultimate chapter, after Camacho's mental breakdown, Varguitas inherits his job and is asked to revise and correct old soap opera scripts: "You are the intellectual type, for you it should be easy" (p. 412), he is told by one of the radio station administrators. In the last chapter, the writer, now reaching maturity in the Paris which had always been part of his dreams, vows to himself what Camacho had believed: "I'll try to be a writer, I'll only accept jobs which will not take me away from literature" (p. 430). It is symbolic that, at the beginning of his work, the "scribbler" borrows the narrator's typewriter, that typewriter which Vargas Llosa sees as a "funeral hearse" (p. 24).

This reminds one of the image of the typewriter as a "small coffin" in *Conversación en La Catedral* (I, 224). This is certainly not the only allusion to the writer's previous works. Numerous echoes of his earlier novels cross the text, fleetingly but insistently, as part of a closed circuit of lived and imagined clues. Figures like Popeye (p. 74), Lituma (p. 77), Javier from *Los jefes* (very important here as the confidant of the narrator), the poet (p. 198), etc., return once again, sometimes under different guises or with different fates, in the best Camacho style. Likewise, places like Grocio Prado, where there is a kidnap as in *Conversación*, or the jungle (p. 168) are visited again. There are whole scenes which seem a reworking of those of other novels: the dialogues between the narrator and his parents could very well compare with those of Alberto or Zavalita with theirs, in *La ciudad y los perros* and *Conversación*. And even Camacho's obsessions have antecedents in critical opinions held by Vargas Llosa: the anti-Argentine feeling of the "scribbler" could be the humorous development of a dictum ("the massive Río Plata pedantry of Homais") which we find in *La orgía perpetua* (p. 17).

It is precisely to this intellectual level that the bulk of the novel points: this condition of literature absorbed by literature itself, which makes *La tía Julia y el escribidor* captivating, besides making up for the absence of practically any other technical innovation other than the profuse and systematic use of the "vasos comunicantes." The apparent simplicity of the book is deceiving: it appears to be an autobiography, but it is the negation of autobiography; it appears to have two distinct levels of the story, but it has many more, of great complexity; it appears to be a double melodrama, but it is quite a different thing—a persistent working out of Vargas Llosa's theory of the "demons" and a glance into the incandescent center in which the experience of a writer becomes imagination. The book not only answers the question of *how literature is written*—with obstinacy, madness, and a reiterated betrayal of reality—it also explains *why it is written*, that is, in an effort, always thwarted, to find reality and from there invent compensatory fictions in which readers can find themselves. The literary effort is a madness, a method, and a verbal communion between the author and his readers. Barthes says that "l'écriture commence là où la parole devient *impossible*."[3] This novel is at the precise point where the writer no longer speaks through his books but, rather, his books speak for him.[4]

Notes

1. *La tía Julia y el escribidor* (Barcelona: Seix Barral, 1977), p. 11. All further references will be cited to this edition by page number within my text.

2. "'Ecrivains' y 'Ecrivants,'" in Roland Barthes, *Ensayos críticos* (Barcelona: Seix Barral, 1967), p. 178. All further references will be cited to this edition by page number within my text.

3. "Ecrivains, intellectuels, professeurs," *Tel Quel*, no. 47, 1971, p. 3.

4. Translation of this essay by Marcela Loiseau de Rossman.

A Mario Vargas Llosa Chronology

1936   Born in Arequipa, Peru, to parents divorced before his
birth. Soon after, he moved to Cochabamba, Bolivia, to
be brought up by his mother and grandparents.

1945   Moved back to Peru—to Piura, which later became one
of the settings of his second novel, *La Casa Verde*. Vargas
Llosa has described it as a horrible year.

1946   With his parents reunited, Vargas Llosa moved to Lima.

1950   Sent to Leoncio Prado Military Academy as a resident
student, where he remained for two years (a year less than
the three required for graduation), and which became the
chief setting of his first novel, *La ciudad y los perros*.

1952   Returned briefly to Piura to complete his last year of high
school. While still a high school student, he began working
as part-time editor or writer for several newspapers, and
saw his play, *La huída del Inca*, produced.

1958   Published his first book, *Los jefes*, a collection of short
stories which is still not completely available in English.
Vargas Llosa made his first trip to Paris, as the prize in a
short-story contest run by *Revue Française*, as well as his
first trip to the jungles of Peru—to the region of the upper
Marañón River, which later became a setting for *La Casa
Verde*.

1959   Abandoned studies for the doctorate at the University of
Madrid, which he attended on a scholarship, after having
completed his bachelor's degree in 1957 at the University
of San Marcos in Lima. Vargas Llosa moved to Paris, where
he lived until 1966.

1963   Publication of his first novel, *La ciudad y los perros*, following a year-long dispute with an editor who objected to
certain lines in the novel. The book won several literary
prizes, including the Premio Biblioteca Breve for 1962, the
Premio de la Crítica for 1963, and second place in the Prix
Formentor for 1963. It also gained the attention of less

appreciative readers, some of whom burned one thousand copies at the Leoncio Prado Military Academy. *La ciudad y los perros* has been translated into some twenty languages.

1964   Returned to Peru for a brief visit, during which he traveled to the jungle for a second time.

1965   Made a trip to Havana in January, as a judge for the prizes of the Casa de las Américas--the first of several such trips to Cuba as literary judge or as a member of cultural gatherings. (Vargas Llosa has proclaimed his deep belief in the principles of the Cuban revolution.)

1966   *La Casa Verde* published in March. Vargas Llosa traveled to New York at the invitation of the PEN Club. Near the end of the year, he moved to London, where he lectured at the University of London, while writing frequently for magazines and newspapers. *La ciudad y los perros* translated as *The Time of the Hero.*

1967   Publication of his novella, *Los cachorros (Pichula Cuéllar)*, which later became a sensational movie. *La Casa Verde* won several important literary prizes: Premio de la Crítica Española, Premio Nacional de Novela (Peru), and, most importantly, the Rómulo Gallegos Award for the best novel in Spanish published during the preceding five years, carrying a prize of $22,000.

1968   Writer-in-residence at Washington State University. *La Casa Verde* translated as *The Green House.*

1969   Publication of his third novel, *Conversación en La Catedral.*

1970   Took up residence in Barcelona.

1971   Published his study of García Márquez, *Gabriel García Márquez: historia de un deicidio.*

1973   Publication of his fourth novel, *Pantaleón y las visitadoras.*

1975   Published a second book-length critical work, *La orgía perpetua: Flaubert y "Madame Bovary." Conversación en La Catedral* translated as *Conversation in The Cathedral.*

1977   Lectured and participated in a symposium dealing with his works at the University of Oklahoma. Now president of PEN Club. *La tía Julia y el escribidor* published in Barcelona. Vargas Llosa teaches at Cambridge University.

Notes on Contributors

Rilda Baker completed her Ph.D. at the University of Texas at Austin and currently teaches at the University of Texas at San Antonio. This is her first publication.

Robert Brody is an assistant professor of Spanish at the University of Texas at Austin. He is the author of a book-length study of Julio Cortázar's *Rayuela*, as well as numerous articles and reviews on contemporary Spanish American literature.

Alan Cheuse has taught comparative literature at Bennington College for the past eight years. His articles and reviews, dealing with contemporary Latin American authors, have appeared in such journals as *The Nation, Caribbean Quarterly, Review*, and *The New York Times Book Review*.

Mary Davis wrote her Ph.D. dissertation on Cortázar, Sábato, and García Márquez. Currently assistant professor of Spanish at the University of Oklahoma, she has previously taught at the universities of Nebraska and Kentucky. Her published works treat García Márquez and Vargas Llosa.

Luys Díez, a Spaniard by birth, was a student of Vargas Llosa's at the University of London, where he took his Ph.D. He presently teaches at Queen's College of the City University of New York, has edited a collection of essays in Spanish dealing with Vargas Llosa, and is the author of numerous articles, reviews, and commentaries on Vargas Llosa, Onetti, Carpentier, Rulfo, García Márquez, and other hispanic writers.

Joseph Feustle is chairman of the Department of Foreign Languages at the University of Toledo. His essays, dealing with such Latin American writers as Rubén Darío, Sor Juana Inés de la Cruz, Amado Nervo, and Ezequiel Martínez, have appeared in *Hispania, Insula, Revista Iberoamericana, Cuadernos Hispanoamericanos*, and other journals.

Malva Filer, associate professor of Spanish at Brooklyn College of the City University of New York, is the author of a book on Cortázar, *Los mundos de Julio Cortazar*, as well as articles on Mallea, Cortázar, Di Benedetto, and María de Villarino.

Alan Warren Friedman, professor of English at the University of Texas at Austin, currently teaches as a Fulbright lecturer at the University of Lancaster in England. He is the author or editor of four books dealing with various authors and aspects of modern literature. His critical essays on modern authors have appeared in numerous scholarly journals.

Jean Franco is chairwoman of the Department of Spanish and Portuguese at Stanford University. Born in England and educated at the University of London, she has written numerous books, essays, and reviews on a wide variety of Latin American authors and subjects.

Luis Harss currently teaches in the Spanish Department at West Virginia University. An Argentine born in Chile, he has published widely, including his own novels as well as numerous critical studies of Spanish American novelists, among them the seminal *Into the Mainstream.*

Michael Moody, who has previously taught at the universities of Washington, Arizona, Juarez (Mexico), and Cuenca (Ecuador), is currently associate professor of Spanish at the University of Idaho. His publications dealing with Spanish-language authors have appeared in a variety of professional journals, both in the United States and abroad.

José Miguel Oviedo is a Peruvian critic and professor of Spanish at Indiana University. His book on Vargas Llosa, *Mario Vargas Llosa: la invención de una realidad*, is about to appear in a second edition. He has published several articles on Vargas Llosa, García Márquez, Octavio Paz, Manuel Puig, and others.

Marcela Loiseau de Rossman was born in Lima, Peru, and has lived in Ecuador and Mexico. She has had extensive experience as a translator, both in South America and in the United States. She did graduate work in Spanish at U.C.L.A.

Charles Rossman, associate professor of English at the University of Texas at Austin, has taught at U.C.L.A., the University of Southern California, and the University of Mexico, where he was a Fulbright lecturer. His essays and reviews, chiefly on James Joyce and D. H. Lawrence, have appeared in a variety of books and scholarly journals.

William Siemens is associate professor of Spanish at West Virginia University. His publications include articles on Cabrera Infante, García Márquez, Carlos Fuentes, and Julio Cortázar.

Raymond Williams is an assistant professor of Spanish at the University of Chicago. He has published articles and reviews on contemporary Latin American authors, and a book on the modern novel in Colombia, *La novela colombiana contemporanea*.